architecture
an introduction

Introduction

1. The Setting

2. Education and Qualification

3. The Client and The Brief

4. From Brief to Project

5. The Project and The Process

6. The Practice

7. The Future

Related study material is available on the Laurence King website at
www.laurenceking.com

*For Dylan, Amelia, and, most of all, Sarah—
without you there is nothing.*

Published in 2010 by Laurence King Publishing in
Association with Central Saint Martins College of
Art & Design

The content for this book has been produced by
Central Saint Martins Book Creation, Southampton
Row, London, WC1B 4AP, UK

Laurence King Publishing Ltd
361–373 City Road
London EC1V 1LR
United Kingdom
Tel: +44 20 7841 6900
Fax: +44 20 7841 6910
e-mail: enquiries@laurenceking.com
www.laurenceking.com

A catalogue record for this book is available from
the British Library.

ISBN-13:   978-1-85669-623-4

Designed by Karen Wilks

Printed in China

Front cover: Winter view of Delta Shelter, Mazama,
Washington, USA. Tom Kundig (Olson Sundberg
Kundig Allen Architects)

Back cover: Upper-level plan, Sagaponac House,
Long Island, New York, USA. Reiser + Umemoto

Frontispiece: View of roof terrace, COR, Miami,
Florida, USA. Oppenheim Architecture + Design

LAURENCE KING

Architects and development

The practice of architecture is not new. While the profession, as we recognize it today, has only been around since the seventeenth century, there is evidence of "designed" structures, and drawings of these, dating as far back as the sixth or seventh millennium BCE. As settlements became more complex it became necessary to plan developments rather than rely upon an ad hoc accretion of structures. This increasing complexity called for design—the ability to envision a future and mediate the building process to achieve that future.

The architect was the individual who had the overview of the needs of development, the knowledge of building techniques, and the application of these to specific types of structures. This was the person who understood a set of graphic conventions, which could be used to explain to others the quantifiable elements necessary to make the "imagined" become the "built."

What is architecture?

Ask a handful of architects this question and the odds are we will get a handful of different answers. Why should this be, when the practice of designing the buildings and spaces that surround us has been carried out for millennia? As with the way in which we build—the techniques, materials, and processes—architecture is in continuous transition and transformation. In response to changes in the world around us, architecture and the role of the architect are constantly being redefined.

Ernest Dimnet, a French-American author, is quoted as saying that "Architecture, of all the arts, is the one which acts the most slowly, but the most surely, on the soul." Whether one likes or dislikes a particular building, public space, or room, the experience of interacting with it will forever be a part of oneself. Architecture can inspire or depress, uplift or oppress, and incite a myriad of other emotional responses.

From the "primitive hut" of Abbé Laugier's writings to the "intelligent buildings" of the twenty-first century, architecture plays a vital role in the way we express our personal beliefs and values, and those of our public and private institutions. Cathedral or mosque, terraced house or mansion, corner shop or shopping mall, architecture is the reflection of our cultural identity made manifest in the built environment.

Architecture is both a local and a global pursuit. Every culture has its specific "vernacular" expressions that will be apparent in the buildings that make up its urban and rural fabric. However, as we have become increasingly mobile and international in our outlook the local vernacular has become a part of a global aesthetic. Architects now practice across national boundaries and bring new influences to bear upon the work that they undertake. In this

Above left
Çatalhöyük, Anatolia, Turkey, 7500 BCE
Building can be the basic process of meeting immediate need, but architecture, and the actions of those who are called architects, transcend simple "building" in order to embody a set of ideas about our present and our future.

Above
Marc-Antoine (Abbé) Laugier, *The Primitive Hut*, frontispiece from *Essai sur l'architecture* ("Essay on Architecture"), 1753
Architecture has long been seen as one of the highest expressions of humankind's ability to structure the world around it; to move beyond merely the construction of shelter and provide order and meaning.

Below
Filippo Brunelleschi, the dome of Florence Cathedral, Florence, Italy, 1436
Architecture reveals and represents our cultural identity as well as our deepest beliefs and values.

process architecture becomes an international language. European "International Style" became American "Modernism." The simplicity of Japanese design became Western "minimalism." We have translated and transplanted styles, techniques, and philosophies between countries and cultures. In this way each culture makes these fusions a part of the fabric of their built environment and the process goes on.

Architecture continues to be one of the most popular and challenging disciplines. Each generation brings a new vision to the way that we can transform the world in which we live.

What does an architect do?

Once again, asking a group of architects what they do will most likely result in a range of answers. Some responses will be affected by the scale of projects that are undertaken. Architects involved in large projects will often work in more specialized areas, whereas those working on smaller projects may carry out a much broader range of activities. Differences will also arise due to variations in the types of project. An architect who works primarily on private residential projects will have a very different view of the profession to one who works on commercial projects.

This divergence in the characteristics of what an architect does should not be seen as a weakness of the profession or an inability to define the practice of architecture. Rather, it is one of the unique qualities of the architectural profession. Because architecture is a broad field there are many opportunities to find either a specialism that suits one's particular talents and interests or to choose a more generalist approach. The world needs architects in all shapes and sizes, because the projects themselves come in all shapes and sizes.

One dictionary definition of an architect is "a person who designs buildings and advises in their construction." If we had to take a single definition this would probably suffice to cover what most people would agree the role of an architect to be. As we shall see later in this book, architecture is not simply about buildings—nor is it necessarily about the design and construction of them. But, for most people the role of an architect is connected closely with the process of design and construction.

Reasons to become an architect

Like any profession, there are many reasons why one might choose to become an architect. Some enjoy the interrelation between design and engineering. Others may find it exciting to see something that they have designed become real during the process of building. Yet others may find a challenge in the more theoretical aspects of architecture and become involved in writing and research. The list is endless.

For many people there is a stylized image of an architect. Whether it is the round glasses and bow tie of the 1970s or the black-clad, goatee-wearing young men of the 1990s, such stereotypes belie the fact that architects do not conform to a "type." However, there remains among some people a view of an architect as (usually) a well-dressed man, in a hard hat, with a roll of drawings, standing on a building site. Similarly, the architects of film and television are often portrayed as characters conjuring up the larger-than-life, possibly arrogant figure reminiscent of Gary Cooper in *The Fountainhead*. But these are stereotypes, and seldom does an architect fit neatly into those molds. There are many myths about architecture as a profession and architects in practice—it would be useful to get some of these out of the way from the outset.

Above
Site Meeting
While it may be easy to find a dictionary definition of what an architect is, defining what an architect does is often a more difficult task. As the nature of the profession of architecture expands and diversifies, the role of the architect becomes increasingly broad.

Below
Film Still, *The Fountainhead*, 1949
Stereotypes of architects abound, but the reality is far more complex. Architects come from all walks of life and all corners of the globe.

Architects are rich

Some architects are indeed rich, but most are not. Architecture is not a profession that naturally leads to wealth. According to the US Department of Labor, for the years 2006–7 the average salary for an architect was $46–79,000. Similarly, in 2007, according to the Royal Institute of British Architects (RIBA), the average annual salary for a qualified architect in the UK with 3–5 years experience (after qualification) was £34–42,000 ($50–60,000). Compare this to the average earnings of a family doctor, which in 2002 were calculated as $150,267 in the USA and £80–120,000 in the UK.

Architects are famous

For every architect whom a member of the general public could name (probably relatively few), there are thousands of architects who will never be known beyond a very small number of people (family, friends, clients, colleagues). Architects are not like football players or rock stars. Even the most well-known contemporary architects walk through crowded streets without being mobbed by fans.

Architects command universal respect

Historically architects have not really been valued that highly by either patron or public. In fact, during the Renaissance architects were considered more as tradesmen than professionals. However, we should keep in mind that the greatest painters of the Italian Renaissance were generally considered to be tradesman as well. These days good architects are respected as professionals in their field, just as good doctors or lawyers are respected for their work.

Architects just draw/design things

As we have mentioned above, architecture is an extremely varied profession. Some architects will be engaged in highly specialized activities—they may be designers and not be tackling the more technical aspects of a given project, while others may be working as technicians or drafting staff and not really be doing much designing. However, it is seldom the case that an architect *just* draws or *just* designs. Even if one is engaged as designer, there will be a need to understand and integrate technical issues during the creative process. Equally, the person who is developing technical drawings for a project will often be designing as the drawings progress, in order to work out issues of detail and construction. If there is one thing that can be agreed upon, it is that architecture is never *just* anything.

So, we've addressed some of the myths that surround architects and the practice of architecture, but what are the realities?

Being an architect is hard work

As we will see in subsequent chapters, becoming an architect requires a serious commitment. Equally, once an architect has completed their

Above
Skidmore, Owings & Merrill, Freedom Tower, New York, USA, 2006–
There are numerous myths about architects. Whatever the perception of what an architect is or does, for most practitioners it is their work that speaks for them. Whether it is a small house or the tallest building in the world, architects undertake each project as a new challenge.

Left
Bennetts Associates, Façade Testing Rig, London, UK
Architects are increasingly called upon to work in ways that are unique to the profession. Beyond simply "drawing buildings," they also play a role in developing new ideas and new ways of building.

education and professional qualification there is still a considerable amount of time to be spent developing as a professional. Further, the professional development of an architect is ongoing—it does not stop once qualification is achieved. To be successful, and to maintain professional standing, it is necessary to engage in continuing professional development—to stay abreast of changes to legislation, materials, products, processes, etc. This is all in addition to the day-to-day activities of professional practice.

Architecture is an occupation

Note that we have not written that "architecture is just a job." An occupation is something that becomes "the business of one's life"—that is to say, it becomes more than just a job. For those who succeed in architecture, the world is a different place. As they walk down the street they experience the world around them differently from others, because they see through the eyes of an architect. The same might be said for artists or engineers—they see the world *as* an artist or an engineer.

However, we should also recognize that there are very job-like aspects to the practice of architecture. If one is to earn a living as an architect, there is a necessity to be down-to-earth and realistic about the way in which one approaches projects, meets deadlines, and is aware of one's clients' needs as well as one's own personal goals. This is often one of the greatest challenges for architects—to balance their *occupation* and their *job*.

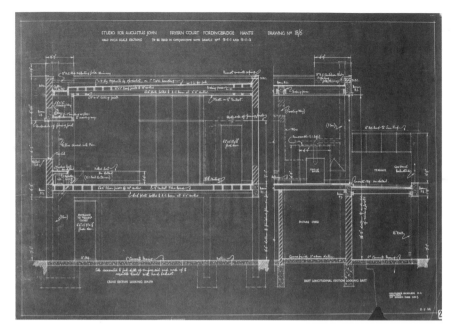

Left
Christopher David George Nicholson, Design
for a Studio for Augustus John, Fryern Court,
Hampshire, UK, 1934
The "blueprint" is no longer the prevailing method
of reproducing drawings. However, the heart of
the activity of architecture has always constituted
more than simply drawing.

Architecture involves a lot more than drawing

For many the image of an architect (besides perhaps the round glasses and the bow tie) is the person with the roll of blueprints under their arm, and this is closely allied to the notion that all architects "draw buildings." However, although in many cases there is an element of truth to this, it belies the complexity of architectural practice.

In a small practice the principal architect may be engaged in almost every aspect of a project, from initial sketches, through technical drawings, to site management. However, in larger practices, where specialization is more common, you will find some architects who do "draw" in the traditional sense. They may be designers, who spend most of their time sketching ideas, or they may be involved in specification writing; others may specialize in site administration and spend their time working closely with contractors and builders.

Architecture is complex—it incorporates many processes and (in the case of large projects) can involve many people, each carrying out a specific part of the work. Drawing is a part of this process—a very important part—but it is not the only thing that an architect does.

Architecture is rewarding

While it is the case that any person who enjoys their job will find it rewarding, architects are often passionate about what they do. For anyone who feels that having a well-designed environment is a vitally important factor in the way that individuals and groups of people feel, then architecture will certainly provide a sense of reward. For anyone who is excited by the prospect of combining creativity, philosophy, science, and engineering (and much more), then architecture can provide a career full of challenges.

Architectural projects, as we have seen, can require many different skills and many types of specialist. This means that there are numerous opportunities for people to become involved in the profession in different ways. Whether you wish to be a designer, a model-maker, a technical drafting specialist, or a site administrator, you can be a part of a profession that is at once ancient and constantly renewing itself.

Who is this book for?

If you are moving toward a career in architecture there are many things you might wish to consider. Architecture is not a profession that you can easily "walk into" without some level of specialist education. Even to be employed in architecture as a technical draftsperson usually requires training in the specific use of CAD software and architectural/building training. In order to choose the right path toward the aspect of architecture that you wish to pursue, you should explore the subject widely. This book is intended to help you in that exploration.

How to use this book

The seven chapters of this book represent a journey from the first principles of architecture through to professional practice and possible future careers.

Chapter 1
"The Setting" provides a grounding in the past and begins the discussion of how one becomes an architect. This includes a historical overview of the profession and a consideration of how theories have informed the practice of architecture.

Chapter 2
"Education and Qualification" explores different forms of education and the issues of professional qualification. The chapter provides an overview of what is required to become a qualified architect.

Chapter 3
"The Client and The Brief" is an exploration of the relationship between architect and client, as well as the process of defining the parameters of an architectural project—from what a client wants to how much an architect might charge for services.

Chapter 4
"From Brief to Project" looks at the way in which architects approach the design phases of a project once a brief has been defined. This includes a review of the steps that are taken in architectural projects and what factors influence the design and production processes, including the environment.

Chapter 5

From initial design ideas through to construction and beyond, an architectural project is a complex process. "The Project and The Process" takes the reader through the stages of an architectural project following on from the design phase; these include drawing, specification, tender, and construction.

Chapter 6

"The Practice" is a review of the different ways in which architects practice and the structure of the teams involved in projects and companies. Just as a project is a multifaceted process, so the relationships between members of the professional team are complex as well. This chapter explores the different types of practice as well as the range of professions involved in architecture.

Chapter 7

"The Future" considers the way in which architects and architectural practice are changing to meet the needs of a changing environment. Whether considering the impact of architecture and building on the planet or the challenges facing the profession in meeting the changing needs of the population, architects must consider the way that the industry is addressing a dynamic world.

Appendices

"Glossary" is a collection of common terms used in architecture, design, and professional practice. "Further Reading" details books that provide further insight into the subjects tackled in each chapter, along with a list of magazines and periodicals that are often found in architects' offices. "Online Resources" emphasizes websites of professional and personal interest to architects, including blogging and networking sites, while "Useful Contacts" provides a list of some of the most important professional bodies and architectural-education institutions.

1.

In this chapter we will take a look at different facets of architecture—exploring the broad sweep of the discipline, the architect through the ages, and the way in which contemporary practitioners look to the past as inspiration for the present.

Architecture is a highly dynamic profession. Every architectural project responds, in some way, to cultural, historic, economic, and theoretical contexts. The balance between these will vary depending upon the specifics of the project, but architects need to consider these aspects carefully. When one looks at large, internationally recognized projects it is easy to see that these issues can become very important. Consider the design of an Olympic stadium: because of worldwide media exposure and the international importance placed upon the Olympics, the buildings created become national symbols for their host country. Add to this the fact that many cities use such major events as drivers for change in their social and urban fabric, and it can be seen that in such cases history, theory, economics, and culture come together in order to shape architectural expression.

Below
Ludwig Mies van der Rohe, S.R. Crown Hall, Illinois Institute of Technology, Chicago, USA, 1956
Architects look to history to inform the present and the future. However, the expression of historic precedent does not always lie in copying an image from the past. Architects may employ the underlying principles of order, proportion, and arrangement, which echo through history, in ways that might be felt rather than immediately seen.

History

Why we look to the past

Architecture does not reside simply in the way in which we build or the manner in which buildings are designed. The buildings that we construct—and, thereby, the communities that we develop—are expressions of culture, with architecture as the medium through which those expressions are made manifest. As a system of symbols, and the rules that govern the manipulation of those symbols, architecture can be used to express a vast range of ideas.

Throughout history there have been architectural styles that were contemporary to their period, but there has also been a tendency to integrate past styles. This could stem from nostalgia or the architect's desire to invoke specific aspects of the past. However, whether through overt reference to historical precedent (as with revival styles) or through more subtle allusions (for example, Classical proportioning or ordering), the past is constantly influencing, and is expressed in, the present. In the same way in which, when developing a new car, designers and engineers do not reinvent every aspect of the automobile, architects equally do not "start from scratch" with every project. There is always some reference to historical precedent—whether obvious or not.

Theory

While history plays a clear role in the way that we design and understand architecture, there is also a *discourse* of architecture. Architectural theory considers the principles and concepts that form the basis on which architecture is thought about. At the most basic level, the consideration of order and proportion can be thought of as architectural theory. At a deeper level, theories relating to the way in which meaning is derived from architecture bring to bear a wide range of other theories and concepts, from philosophy to semiotics and linguistics.

How does theory inform practice?

One might think of architecture as a language (a system of signs, the use of which is governed by a set of rules—or grammar—which, in turn, allows us to read and understand), and building as being the writing of that language. The way in which we deploy that language will determine the meaning that is derived.

It is often said that architectural theory is about "thinking a new architecture," and that in thinking a new architecture we may move toward a position of being able to make a new architecture. So, practice can be influenced by the process of theorizing about architecture—we may come to new ways of expressing meaning through architecture by questioning the way in which we read the language of architecture.

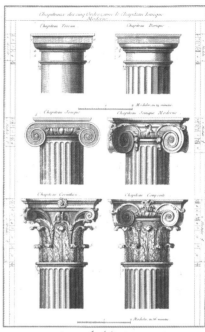

Architecture.

Above
Three Classical Orders (Doric, Ionic, Corinthian)
The visual order of architecture sets the tone of the building. The Classical orders provided not just a coherent set of decorative motifs, but also defined a system of proportion and rules of usage for different building elements—essentially forming a visual "language."

Material, Light, Poetry:
Tadao Ando, Hombroich Museum, Langen Foundation, Neuss, Germany

Gallery block, Hombroich Museum, Langen Foundation.

Materials play a crucial role in the way that we view and understand architecture. Throughout history the development of new materials and methods has allowed architects to achieve new designs that embody the spirit of their time. They also allow us to have different relationships to architecture. The use of brick, for example, often creates buildings that seem more human in scale, because of our ability to see the smaller module of the brick rather than a single continuous surface. The use of wooden siding on a rural retreat can create a sense of a building closely related to nature, particularly as the wood weathers to suggest the passage of time. The selection, specification, and use of materials in architecture is one of the most important aspects of a design.

Concrete is an old material, the Romans being the best known of the ancients to use it, most notably in the dome of the Pantheon. Despite this, many people feel it affords little other than a cold, harsh, industrial feel. We often see concrete used primarily for its structural properties, in highway embankments, retaining walls, and foundations. But for some architects concrete becomes a material of expression and poetry.

Tadao Ando has become known for his use of concrete in buildings ranging from churches to hotels. In most cases his use of the material is very simple: untreated, cast-in-place, and perfectly executed. But concrete is not the only material that Ando uses in his work. Often concrete combined with glass, timber, and (most importantly) light gives Ando's work its beauty and poetry.

In projects like the Church of the Light (1989) we see this combination of material and light in its most striking form. The church, located in Ibaraki (a suburb of Osaka, Japan), is modest in scale. From the exterior we see a plain concrete box; a steel cross gives the only indication of its religious nature. Inside, however, the relationship between concrete and light creates a space of quiet serenity. The precision with which the large cross, formed by a gap between four concrete

Church of the Light, Ibaraki, Osaka, Japan.

Entrance, Hombroich Museum, Langen Foundation.

wall panels, meets the joints between panels on the flank walls speaks volumes about the attention to detail Ando requires. We see how the material and immaterial come together to create something that transcends the physicality of the space.

In his design for the Langen Foundation's Hombroich Museum (2004) we see a poetic composition of form and material. The site, located in Neuss, near Dusseldorf, Germany, is a former NATO missile launch facility. The use of concrete would, initially, seem to be in keeping with the site's history. However, in Ando's hands, concrete, in conjunction with other materials, becomes a constituent of a new picturesque. The building initially appears, through a concrete arch, as a composition of glass, concrete, and water. This plays transparency and solidity against one another, as well as the real and the reflected.

View toward entrance, Hombroich Museum, Langen Foundation.

The building is divided into two sections. A pair of concrete structures partially submerged into the site (thus the 26-foot [8-meter] height can only be experienced inside) house the modern collections. Their solidity is contrasted by the Japanese gallery, which is a 140-foot-long (43-meter-long) concrete box enclosed in a steel-and-glass box.

It is the Japanese gallery wing that gives the project its outstanding views and is representative of Ando's use of material and light. The enclosing of the concrete gallery space within glass and steel serves to reduce the visual impact of the concrete within. Further, the play of shadows cast by the steel supports of the glass enclosure animates the surface of the concrete with a rhythm of shadows.

While some architects become known for the daring of the forms they create, or the scale of projects they complete, Ando has become a recognized master of material and light.

Concrete and glass junction, Hombroich Museum, Langen Foundation.

The profession—history and theory

When considering the history of the profession of architecture we must
recognize that the term "architect," referring to someone who holds a specific
position related to a specific set of activities in a professional capacity, has
only been in use since the seventeenth century. Prior to this there was no
profession of architecture, but simply the making of architecture. In reality, the
vast majority of building throughout history has not involved the architect as a
professional—the individual we call "architect" was a craftsman or the leader
of craftsmen. However, for clarity we will continue to refer to these individuals
as architects—and we are thereby able to understand the relationship that the
architects and their work had to broader society and culture in these periods.

The priest and the pyramid

The Egyptian pyramids are among the most well-known structures on the
planet. Scientists have long pondered, studied, and proposed ways in which
they might have been constructed. There is little actual evidence to suggest
the building techniques employed in the erection of these monumental
funerary buildings. While we do not know the dates of his birth or death, and
much of the information available is indirect, it is held that Imhotep was the
designer of the Pyramid of Djoser (also called the Stepped Pyramid) in
Saqqara. Dating from the Third Dynasty (approx. 2600–2700 BCE), Imhotep
is considered to be the first architect (as well as the first physician)—even if
not in the sense that we know the profession today.

We may assume that there was some status associated with his position.
The pyramid was not simply a place to bury a pharaoh; it represented one
of the most important aspects of the life and afterlife of the most powerful

individual in the kingdom. The burial of a pharaoh was a highly ritualized and profound process; those involved were of the highest standing, and the designer of the pyramid would have, of necessity, been held in high esteem by both the ruling and priestly castes. This may also be attested by the fact that Imhotep was given the honor of becoming a deity in his own right following his death.

There is little evidence that anyone beyond the Egyptian ruling elite employed professionals to design for them. This is not to say that all construction was undertaken in an ad hoc manner. It is likely that individuals were charged with the management of construction, and probably had some role in design, but this would most likely not have been a role that carried with it any particular social standing. Imhotep's role would seem to have been relatively unusual for the period—the titles that he held (Chancellor of the King of Lower Egypt, High Priest of Heliopolis, Builder, Chief Carpenter, Chief Sculptor, and Maker of Vases in Chief) would suggest not only a professional, but a clearly noble status.

The architect and the state

During the period commonly referred to as Classical Antiquity, encompassing the height of the Greek (approximately 1000 BCE to 146 BCE) and Roman (approximately 753 BCE to 476 CE) empires, architects are still found in service to the ruling classes, and being commissioned to design and manage the erection of funerary structures as well as an expanding array of other building types.

We have clear records regarding those credited with the design of some of the major buildings of ancient Greece. The Parthenon, the centerpiece of the Athenian Acropolis, is said to have been the product of a collaboration

Above
Sir Robert Smirke, The British Museum, London, UK, 1827
The influence of the Parthenon can be seen in many of the cultural, financial, and government buildings of the world's major cities.

Below
The Parthenon, Athens, Greece, fifth century BCE
Buildings such as the Parthenon have become templates; many important works have followed the form and language that was expressed in ancient Greece.

between Iktinos and Kallikrates. Initiated during a major building program
undertaken by Pericles—the military leader, orator, and statesman of the
Athenian city-state during the fifth century BCE—the Acropolis became the
cultural center of both the Athenian city-state and the broader Greek collection
of city-states, the Delian League. It was to be the template for important public
and private buildings for centuries to follow.

Similarly we have some sense of those who were the figures of note in the
development of Roman architecture. Much of what Roman architects achieved
in terms of design can be clearly traced to developments in Greece. There
was an obvious sense in which the younger Roman Republic and Empire saw
value in the appropriation and integration of long-established Greek styles. In
part this was a political as well as a cultural endeavor. By taking up the styles
and cultural trappings of Greece, Rome was suggesting that it too was a
culture worthy of longevity and importance on the world stage.

Marcus Pollio Vitruvius, best known simply as Vitruvius, is often cited as the first architectural theorist. In reality we can say only that he was the first Roman architect to leave extant writings on the discipline. His treatise *De Architectura* ("*The Ten Books of Architecture*") is a wide-ranging collection of writings dating from around 27 BCE; some are specifically architectural in content; others cover subjects such as materials, plumbing, water, and more.

While we know little of Vitruvius' actual work as an architect, his writings set out clear principles for architecture. Set out in *De Architectura*, his notions of *firmitas*, *utilitas*, *venustas* (firmness, commodity, and beauty) were some of the earliest articulations of those things that must be present in order to constitute architecture (as opposed, say, to building). It was also Vitruvius' position that architecture sought to imitate nature and strove for the expression of proportion and order. These, in turn, allowed for a reflection on the order and proportion of the human body. To explain this relationship Vitruvius defined the order and proportion of the body through a series of relationships, with the body inscribed within a circle.

The Pantheon in Rome is, again, one of the most iconic and recognizable buildings of the Classical period. It is a unique structure in its design, construction, and political context. The building is essentially a temple dedicated to the seven main gods of the Roman state religion. While it is by no means definite, the design of the Pantheon is credited to Apollodorus of Damascus.

While individuals such as Apollodorus cannot be considered architects in the professional sense that we know, they were referred to as architects. This we know from the many funerary inscriptions that can be found throughout the former Roman Empire. That individuals were recognized at their death by reference to their occupation ("ARCHITECTVS") suggests a change in the role that architecture and its practitioners played within society in general. Although no longer associated with the priestly class, the practice remained the preserve of the upper social orders.

The master builder and the cathedral

During the Middle Ages the power of the Roman Catholic Church and the rise in the monastic orders brought about a change to the role of architectural practitioners. There is little evidence of individuals called architects being involved in the design and construction of the great cathedrals of Europe, but there is a considerable amount of information that shows that the practice was active and well established.

The growth of the Gothic style was as much a change in the conceptual relationship between mankind and God as it was between religion and building. It is difficult to identify clearly who conceived of this new form of architectural expression. It is generally held that Abbot Suger (a Cistercian monk) set out a new vision for the cathedral of St Denis in a treatise of the mid-twelfth century. In his *Liber de rebus in administratione sua gestis* ("*Book of what was done under his administration*"), he offered a theory that set out

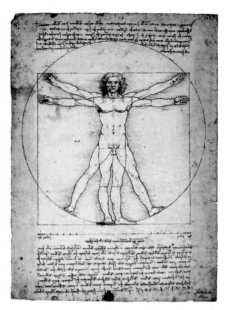

Above
Leonardo da Vinci, *The Vitruvian Man*, c.1490
Vitruvius saw the proportions of architecture as being related to the proportions of the human body. His writings give us some of the first theories of architecture, and define the language of architecture.

Above
Possible self-portrait of Villard de Honnecourt, c.1230
The Master Builders of the Gothic period were often itinerant workers, but their eclectic education and professional experience made them sought after by a range of potential patrons.

to define an architecture that was representative of a new notion of the relationship between humanity and God. While many of the features that were combined at St Denis—the pointed arch, ribbed vaulting, flying buttresses, and the ambulatory with radiating chapels—had been developed during the Romanesque period, by bringing them together with an overarching logic and relationship to a physical manifestation of the Heavenly Jerusalem, Suger defined a new theory of architecture.

Where we do have evidence of specific individuals associated with the design and building of the great cathedrals they are most often referred to as Master Builders. These were often people with a set of skills that allowed them to undertake the geometric, mathematical, and engineering tasks necessary to facilitate the cathedral's construction. There is no evidence of any specific education, and it is likely that any such learning would have been via an apprenticeship—most often as a mason. Many were probably itinerant, traveling from town to town where cathedrals were being planned or were under construction, offering their services to the church or monastery concerned.

It is difficult to assess the full role that such individuals would have played in the design and construction process—in part owing to the fact that there were no "sets of drawings" produced for the cathedrals. Much of their design and development seems to have happened on site. As this was a new form of building (both in concept and in construction), it would have been necessary to establish solutions to structural and construction issues as they arose.

What makes the Gothic practitioner unique is the fact that theirs was a vocation that still grew from the process of making (stone-cutting or carving). There was still a very definite connection between the act of conceiving a design and that of making. We might imagine that the Master Builder could, when walking through the building site, be equally as comfortable with hammer and chisel in hand as with pencil and rule.

Patron and artist

The "discovery" of a manuscript of Vitruvius' treatise, *De Architectura*, in the library of the St Gall Monastery in 1415—part of the general reconsideration of "antiquity" known as the Renaissance—provided a clear indication of the qualities and image of Classical architecture, but also a definitive description of the role of an architect that bore little resemblance to that of the Master Builder. For Vitruvius, an architect must possess the ability to practice as well as theorize:

> *Wherefore the mere practical architect is not able to assign sufficient reasons for the forms he adopts; and the theoretic architect also fails, grasping the shadow instead of the substance. He who is theoretic as well as practical, is therefore doubly armed; able not only to prove the propriety of his design, but equally so to carry it into execution. (Vitruvius, De Architectura, Book 2, Passage 2.)*

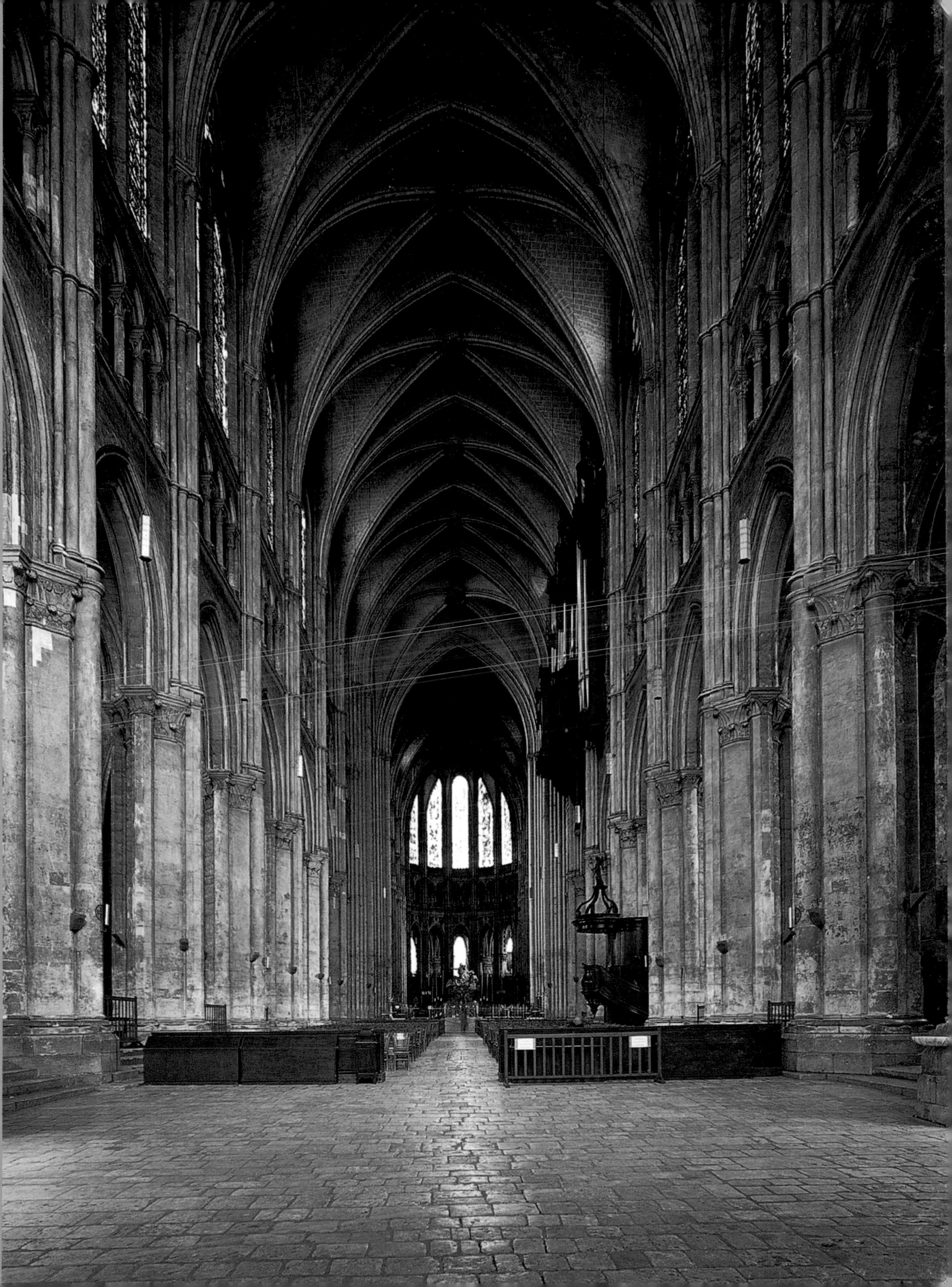

Based on Vitruvius' definition it became possible, within the intellectual and social structures of the time, for the architect to be seen as on a par with other artists, and also as the possessor of a level of theoretical and Classical knowledge. The broader study of Classical Antiquity carried into architecture as well. Sketchbooks extant from a great many artists and architects show an appreciation of the visual detail and complexity of Classical form and ornament, but also a distinct study of the quantification of those forms. Many have detailed studies, with dimensions, of architectural forms and details. There is, then, a sense in which new "pattern books" were being developed, but from a theoretical as well as an aesthetic position.

During the Renaissance, the architect was often also an artist. Apprentices would receive educations in the humanities as well as the arts, augmenting basic reading, writing, and mathematical studies. We should remember that in the fifteenth century most artists would have been seen as craftsmen—it was only the master artist who had social standing of note.

Filippo Brunelleschi is a good example of the artist's transition to architect. We have solid evidence of Brunelleschi's work, both by his own hand and through various biographies. He trained as a goldsmith, becoming a master in the Silkmakers' Guild (which included metalsmiths) in about 1398.

In Brunelleschi we see an individual who was possessed of a certain amount of practical knowledge (although not directly linked to the building process) coupled with a level of theoretical knowledge. We may assume that, beyond a natural talent, his training in the arts and humanities gave Brunelleschi the ability to lend his hand to architecture. His study of Classical architecture gave him the basis for his later reinterpretation of Classical form in his own projects. Thus the architect is now engaged in a practical pursuit, but from a position of scholarly study of geometry, mathematics, and aesthetics—theory and practice are beginning to come together.

Another change was in the relationship between the architect and the commissioning body, whether this was an organization or individual. The Renaissance saw a rise in secular bodies (both in terms of social classes and commercial enterprises) who were in a financial position to employ artists, designers, and architects. The role of the architect, from being one largely allied to the ruling elite or religious orders, therefore expanded to include private clients.

There was also a formalization of the role of the architect: by the middle of the sixteenth century—and particularly in northern Italy—treatises began to appear that articulated both the development of the architect as a profession and also a reasoning of the difference between the architect and the master mason or other skilled craftsman. The sixteenth-century French architect Philibert Delorme wrote that clients should hire an architect because other practitioners were schooled only in the art of manual labor, whereas the architect was possessed of both theory and practice. To rely upon other craftsmen to design a pleasing building would result only in "a shadow of a real building." Delorme also conceived of a self-regulating profession with standards of education, responsibility, and practice—foreshadowing the professional arrangements found in architecture today.

Perhaps the most marked change in the nature of architectural practice during this period was the shift toward design as a service in itself. Some architects became so busy with the process of designing for a large number of clients and projects that they were little, if at all, involved in the actual building process. This stands in marked contrast to the earlier periods, in which the practice was clearly weighted toward those who were closely engaged in the building process.

The architect

By the latter half of the sixteenth century we begin to see practitioners solely engaged in architecture as a design discipline. While it was still the case that many apprenticed within a traditional trade, the bulk of their career now lay in

Below left
Andrea Palladio, Villa Almerico-Capra ("Villa Rotunda"), Vicenza, Italy, 1591
Trained specifically as an architect, Palladio became influential in his own time as well as down the ages. His villas, built for the wealthy elite of Venice and intended as a reflection of the taste and intelligence of his clients, became a new model for architects' relationship to their patron.

Below right
Andrea Palladio, *I Quattro Libri dell'Architettura* ("*The Four Books of Architecture*"), 1570
As well as being instrumental in changing the relationship between architect and client, Palladio continued to develop new architectural theories. His *Four Books of Architecture* offered a set of rules that defined the parameters for architecture.

designing, drawing, and managing the process of building, rather than being directly engaged in construction.

Andrea di Pietro della Gondola, or Palladio, was born in Padua in 1508, and later apprenticed as a stonemason until he ran away to continue his studies in Vicenza. It was not until his mid-thirties that he was "discovered" by Count Gian Giorgio Trissino, who sent his protégé to Rome to study geometry, proportion, Vitruvius, and the Roman monuments. In essence Palladio (despite a background in the building craft) was educated, specifically, to be an architect.

Palladio went on to become one of the most influential architects. His work, during a career that lasted 40 years, came to represent a new direction in the fledgling profession. His success (although he was never a wealthy man) was due to the fact that his designs resonated with the social aspirations of his clients. His designs for rural villas in northern Italy combined a reinterpretation of Roman Classical tradition with new forms and layouts. By having a villa design that not only referenced the Classical but also used it as a new expressive language, Palladio was highlighting the intelligence and quality of his patrons.

Palladio's *I Quattro Libri dell'Architettura* ("*The Four Books of Architecture*"), of 1570, set out nine rule-sets that defined the principles and regulations upon which architecture should be based. In some cases these rule-sets are based on the construction process, while others are grounded in geometry, shape, and proportion. Through this combination of rules, building upon those set out by Vitruvius, Palladio set out to create a clear and coherent "grammar" for architecture.

Inigo Jones, the first architect in England to have followed the late-Renaissance model of an education directed specifically toward architecture, became Surveyor of the King's Works in 1613. Through the Office of Works, architects such as Jones, Christopher Wren, Robert Adam, and many more

Far left
John Smith after Sir Godfrey Kneller, *Sir Christopher Wren*, 1711–13
Although there were many who were being trained specifically as architects, the tradition continued of the "gentleman architect." Christopher Wren, for instance, as well as being an architect, was a geometer, astronomer, and member of the Royal Society.

Left
Sir Christopher Wren, St Paul's Cathedral, London, UK, 1711
Although only one of a total of 53 churches designed by Wren, St Paul's is considered to be the greatest of his achievements and still dominates London's urban landscape.

Above left
Inigo Jones, Queen's House, Greenwich, London, UK, 1616
While the relationship between architect and client continued to evolve through the seventeenth and eighteenth centuries, the expression of an architectural language continued to rely upon reference to a Classical tradition.

Above right
William Hogarth, *Inigo Jones*, 1757–8
The Office of Works, part of the Royal Household in England, became a hothouse for the development of architects. As one of the first places to develop a systematic program of education specifically for architects, it was to be the proving ground for Inigo Jones and for many others.

were engaged in the design and construction of many of the most prominent buildings in England during the seventeenth and eighteenth centuries.

From the eighteenth century onward there was a continued growth in the importance of the professional architect, and also a continued move away from the patronage model. With the increase in prosperity, based on the growth of industrial production, the middle class was becoming more affluent, and there was a greater demand for design and building services to support the expression of this in their business and domestic environments. Architects were now in greater competition with each other; therefore, the role of the architect developed to include a more business-oriented view of practice.

Client and consultant

Our modern conception of the professional architect, although a development from as early as the fifteenth century, is largely defined by changes during the nineteenth century. From the eighteenth century, as the profession became more distinct in its scope and practices, there had been attempts to establish organizations to protect the interests of practitioners, improve their standing, and develop a coherent and formal educational canon. In France we see the Académie de l'Architecture (formed in 1671 by Jean-Baptiste Colbert) and the later atelier system within the École des Arts (1743), both of which served to formalize architects' education. Similar developments were found in Rome.

In England, however, it remained largely a process of apprenticeship within an established office. Some joined the Society of Artists, set up in 1761, and later the Royal Academy, but architects' membership within these societies was relatively low and had more to do with social standing than a concerted effort to formalize the profession. The Institute of British Architects was formed in 1834, for "promoting and facilitating the acquirement of the knowledge of

the various arts and sciences connected therewith; it being an art esteemed
and encouraged in all enlightened nations, as tending greatly to promote
the domestic convenience of citizens, and the public improvement and
embellishment of towns and cities ...." In the United States the American
Institute of Architects (AIA) was formed in 1857 along much the same lines.

We should not, however, assume that architecture was thus established
as a coherent profession. In fact, the membership of these organizations
represented only a small fraction of those practicing within the industry.
The need for such organizations was seen as increasingly important, as the
complexity of projects and the relationships between client and architect, and
architect and builder, became more specialized. Under such circumstances
the role of the architect carried increasing levels of responsibility. Sir John
Soane, the first President of the Institute of British Architects, said in 1788:

> The business of the architect is to make the designs and estimates, to direct
> the works, and to measure and value the different parts; he is the intermediate
> agent between the employer, whose honor and interest he is to study, and
> the mechanic, whose rights he is to defend. His situation implies great trust;
> he is responsible for the mistakes, negligences, and ignorances of those he
> employs; and above all, he is to take care that the workmen's bills do not exceed
> his own estimates.

Where the membership of the nascent professional organizations had
often been dependent upon the amount of time one had been in practice,
or on the payment of a fee, it is only toward the close of the nineteenth
century that we begin to see examination become a requirement. And it
would be only in the twentieth century that legislation was enacted formally
to define the architectural profession. In 1931 legislation was introduced in
Britain resulting in a closed profession, with the title of "Architect" conferred

Left
Sir John Soane, Breakfast Room, Soane Museum,
London, UK, 1824
As the first President of the Institute of British
Architects Sir John Soane presided over the early
stages of moves toward a defined profession of
"architect," as well as designing the inventive
townhouse that was to become his own museum.

upon those who had achieved specific qualification through education and
professional practice.

In the United States the formalization of qualification and professional
standing came somewhat earlier. Programs of education directed specifically
toward architecture were more widespread than in Europe, and by the end
of the nineteenth century there were a number of large institutions with
established architecture programs. Based on the French École des Beaux-
Arts tradition, these were to become the model for architectural education for
much of the twentieth century. The first laws regulating the profession were
established in Illinois in 1897. However, it was not until 1951 that all 50 states
had achieved licensing laws for architects.

In many countries there is now a rigorous process by which professional
qualification is achieved, which can take a number of years of specialized
study followed by a period of directed professional practice.

Contemporary practice—contemporary theory

The role of the architect in the professional sphere continues to grow and
diversify. In many cases an architect may be part of a large multidisciplinary
team. Different modes of practice parallel a diversification of the theories that
affect architectural design. New ways of working and new ways of thinking
about architecture often go hand in hand.

The upheaval following the First World War led many architects to see a
new role for architecture and the expression of society and culture through
their work—a new social order was now possible, and the idea was that
architecture should express a new relationship among people that was no
longer about aristocracy and class, but about equality and democracy. For
others, new materials and technologies, mass production, and economic

Left
Le Corbusier (Charles-Édouard Jeanneret-Gris)
Villa Savoye, Poissy, France, 1929
Modernism as a theoretical position embraced the notion that traditional forms of art, architecture, literature, and social organization were moribund while change was happening through science, technology, and social upheaval. It began as a European movement in architecture but soon spread to become a worldwide phenomenon, and its effects were felt in art, culture, politics, music, and literature. These wide-reaching shifts in the social and cultural landscape set the stage for advances in architecture (both in theory and practice) that are still with us today.

Left
Walter Gropius, The Bauhaus, Dessau, Germany, 1925
Combining architecture, arts, and design, the Bauhaus opened up new avenues for architecture and education. The radical change in the way that architecture and design education was approached continues to affect the profession today.

realities meant that there was a new range of possibilities for designers to exploit. It is likely that it was a combination of these and other factors that led to the rise of *Modernism*.

Often cited as the most important school in the early Modernist period, the Bauhaus has become a model of multidisciplinary education and practice. While the philosophy of the institution saw architecture as the most valuable of the arts, it engaged students and teachers in a program that encompassed fine art, ceramics, performance, product design, and applied arts. Many architecture schools today still base their early years on the program defined by the Bauhaus, and many modern practices also embrace a similar multidisciplinary approach.

Postmodernism was a reaction to, or growth from, Modernism. In architecture it was seen as a move against the "nondescript" nature of Modernism and a return to architecture that could be open to carry social

and cultural significance to the people who used or viewed it. For many, the Postmodern era in architecture began in the 1980s with work by Michael Graves and Philip Johnson, but its seeds were sown by Robert Venturi, Denise Scott-Brown, and Steve Izenour when they published *Learning from Las Vegas* in 1970. In this study there is an analysis of the architecture and representation of the Las Vegas strip. It identified a taxonomy by which architecture may represent its use to the viewer.

Deconstruction and *Deconstructivism* are terms that are often used interchangeably, but they have considerable differences. The former refers to, arguably, the twentieth century's most controversial philosophical development, which found expression in architectural theory. It began as a set of practices in philosophy, literary criticism, and social sciences involving close reading of texts. Through this reading the actual meaning of the text becomes more and more difficult to pin down as inherent gaps and assumptions are revealed.

In terms of architecture, deconstruction is even more problematic. If we accept that architecture is a language of signs and symbols, which create a meaning by their arrangement and usage, we should be able to apply principles of deconstruction in order to explore the range of potential meanings. However, as architecture is not a textual or spoken language it is difficult to recognize a common reading.

Deconstructivism is a term coined by Philip Johnson and Mark Wigley for the 1988 exhibition "Deconstructivist Architecture" at the Museum of Modern Art, New York, which brought together diverse architects from the USA and Europe. Some, including Peter Eisenman and Frank Gehry, were well established in the architectural community, while others, such as Daniel Libeskind and Zaha Hadid, were yet to complete any built projects.

The architects included were not to be considered as practitioners of deconstruction, but their seemingly unconnected work was presented as exhibiting some of its qualities. Wigley suggested that the work of these

Above left
Robert Venturi, Vanna Venturi House, Chestnut Hill, Pennsylvania, USA, 1964
Early Postmodernist works combined the simplicity of Modernism with a reconsideration of form and ornament; seeking to reflect the eclecticism and complexity of contemporary culture.

Above right
Michael Graves, Disney Dolphin and Swan Hotels, Orlando, Florida, USA, 1990
Postmodernist architecture is most often characterized by the use of historical building forms, cultural references, and decorative motifs. These are usually intended to be iconic, giving the viewer some understanding of the significance or meaning of the building.

Above
Morphosis, Diamond Ranch High School,
Pamona, California, USA, 1999
While not part of the deconstructivist exhibition
at the Museum of Modern Art, New York, practices
such as Morphosis make similar challenges to the
traditional form and language of architecture. The
impact of the 1988 exhibition continues to affect
design around the world.

Left
Daniel Libeskind, Royal Ontario Museum, Toronto,
Canada, 2007
Whether "deconstructivist" or "deconstructionist,"
the work of architects such as Daniel Libeskind
continues to push the boundaries of both the
physical expression of architecture and the
theoretical basis upon which we understand
built form.

"deconstructivists," which combined influences from the avant-garde work
of the Russian Constructivist movement of the early twentieth century with
the aesthetics of high Modernism, resulted in an instability of the traditional
formal structures of architecture. It was this apparent assault on the tradition
of form and order that resulted in the grouping together of these particular
architects, and which allowed further questioning of the way in which
the language of architecture could be read and of the meaning that might
thereby be derived.

Greg Lynn,
Cardiff Bay Opera House Competition, Cardiff, UK

Aerial view.

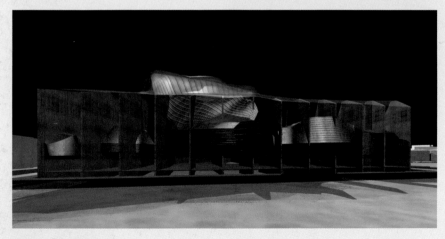

View of portal framing.

Section through performance hall.

For some architects the theoretical development of an architectural language becomes one of the prime influences on their work. While this may not always be obvious in the final outcomes of their design process, it can have a fundamental impact upon the way in which they think about and address architecture.

For Greg Lynn two of the starting points of the competition brief for the Cardiff Bay Opera House in Wales gave rise to a series of theoretical steps that resulted in a proposal that is both emblematic of the complexity that can arise from "folding" in architecture, as well as a building that appears to be recalling natural forms.

The competition in 1994 called for a symmetrical horseshoe-shaped performance hall and a strong relationship to the historical site of the Oval Basin dock. The intention of these directives from the competition organizers was to encourage the teams taking part in the competition to recognize and integrate the specific context of the site. For Lynn, this requirement for symmetry in the main space of the building caused him to reconsider the ways in which "symmetry" and "oval" might lead to other kinds of context.

Rather than see the stated requirements as an indication that the design should follow a traditional understanding of symmetry, Lynn used this as a way of challenging the brief itself. How could one include the themes of symmetry and oval to such an extent that it no longer appeared to follow a recognized context, but might nonetheless suggest that there was an underlying, recognizable, set of references that define the building?

Symmetry in architecture is usually identified in buildings that appear to be identical about an axis. As in the plan of St Peter's Square in Rome, we can see that symmetry typically brings order and regularity. What Lynn began to explore was a notion of symmetry developed by the nineteenth-century geneticist William Bateson. This led him to uses of symmetry related to mutation and variation rather than order and similarity. Thus, the arrangement and forms of the building elements show both localized symmetry and variation. These are principles that derive from evolutionary processes rather than architectural form.

View from basin.

In the design for Lynn's entry to the Cardiff Bay Opera House competition we see one of the ways in which architectural theory is developed and informs a design process. In this case, Lynn has brought a set of processes from genetics and evolutionary biology to bear upon his ideas about architectural form and order. Such a transfer of another type of thinking into the discipline of architecture is often the basis for new theoretical positions. Bringing these biological and genetic processes into play during the design of the proposal allowed the team to work within a set of parameters that, while highly defined in their action, could not be predictable in their outcome.

The resulting building, based on two structural systems (portalized fin walls and rib-structured hulls), brings together the context of the site with an innovative design for a new cultural institution. Through references to both the Oval Basin and in the ship-like hulls, which recall the site's historical past, the project contains identifiable elements of its surroundings. However, the overall scheme suggests a building that has been grown as much as built.

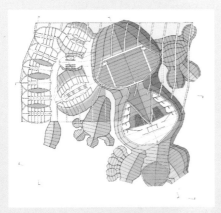

Roof plan.

Ground-level plan.

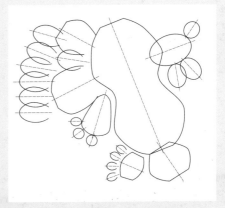

Diagram of relationship of local symmetries.

The "fold" and the digital

The 1993 translation of Gilles Deleuze's *Le Pli* ("*The Fold: Leibniz and the Baroque*") gave rise to a new theoretical debate among architects. The "fold" is representative of systems in which complexity is held within the overall by being contained within and between the folds. "Folding" in architecture is a theoretical debate, which has found expression through works predominated by advanced use of computation.

There is little doubt that the computer has revolutionized the production of architectural information. The use of computer-aided design (CAD) software is now so commonplace that to find traditional drawing boards in an architect's office is rare. However, the use of computers in order to design is more controversial. Some might argue that the computer hampers the design process by limiting the way in which one can conceive of architecture, as the conception is bounded by or mediated by the software and the user's ability to utilize it.

There is, however, a growing movement of architects who use the computer as a way of generating form in new and innovative ways. Rather than see the computer as a tool to be used as a substitute for traditional pencil sketching of concepts and ideas leading to a "final" design, the computer is used as a generative process. Through the use of programming and parametric systems, these architects are developing forms that could not have been created easily (if at all) without computers.

As we are now able to move away from the traditional methods of conceiving and producing architectural forms, we may also be able to see architecture in a new way. The "reading" of the language of architecture becomes one in which complexity is inherent in the process as well as the outcome. The meaning becomes something that embraces complexity and contradiction, and also variability and change. The language of architecture is again redefined.

Above
Peter Eisenman, Max Reinhardt Haus, Berlin, Germany, 1991–3
"Folding" in architecture reflects both a new theory and a new formal language. Through the use of computers, to manipulate form via a series of mathematically derived processes, such architecture seeks to reflect physical as well as metaphysical aspirations.

2.

As we have seen in the previous chapter, the profession of architecture is a relatively new one. While the role of the architect has been developing constantly for hundreds of years, the profession itself has only been distinct and recognized (legally) for less than a century. However, in that time the requirements and responsibilities of the architect have become increasingly complex. In order to meet this challenge, architectural education and professional qualification have developed specifically to ensure that those who enter the profession are well prepared.

How long will it take?

The education of an architect is unique in many ways. While it is clearly engaged with the integration of contextual (often historical or theoretical), technical, and aesthetic issues, there is a great deal in the design process that is fundamentally about creative problem-solving. Architects do not approach challenges in the same way as, say, an engineer. They do not necessarily have a set of predetermined rules that can be followed in order to find a solution. For each project the architect must reconsider the issues (the context) and find the best way to approach the problems that are posed. Although the design process may follow similar steps each time (research, analysis, synthesis, concept, development, etc.), the way in which each step is carried out and affects the next step will vary with each project and may even change within a project.

Left
Julian Konti, Multicultural Housing Tower, London, UK
Education is only the first step in becoming an architect. In most countries there is a requirement of at least five years of education, followed by at least two years of professional experience and then the passing of an examination. As students progress through their education, the types of project they undertake become more complex and begin to reflect future professional aspirations.

Left
Stuart Alexander, The House of William Curtis, London, UK
Every project, whether in education or professional practice, will bring a wide range of skills to bear on the process of design. The utilization of those skills, along with inspirational thinking, brings about new ideas that will transform our built environment. An architect must also be able to integrate design ideas with technology and cultural context and be able to express this through drawings, models, and other forms of communication.

It is this unique sense of creative problem-solving that makes an architectural education a grounding that can prove useful in a wide range of fields. Many who study architecture do not necessarily end up practicing as architects, and the field of architecture can involve people in a very broad range of positions. While qualified architects are clearly required in the process, there are a great many other roles that play a vital part in making architectural ideas a reality. Whether a given individual goes on to specialize in construction drawings, site management, or practice management, an architectural education will prepare them to work within a collaborative, creative team. We will explore the range of related roles and professions in later chapters.

There are over 40 architecture schools in the UK, 67 in the USA, 12 in Canada, 12 in China, 15 in Australia, and many more across Europe and the rest of the world. Competition for places in architecture schools is often high, and in some cases there may be many applications for a small number of places. With competition for places so fierce it is wise for students to give careful thought as to which schools they will apply.

When deciding at which university or college to study architecture there are many factors that should be considered. Each course will have its own particular approach to architectural education, professional practice, design, and other issues. Prospective candidates should do as much research as possible to find out the details of the course that they are considering. Many schools offer "open days" on which those interested may visit and see the facilities, and perhaps talk with staff and students. These are a very good way to find out about a course and a school. Speaking to current students can often be the best way to discover whether a course is right for you, and most students will be happy to discuss their experiences.

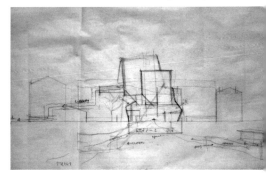

Above
Lewis Scott, Women's Institute, London, UK
From the sketch to the finished building, architecture is a process of creative problem-solving. Each project will present a different set of challenges and rewards.

Each school will have its own set of entry criteria for its course. In some cases the professional bodies, for instance the American Institute of Architects (AIA) and the National Council of Architectural Registration Boards (NCARB) in the USA and the Royal Institute of British Architects (RIBA) and the Architects Registration Board (ARB) in Britain, will have recommended minimum requirements for entry. Some will have very specific guidelines, looking for levels of achievement in particular subjects (typically math, sciences, and art/design), while others will simply require an overall achievement in secondary education (based on grade-point average). Such entry criteria are intended to ensure that the student is prepared to undertake the rigors of technical, theoretical, and graphic work that are required in architectural school.

For many architecture programs, there is also a requirement of the candidate to submit a portfolio of work for review. This may also be accompanied by an interview. The portfolio is intended to allow staff on the prospective course to see how the student's skills in working and thinking are developing. In the competitive environment of applications to architecture schools the portfolio gives the school a way of identifying those candidates who are ready and will have the best opportunity for succeeding in the demanding environment of architectural studies.

Differences in entry requirements often relate to different structures of higher (or *tertiary*) education in countries. In the USA there is a significant degree of variation between routes through architectural education. The most common routes are to study for a five-year professional degree (*Bachelor of Architecture*) or a four-year degree (*Bachelor of Arts* or *Bachelor of Science*), followed by a two-year postgraduate degree (*Masters*). In the UK (and, increasingly, across Europe) it is more typical for students to enter directly into architectural studies, and work toward a three-year undergraduate (or *honors*) degree.

Above
Harry Cassell, prototype wall detail, Collective Eco Housing
Each architecture school or course will have its own unique character. Some will be more technical, while others will stress design. Choosing the right program to match their interests and ambitions is the first (and probably most important) step for students planning to become architects.

Left
Conceptual Models
The range of skills that are required for entry into architectural education is very broad, from drawing and model-making to writing and speaking. The skills expected of candidates will vary from school to school.

Opposite
International Requirements for Architects.

Country	Years of Education	Years of Practice	Professional Body	Registration
Australia	5 years	2 years	Royal Australian Institute of Architects (RAIA)	Compulsory to use the title "Architect." Administered by state boards
Austria	5 years	3 years plus examination	Bundeskammer der Architekten und Ingenieurkonsulenten (BAIK)	Required membership in BAIK
Canada	5 or 6 years	5600 hours in specific areas of practice	Royal Architecture Institute of Canada (RAIC)	Compulsory to use title "Architect." Registration (licensing) is administered by provincial councils
France	6.5 years (divided into 2-year blocks with compulsory 6-month final block)	Dependent upon the type of degree awarded	26 Regional Councils of the Association of Architects	Required membership in one of the Regional Councils
Germany	4 or 5 years	Minimum 2 years	Architects are members of regulated register	Compulsory to use the title "Architect"
Ireland	5 years, or 3 plus 2 with an optional 1-year stage after the first cycle	2 years	Royal Institute of Architects in Ireland (RIAI)	Registration as part of RIAI
Italy	Section A: 5 years Section B: 3 years	None required	Architects are organized in Provincial Registers within a National Council	Compulsory for each category (Section A and Section B)
The Netherlands	5 years (technological universities); 4 years (academies in conjunction with architectural sector)	Not compulsory for registration, but 2 years required for enrolment in BNA	Bond van Nederlandse Architecten (BNA)	Compulsory to use the title "Architect"
New Zealand	5 years	2 to 3 years	New Zealand Institute of Architecture (NZIA)	Compulsory to use the title "Architect." Registration is administered by the New Zealand Registered Architects Board (NZRAB)
Poland	5 years	Minimum 3 years	Stowarzyszenie Architektów Polskich (SARP)	Compulsory registration through SARP
Spain	5 years	None required	Colegio Oficial de Arquitectos	Required membership of Colegio Oficial de Arquitectos
Sweden	4 or 5 years	None required	Sveriges Arkitekter	Voluntary membership of Sveriges Arkitekter
United Kingdom	5 years	2 years	Royal Institute of British Architects (RIBA)	Compulsory to use the title "Architect." Registration is administered by the Architects Registration Board (ARB)
United States	5 or 6 years	700 training units (each = 8 hours) in specific areas of practice	American Institute of Architects (AIA)	Compulsory to use the title "Architect." Registration (licensing) is administered by individual States within National Council of Architectural Registration Boards

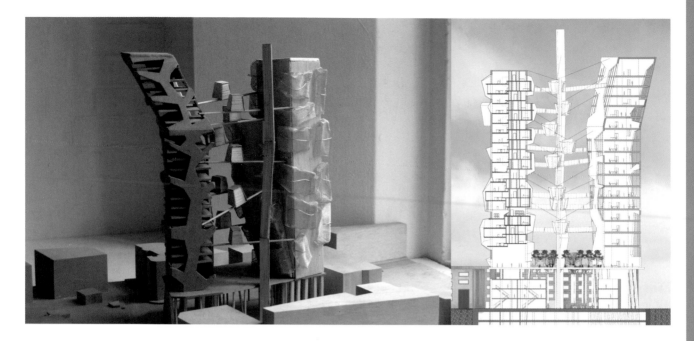

An undergraduate degree is not sufficient to make one eligible for professional qualification. In most of the countries that offer a three-year undergraduate degree there will be a further two years of postgraduate education in order to complete the educational requirements of the profession. In those countries that typically have a four-year undergraduate degree there is sometimes a one-year *professional* degree available—or a student may choose to complete a two-year *Masters* degree.

Following the completion of (usually) five years of architectural education, there is still (in most countries) a requirement for work experience before one can be considered a candidate for professional qualification. The requirement for professional experience prior to qualification stems from an understanding that the complexities of architecture in the real world make it difficult for someone to understand the nature of the profession unless they have actually engaged in the day-to-day practice of an office and the process of working on real projects.

Each country will have slightly different requirements. Some will require a longer time spent in formal education, but will then require little or no professional-practice experience prior to qualification. Others will have different periods of time for professional practice, based on the type of education that has been undertaken. It is, however, generally the case that the average time to achieve professional qualification is seven years.

Getting there by other routes

While a set number of years of education followed by professional experience is the most common path to qualification as an architect, it is not the only way. Just as our exploration of the history of the profession showed that there is a long tradition of architects progressing from an involvement in the building trade, so it is possible for a person to become an architect through professional experience.

It is important that the profession of architecture remains open to alternative methods of entering practice. While it is vital that an architect be able to meet the requirements of the profession, particularly in terms of health and safety, it is equally important that the profession is able to embrace a diversity in the kind of people who offer architectural services. It is also important to recognize that there may be social and economic reasons as to why individuals enter architecture through alternative routes. Five years of university education can be an extremely expensive undertaking, and this may mean that individuals from less affluent backgrounds are unable to enter or complete a traditional educational route to the profession.

Most of the professional organizations offering qualification status allow for the possibility that an individual may possess the requisite skills and abilities without having been formally educated as an architect. Through working in architectural practice it is possible for a person to have gained sufficient understanding and experience in the specific requirements, legal responsibilities, professional practice, design, construction, etc., to be able to function as an architect. In such circumstances the qualification body may have guidelines as to the requirements that such candidates should have achieved. Similarly, in some cases there will be an examination and/or review of a portfolio of professional work that is deemed necessary to achieve the qualification.

Left
Drawing and Modeling Workshop
The development of a design process is often one of the key elements of an architectural education. Through drawings and model-making students develop strategies for taking ideas and making them into communicable designs.

What to expect from courses

Every architecture school and course will have its own particular approach. It may be that some schools have a more technical attitude, in which an understanding of the "hard" aspects of architecture (structure, mechanical systems, professional practice) are emphasized, and the teaching may consequently be geared toward this approach. In other schools a more design-led stance may be taken, in which the conceptual development and theoretical exploration of architecture is given more prominence.

We should not assume that one kind of architectural education is better than another. Architecture is a very large subject and, in professional practice, there is a need for a wide range of skilled individuals. Those who choose to study on a program with a technical focus may find themselves particularly suited to some aspects of professional practice. There is always a high demand for architectural technicians—those individuals who are particularly conversant with the production of construction information and with the building process.

Whether within a technically-focused or design-focused approach, there is a range of subjects that should be included in any architecture course. While each course or school may emphasize these to varying degrees, the student should expect to find:

- Design projects
- Structures (the study of structural systems and materials)
- Construction (the process and methods of building)
- Historical/contextual studies (history and theory of architecture and related disciplines)
- Environmental design (the study of materials and systems for heating, cooling, ventilation, and lighting)
- CAD (computer-aided design)/visualization (computer-assisted drawing and modeling)
- Professional practice (business practices associated with architecture)

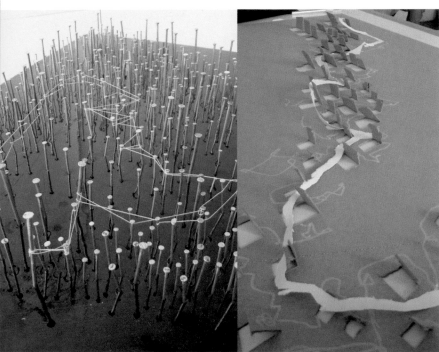

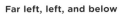

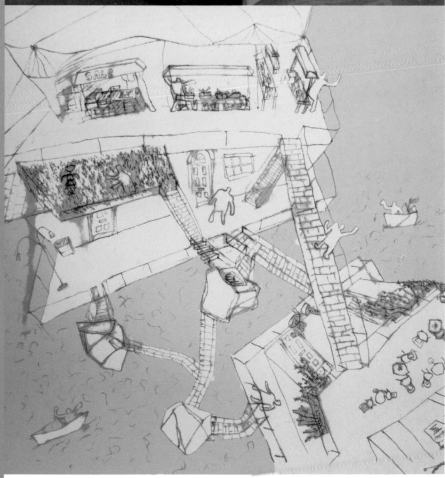

Far left, left, and below
Conceptual Models and Drawings
Some architecture courses will have a more
conceptual approach—seeking to explore
architecture through ideas—while others will
take a more pragmatic or technical stance. Most
will combine aspects of a range of approaches,
with the aim of supporting students in becoming
well-rounded professionals.

The way in which these subjects are taught will also vary from school to school. Some of the methods may be familiar, as they will be similar to what is found in secondary/high school. Other methods may be a new kind of experience. Generally speaking, the difference between secondary/high school and higher education will be most clearly seen in the level to which students are expected to take responsibility for their own learning. In school, learning and teaching is a more prescribed process (students are given an assignment and directions on how to carry it out), whereas in university students will be expected to take more of an active role in deciding how they will approach the assignment/project. Some students can find this shift difficult, but it is imperative that they are able to make this transition so that they are developing their own approach to architecture.

Traditionally architecture was taught in an apprenticeship or *atelier* model, as we saw in Chapter 1. Prior to the establishment of architecture schools a young man (and for a long time it was only men that were allowed to study such subjects) would be apprenticed to an architect, work in the architect's office, and learn the way in which that architect approached the subject. Even after the formation of architecture schools this model remained common, except that the architect now came to the school to meet with students. However, it was still the case that students were "learning from the master." While the relationship between student and teacher has changed, there is still a role for the interaction between established practitioner and student, as the practitioner will bring unique insight to a discussion or a tutorial/crit and students will gain from the knowledge of how the practitioner approaches certain types of design problems.

There are a number of different approaches to architectural education; each has a slightly different focus and will support different types of learning. It is often the case that a school will employ several different types of learning and teaching strategies at different times.

Many schools in the USA and UK have modular programs. This is a system wherein a student's education is built up of a series of modules that each carry a credit weighting. Generally, a module equates to a specific class—students would have a design module, a structures module, a history module, etc. To achieve their degree a student will have to accumulate the requisite number of credits. In such a system students will spend part of their time in the studio working on design projects, part in a lecture theater receiving presentations on history, theory, or professional practice; and part in a classroom, carrying out work on structures or mechanical systems.

In larger schools of architecture each of the modules may be offered at different times throughout the year. Therefore, a student will have some flexibility in how they "assemble" their curriculum for any given year. There may be some prerequisites that mean that modules can only be taken in a specific order, but the flexibility of such systems can be attractive for students. The potential drawback of the modular program is that it does not necessarily encourage the integration of different areas of study. Because each module is

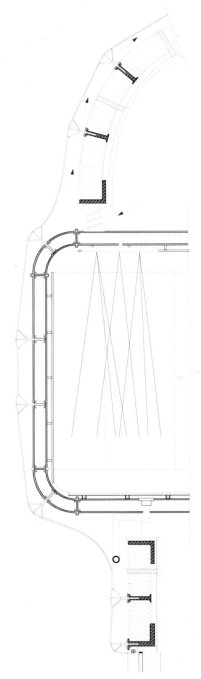

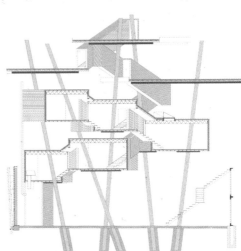

presented as a discrete learning experience, some students may find it difficult to bring the different strands of their learning together.

A new form of architectural education was introduced by the Architectural Association (AA) in London in the early 1970s. The *Unit System* is based on the idea that a group of students (usually less than 20) will work with the same tutor(s) for an entire academic year. The unit is led by a Unit Master, who sets out the general area of study that students in that unit will pursue. The main focus in the Unit System is the design projects, with the other areas of study acting in support. The emphasis within the Unit System is on the integration of technical and contextual studies into the design projects.

The unique character of the Unit System is that it relies very little on traditional classroom teaching. The delivery of technical areas of study is related to the students' specific unit and project, often through tutorials with a practitioner—each unit having its own set of support tutors. From the 1970s up to the present day the Unit System at the AA has seen a range of well-known architects (Zaha Hadid, Will Alsop, Peter Wilson, Peter Cook, Jeff Kipnis, Daniel Libeskind, Cedric Price, Bernard Tschumi, Ken Yeang, and many more) act as Unit Masters. It has always been the case that the Unit Master sets the tone of the unit, and the work produced by students will often reflect as much on the Unit Master as the particular student.

The popularity of the Unit System has seen it adopted by many architecture schools across Europe. Its ubiquity does not necessarily mean that it is the best way of learning architecture. Its strengths are the intensity of the experience of working on a single "topic" with a small group of students and tutors. There is a strong emphasis on the design aspects of architecture, with the other areas being more subordinate. The drawbacks are that for some students the lack of a structured curriculum can make it difficult to gauge progress, and the need for strong self-directed study and work skills can make it a challenge.

The most common form of architectural education is often referred to as the *Studio System*. Many of the schools that follow a modular structure will be based around a Studio System. In this, the design-studio activity will be one module among others that a student will be engaged with during the course of a semester or term. Each will be overseen by a studio critic/tutor (or studio critics, depending on the size). The projects may vary between studios, but will adhere to a structure of what is to be achieved in the particular module. In such systems students may be in different studios, with different studio critics, undertaking different projects, but the intended learning will be the same.

Like the Unit System, the Studio System places the majority of the emphasis on the design elements of architecture. This can be seen in the fact that most modular studio-based programs will have a much higher credit rating for studio modules than for technical ones, as well as more hours allocated to the teaching time for studio activities.

In most of the examples explored so far we have been looking at groups of students who are generally working at the same level or in the same year of study. "Vertical" groups, in which students at different levels work together, can be facilitated in both the Unit or the Studio Systems—and there are great benefits for students in such educational experiences. Students at the earlier stage of their education benefit from the interaction with more-advanced students, seeing how the latter students approach the design problems that

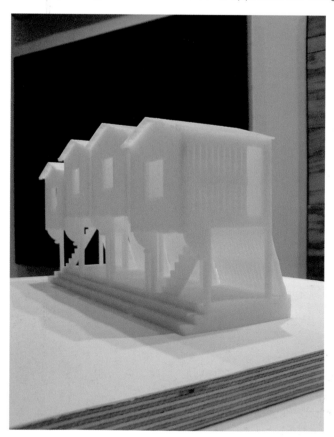

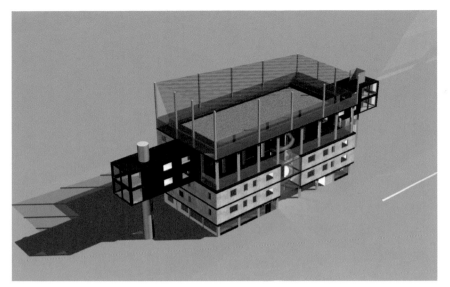

Left
Matteo Mantovani, Youth Hostel and Day Center, Bucharest, Romania
Whether in a Unit or Studio System, students' design development will often be at the center of all aspects of their education. Through a holistic approach—one that seeks to integrate the technical and creative aspects of architecture—students will develop both skills and creativity.

are presented, as well as engaging in the level of discourse that accompanies the work. For those students higher up in the program, the interaction with the newer students gives them opportunities to reflect upon their own practices. In having to articulate their process to others less familiar with the design process, the more advanced students must ask themselves internal questions about what they do and how they do it. In addition, their use of a language of criticality becomes more developed as they seek to articulate their work to others.

In the vertical studio the role of the studio critic is to facilitate the interaction between groups of students and to set up situations in which a debate on working methods and concepts can be of benefit to all students. While on the surface it may seem that there is less teaching taking place, in fact there is more careful consideration of the way in which the teacher interacts with the students. At one level the studio critic must ensure that the information and practices being shared are positive for the students. At another level the teacher will need to be designing projects and activities carefully in order to meet the needs of students at different levels in their educational and professional development.

The project and the charrette

For many students the most exciting part of architectural education will be design. This is where they will have the opportunity to explore their ideas about buildings and space, drawing, and presentation. The development of design skills and conceptual thinking can be vital to successful architectural education and later professional practice. It is also through design work and the integration of other areas of study that students find the opportunities for the development of critical thinking about their own work and the work of others.

Architecture and design education is predicated on "problem-based learning." This is a form of learning and teaching that seeks to create

Kyu Sung Woo Architects, Nerman Museum of Contemporary Art, Johnson County Community College, Kansas, USA

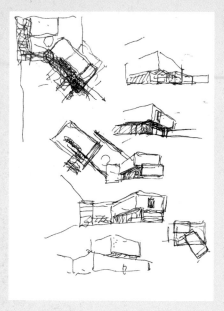

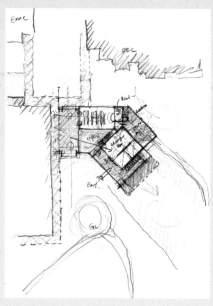

Design sketches.

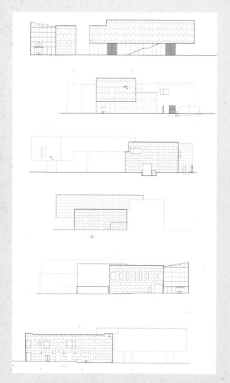

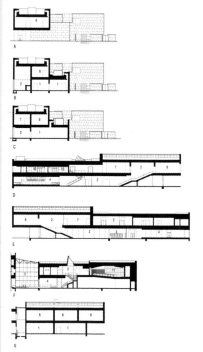

Presentation drawings.

In architectural education there is a consistent stress on the importance of developing a clear "design process"—the ability to carry a project from initial ideas through a series of stages of testing and re-evaluation until a final design is achieved. This is not simply a matter of educational necessity; it is an important aspect of the professional practice of an architect as well.

The importance of this "process" is both because of its value in problem-solving (thinking clearly and working through sketches and models means that you are able both to visualize and to consider the design) and because the architect is able to explain the design to clients and other parties. This ability to communicate the design process can be vital in helping a client to understand a design proposal that challenges their preconceptions.

The early phases of a project will have a lasting influence on the final outcome. From initial sketch, through feasibility, and on to design development, the architect will be engaged in an iterative process aimed at refining the proposal through each step.

Through their earliest sketches, through more defined presentation drawings, and then in the finished building, it is possible to see the development of Kyu Sung Woo's design for the Nerman Museum of Contemporary Art (NMOCA). In each sketch one can see the changes that are being developed and explored. As these ideas begin to firm up the architect produces more refined sketches and then final presentation drawings.

Conceptually the building, completed in 2007, seeks to be not simply a repository for art, but the start of a journey to explore the art collection across the campus of Johnson County Community College. The orientation of the glass-enclosed lobby invites visitors into the building, while the 13-foot (4-meter) cantilever becomes a work of art itself through the installation of an LED surface by the artist Leo Villareal.

Interior lobby view.

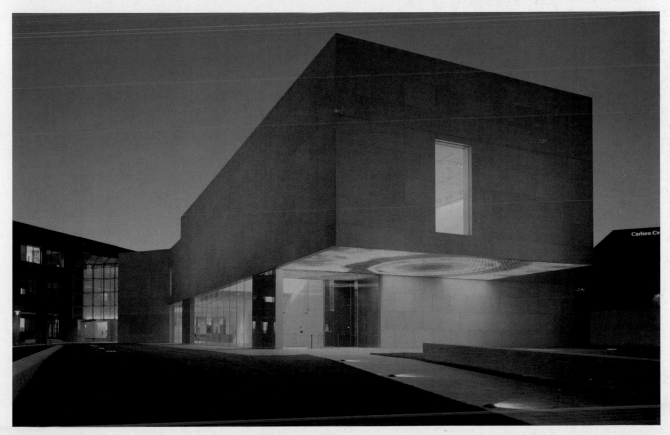

View of extension.

situations where the student engages with issues that are like those that exist outside of the educational environment—modeled on "the real world." In order to deal with the problem the student will be required to behave and think *like an architect*. Architecture, like all design disciplines, has the property of being a discipline in which simply reading or hearing about issues cannot provide the necessary learning to ensure that one is capable of actually *doing*. To understand what it is to be a designer or architect, you need to design.

The way that projects are structured for students will vary depending on both the school and the aims of the project. Some projects may be designed to encourage students to engage in conceptual thinking, while others may be intended to explore materials or structural solutions. In all cases the project will start with a *brief*, or description of what is to be undertaken in that project. Early in an architect's education the brief will tend to be quite prescriptive and define the scope of the project very tightly. As a student progresses the information provided in the brief will likely become less and less prescriptive but require more exploration and research by the student in order to define the context for their design. We will see in a later chapter that the brief is also an element of professional practice, in defining the needs of the client. Again this points to the fact that in architectural education we are seeking ways in which we can model the teaching and learning activities on the types of activity that will take place in the professional environment.

The amount of time given to a project can vary from a day to a year (or more), depending on the school and the nature of the project. In many

Above
Model-Making Workshop
Many schools of architecture bring students together from different stages in their education. Such "vertical" studios support students through peer learning, with the more advanced students offering support to students earlier in their education. Through such teaching and learning methods both groups benefit—one from interaction with more advanced students, the other from having to engage in a discourse about their design process.

Left
First-Year Ideas Workshop
At the heart of architectural education is the notion of "problem-based learning." This is to say that students learn by tackling problems that model those they may encounter in professional practice. For many schools this is expanded to include working on real, "live" projects.

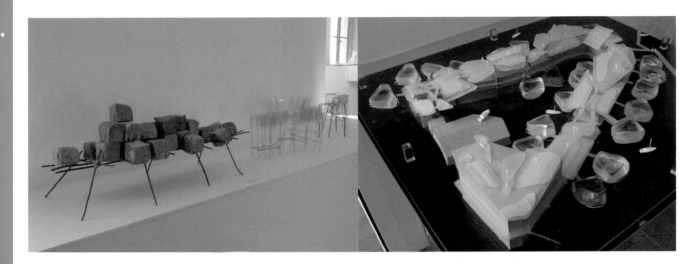

Above, left and right
Conceptual Designs
Whether through a long project or a short, intense
"charrette," the outcome of a design process is
not always a specific building. Architecture is often
about exploring ideas or concepts. Through work
that seeks to question architecture and design,
students are able to discover their own particular
approach to their work and their working method.

schools that follow the Unit System there may be a single project for the year, with smaller sub-projects that support the development of the larger, overall scheme. Again the nature of the learning experience that is sought will determine the length of time allocated to a project.

A short project is sometimes referred to as a "charrette." The term comes from the French for a small cart, and refers to the fact that students of the École des Beaux-Arts were to be found still working on their drawings as they rode the carts to the École on the morning that their work was due. Today the word charrette refers to a short and intense project—in some cases, an opportunity for students to work alongside a well-known architect. It can also be the case that a charrette can take place outside of the normal studio environment, either on the site where the project is proposed or in an architect's office or a space specifically chosen for the event. Some schools arrange trips to locations around the world where students work with professionals or students from another architecture school on a charrette. The crucial thing about a charrette is that it is very *active*—everyone will be working together. Because the charrette will usually be a completely self-contained event (that is to say, students will not be doing any other study during the period of the charrette), the entire process of a design project is condensed into a short space of time. This can make for a very exciting experience and can lead to interesting outcomes. It is also good practice for developing strategies and design methodologies in response to short deadlines.

Projects are not always "simulations" of real-world activities. In some cases students may have an opportunity to work on a real project for a client as part of their studies. These are sometimes referred to as "live" projects. It may even be the case that the client is paying a fee. In such projects students will have the client's brief to work to, and will have regular meetings with the client. This form of project takes the students' experience of education one step closer to that of professional practice. From the client's point of view there are some real benefits as well. If a group of, say, 20 students are all working on the project, then the client has a much greater potential of finding some very creative solutions to the brief—more so than if they hired a single architectural practice. Additionally, students may not have the same set of concerns that a professional would have, and are therefore less likely to be hampered by constraints.

The crit, the tutorial, and the jury

We have seen that the primary teaching and learning activity within architecture schools is the studio-based project. This gives students the opportunity to develop their own ideas and approach to architectural design and problem-solving. However, this does not happen simply through the work on the project. Students will also be meeting with their teacher or tutor/studio critic, to discuss their progress and debate ideas.

Whether such meetings are called *crits* or *tutorials*, they are intended to be an opportunity for the studio critic to see how a student's work is developing and provide guidance on whether the work suggests that the student is headed in the right direction and the intended learning is being achieved.

In most architectural schools these meetings between studio critic and student will be very regular (often weekly). The frequency will depend both on the nature of the program and the level of the student. It is often the case that students require fewer contacts with their critic as they progress in their studies, with students in their final years acting, largely, independently.

Another variation that one may see between different programs is the approach to crits and tutorials in terms of the nature of contact. There is a tradition in architecture schools that much of the contact between students and teachers is one-to-one. This clearly means that students get very individualized input from the studio critic in regard to their work. However, based on research in the last 15 years, many schools of architecture have begun to explore ways in which tutorials and crits can be more group-focused. Research has shown that the one-to-one tutorial format does not always provide the student with the best learning opportunities. A more group-oriented activity offers students greater opportunities to develop a critical language for discussing their work. In this group-tutorial format the onus is placed upon the students to discuss work, with the studio critic acting to facilitate their discussions. We can see that this moves us some distance from the notion of master and apprentice, with the students now taking greater control of their learning. This is not to say that the critic does not still play a very important role, but that that role is now one in which students are supported in order to develop their learning as individuals and to develop their own particular view of architecture and design. Another positive aspect of group tutorials is that they encourage students to see and discuss each other's work; in so doing, any individual student can benefit from the experience of his or her peers.

While the day-to-day development of a student's design work is often undertaken through crits and tutorials, in which they are meeting with their

Above
Presentation/Jury
While students may work individually or in groups, a formal presentation before an audience of peers and studio critics often forms part of the educational process. Through such activities students learn the skills necessary to present work to clients, and discuss, debate, and defend their ideas.

Left
Alexandra Toomey, Raleigh House/Windrush
Square Project, London, UK
The ability to communicate is crucial to an
architect. Whether through models, drawings,
writing, or speaking, students will need to develop
the skills necessary to express their ideas in a
range of contexts.

individual studio critic, there is also a form of learning and teaching that
requires the student to present and defend their work before a panel. The *jury*
or *review* is a more formal structure of discussion and feedback around the
student's work. Such events can be used as a form of final assessment
(where a student is awarded a grade or mark for their achievement in the
project) or as a "milestone" in the development of the project. While there is a
level of pressure that a student may feel when having to stand before a group
of teachers and practitioners to present and defend their work, the aim of the
jury is to give the student an opportunity to receive critical feedback from a
range of different people.

Communication

One of the most important skills for an architect is the ability to communicate.
Whether through drawings, models, computer-visualization, written reports, or
verbal presentations, the need for an architect to communicate is essential in
dealing with clients, meeting with contractors, or discussing work with peers.

The ways in which architects communicate through drawing, modeling,
and visualization are relatively easy to identify. Equally, the ways in which
they learn as students to communicate through these mediums is fairly
straightforward. Students may attend seminars and workshops. They may
sit through demonstrations of how to use a particular software application.
More than anything else, they must practice and experiment. Through
repeated use of any tool (be it a pencil, a computer, or a machine in a
workshop) we become more and more fluent in its use and are able to
deploy it more effectively. Through continued use of the tool we may begin
to identify how it can be used in new ways.

Left
First-Year Presentation
Verbal skills are often overlooked or underestimated by students, but it is the ability to speak about their work that will often prove vital throughout their education and professional practice.

Written skills are equally important. Whether in professional practice or in further academic study, an architect's ability to write about their work or methods is important. In the professional environment architects are called upon to write for a number of different reasons. At one level there is a clear need to be able to write letters (to clients, contractors, consultants, etc.) that are clear and precise. Additionally there will often be situations in which a report may be required—for submission either to the client, a statutory authority, or another professional body.

Throughout the experience of studying architecture students are required to submit written works. These may be short essays related to history and theory, reports on research undertaken in relation to a design brief, or a piece of reflective writing to accompany their design project exploring what has been learned in the project. In some institutions a major piece of writing—for example, a dissertation—may be required in order to complete a degree. All of these help to support the development of good writing and critical skills, which are going to be needed in the future.

Verbal skills, however, are also very important. Architects are often called upon to speak about their work, either to an individual or to small and large groups. Whether in a one-to-one meeting with a client or a presentation to a large group of people for planning consideration, having good verbal skills is essential. Not only does the ability to talk about their work support architects' interactions in professional practice, it is also invaluable in the development of their design work. The language of criticality is part and parcel of both education and professional practice.

The development of verbal skills in presenting, defending, and debating a student's work is supported through a number of different types of teaching and learning activity. On a fairly regular basis students will have interaction with their peers and their teacher through tutorials and studio crits. However, it is in the more formal events, involving a student presenting to an audience, that verbal presentation skills are truly tested. It is important to remember that this is, again, a skill that will be required in professional practice. When competing with other designers for a large commission an architect may be asked to present a set of ideas to a client team. Or they may be called upon to present and defend their designs at a planning committee meeting in order for their client to obtain planning permission. Clearly these are different audiences and therefore different types of presentation will be required, but it is vital that an architect is able to communicate both through the drawings and models that describe their design proposal, and through explaining their work to both specialist and non-specialist audiences.

Professional experience

As we have seen, in most countries it will take about seven years to become a qualified architect, including some period of required professional practice. However, simply getting a job and working for a couple of years will not necessarily provide a candidate with the experience required. It has long been recognized that for an individual to be prepared to practice architecture, there is need to ensure that their initial experiences in the profession provide them with exposure to the range of issues that architects must address in their professional lives. To this end, many countries have now put in place specific systems to ensure that anyone progressing toward professional qualification will have had the necessary experience both to pass the examination (if that is a requirement) and to be familiar with the professional responsibilities associated with architectural practice.

In order to explore the importance of professional experience we will look in detail at the US and UK models for an architect's qualification. These systems have some similarities, but there are enough differences to allow us to see different approaches to effective development through professional experience. Many other countries will have similar structures in place, and anyone considering qualification in a specific country should study its requirements carefully.

Professional experience in the USA

The structure in the USA for the study of architecture is typical in the amount of time that it takes to become an architect, but the breakdown of years and the subsequent professional experience can take various, slightly different forms. As we have mentioned before, the model for most of the educational institutions in the USA is two years of liberal arts followed by two years of architecture in order to achieve a Bachelors degree (BA, BSc) in architecture. This is followed by either a one-year "professional degree" (BArch) or a two-year Masters degree (MA or MSc). There then follows a period of professional experience before taking the Architects' Registration Examination (ARE).

The US model tends to keep all professional-qualification-related activity until the completion of both education and professional experience, unlike the Royal Institute of British Architects (RIBA) equivalent in the UK described below. Rather than set a number of years as the target for professional experience, the American Institute of Architects (AIA) sets the target as a number of "training units." The required 700 units are spread across 16 areas representing the range of activities an architect is normally required to undertake in professional practice. This Intern Development Program (IDP) is a joint initiative by the AIA and the National Council of Architectural Registration Boards (NCARB). Similar to the RIBA scheme, it is a structured way in which the registration body can ascertain that candidates for professional qualification have engaged in the appropriate professional activities.

The IDP scheme also calls upon the profession to support candidates through the process of preparing for qualification. In this case there will be two individuals from professional practice who will be responsible for supporting the candidate. The Supervisor will be a qualified architect within the office in which the candidate will be working, and this individual will have daily contact with the candidate. The Mentor, who will usually be outside of the office, will act to monitor the candidate's progress throughout the period of the IDP with meetings held every six months, and will also sign the candidate's records.

Through the Intern Development Program candidates for professional qualification in the USA are prepared for both the rigors of architectural practice and for the Architects' Registration Examination (ARE).

Professional experience in the UK

In the UK the normal pattern for the study of architecture is three years of undergraduate study, followed by one year of professional experience, then a further two years of postgraduate education, and finally another year of professional practice. In courses validated by the Royal Insititute of British Architects (RIBA), students will achieve RIBA Part 1 exemption upon successful completion of their three-year undergraduate degree. Upon completion of a further two years of postgraduate study the student will have achieved RIBA Part 2 exemption. With the requirement for two years' professional experience completed, the candidate is able sit the RIBA Part 3 examination. Many take a further short course to prepare for this final exam.

During the periods of professional practice, prior to RIBA Part 3, students will be required to keep a record of the types of activity that they are undertaking in practice. The RIBA Professional Experience and Development Record (PEDR) provides a structured way for students to present evidence of their engagement with the different areas of work required to fulfill the professional-practice element of their progress toward qualification.

The PEDR system divides professional experience activities into seven areas. In each of these areas a candidate will record the number of hours spent as a participant or an observer of specific aspects of professional practice. Further, the PEDR forms require that candidates reflect upon their experiences in order to identify what they feel they have learned in the process. By recording the details of the types of work that have been undertaken, and reflecting on this experience, the PEDR system encourages the candidate to put into context their learning through experience. It is intended that this will support the development of good practice.

Support for candidates to achieve the necessary professional experience comes from the schools of architecture as well as the profession. Each school provides a Professional Studies Advisor (PSA), whose role is to act as an advisor to the student and the employer, and to ensure that all parties are clear in how they are meeting the requirements of the RIBA and the Architects Registation Board (ARB) in providing the candidate with appropriate professional experience. The PSA is also required to review and sign records from the candidate every three months. The PSA has a very important role in making sure that the candidate is on the right track to complete the necessary range of professional-practice experiences that are required, and to ensure that the employer is also working in the candidate's interest.

From the employer's side the RIBA asks that the practice identifies an Employment Mentor, usually a qualified architect, to act as the candidate's advisor, guiding them through the various parts of professional practice and helping them to complete their experience in necessary areas. The Employment Mentor will be required to sign the candidate's quarterly record, verifying that he or she has completed the required hours in specific areas of practice. This may sound like a complicated process, and employers might be reluctant to engage candidates as a result. In reality, it is usually in the interest of the office to provide the candidate with support and guidance, as this will ensure that the work done by the candidate clearly relates to the needs of the practice.

This might sound like a very involved process simply to get a couple of years of professional experience before sitting the RIBA Part 3 examinations. In reality the use of PEDR should be relatively easy in the context of any office that is providing the necessary support to the candidate. With the support of the Employment Mentor and the Professional Studies Advisor, those progressing toward qualification will have the best opportunities to prepare themselves for the RIBA Part 3 exam and for professional practice.

Above
During the period of professional experience prior to qualification, structured programs such as the AIA's IDP or the RIBA's PEDR require both educational institutions and practices to work in supporting candidates to ensure that they are receiving the necessary range of experiences to prepare them for qualification.

Choosing an office

As may well be imagined from the issues previously discussed, choosing the
right office will be crucial in ensuring that a candidate is able to achieve the
necessary professional experience. With the structure of the IDP or PEDR
schemes there is a strong sense of support from the profession, and therefore
candidates are more likely to achieve the required experience. However, it is
still important for the candidate to make sure that they choose the right office
in order to gain the experience that will be most valuable to them, as well as
achieving the requirements. What should candidates look for? And what
should they avoid?

One of the perennial questions is whether to work in a large or a small
office. This is often a matter of preference. A large office will provide
opportunities to work on large projects, but may mean working on only one
scheme—although one may work on many different aspects of that scheme.
In some respects this can be a positive experience, as it will allow some
continuity (if a candidate is able to follow the project through a number of
different stages). However, large projects can take a very long time to move
forward, and some candidates may find that they are not able to get the full
range of experience in the time available. There is no limit to the amount of
time that a candidate can take to achieve their required experience—although
most will aim to finish it as soon as possible, they may choose to extend the
time period in order to follow a project through a number of stages.

Working in a small office can be a very rewarding experience, and will
often allow a candidate to experience a very broad range of professional
practice aspects. However, small offices will often have projects that are of
a similar character and may not cover all the types of work that one might
hope to encounter. For example, a candidate may find that a small office is
predominantly engaged in residential extension projects. In this case, the
range of clients with whom a candidate may come into contact and the types

of construction that they would be able to observe would be limited. However, in contrast to a larger firm working on large projects, in a small office it is more likely that the candidate would actually have contact with the client, be able to take a more active role in site visits, and so on.

Choosing the right office for professional experience is really a question of being forward-thinking in terms of the direction in which a candidate would like to see their career develop. Large and small offices each have benefits and potential drawbacks if a candidate wishes to see their career develop in a certain way. If they really want to work on large buildings and see themselves progressing within a large firm, then working in a small office may not be the best overall strategy for pre-qualification experience or longer-term ambitions. However, if they are interested in establishing their own practice as soon as possible, then the experience of a small office would most likely be invaluable. Thinking about pre-qualification experience in relation to the future will help to identify the kind of practice that will best serve both qualification needs and longer-term ambitions.

Professional examination and registration

Following the completion of the required professional experience, the final step in achieving qualification is usually that of sitting an examination. Again, each country will have a specific type and character of examination that is required. Some will be very complex, with many different aspects being tested, while others will take a more focused approach. Taking the USA and the UK as our examples once again, we can see two different approaches to the examination for professional qualification.

The examination in the USA—the Architects Registration Examination (ARE), which is administered by NCARB—is divided into nine sections. Six of the sections are multiple choice, while the remaining three are "graphic." The nine sections are:

- Multiple Choice:
  - Pre-Design
  - General Structures
  - Lateral Forces
  - Mechanical and Electrical Systems
  - Building Design/Materials and Methods
  - Construction Documents and Services
- Graphic:
  - Site Planning
  - Building Planning
  - Building Technology

The aim of the ARE is not to attempt to examine a candidate on every aspect of the profession of architecture. Clearly, this would not be possible given the range of issues that may come up in practice. Instead, the ARE is designed to test candidates on those areas in which architecture impacts on public safety, health, and welfare.

The multiple-choice sections of the examination cover the areas of professional practice where procedures, legal matters, calculation, and processes are of particular importance. The "graphic" parts of the examination are intended to test a candidate's ability to design and detail in accordance with legal restrictions (planning rules, building regulations) and to use appropriate technologies and techniques to achieve a suitable solution. In design terms this exam is not intended to judge whether the candidate is a good designer, but whether they are able to design within the requisite parameters and also to produce designs that are safe and that comply with regulations.

The UK examination process is different, both in terms of the type and the aim of the examination. After the requisite period of professional experience has been completed, the candidates will usually undertake a further course that is recognized as providing RIBA Part 3 exemption. Many of the schools of architecture offer such courses as part of their architecture curriculum. The nature of these courses varies widely, with some of them lasting only a few weeks (and requiring full-time attendance), while others may be a course spread over one year requiring only part-time attendance. Generally speaking such courses do not engage in design projects, rather they will concentrate on the business and legal aspects of professional practice (such as practice management, project management, planning legislation, contracts and contract law, etc.).

The examination to achieve RIBA Part 3 comprises three elements:

- Professional Experience Development Record
- Documentary Submission
- Interview

The evidence of appropriate professional experience, as documented through the PEDR discussed previously, provides the examination board with the confidence that the candidate has engaged in professional practice across a range of areas and is sufficiently familiar with these to be ready for qualification.

The Documentary Submission is the largest element within the RIBA Part 3 examination. This body of evidence is intended to provide the examination board with a context within which to evaluate the candidate's experience and familiarity with architectural practice. The submission must include:

- A curriculum vitae, which outlines the candidate's professional experience (both in architecture and in other occupations) and education.

- A professional experience evalution—this is a self-reflection on the candidate's experience in architectural practice, and may include drawings, photographs, and letters. The aim is for the examination board to be able to evaluate the candidate's own view of their progress and experience.

- A case study, which documents the candidate's experiences and evaluation of the process of working on a single project. This will normally take the form of a written document (supplemented with drawings and photographs, as necessary). Where a single project does not provide the candidate with sufficient material to evidence engagement with the full range of experiences (as required by the PEDR), a candidate may choose to write about their involvement on a number of projects with specific experience gained in each case.

- Assessed coursework, examinations, essays, etc. The content of this part of the submission will vary depending on the course and the institution. Many courses rely on the sitting of a written examination for candidates to evidence their knowledge and understanding. Some schools will set "scenario-based essays" as a means of assessing the candidates' knowledge. In the case of either a written examination or an essay, candidates will be expected to present their answers in clear and concise language. It is not necessary that a candidate "have all the answers," and it is expected that, where necessary or advisable, a candidate is aware of when to seek advice from a senior member of a practice or from other professional consultants (such as an engineer, project manager, etc.).

The interview is conducted in relation to the submitted evidence. There will normally be two interviewers. One is a "professional examiner," appointed by the university or college from a list of examiners provided by the RIBA, who will be asked to comment on the candidate's achievement of the RIBA Part 3 criteria. The other interviewer usually will be from within the awarding institution, and will be tasked with reaching a consensus decision with the professional examiner. Both interviewers will be qualified architects with considerable professional experience.

The interviewers may choose to pursue some specific aspects of the candidate's experience where the submitted evidence is not sufficient to fully express the candidate's understanding of the issue. Similarly, the interviewers may wish to invite the candidate to talk more about their own sense of development and learning through professional practice. Above all, it is important for candidates to remember that the interviewers are not looking for ways to "trip them up" or "catch them out," but are looking to assess the candidate's ability to discuss their work and experience in an informed manner. As discussed above, an architect's ability to communicate verbally is an important part of the way in which they are able to interact with clients, consultants, and others. Therefore, the interview is also a way of assessing a candidate's readiness to engage in a discourse about their profession.

3.

Most of the work done by architects is undertaken for a client. While, as we will see later, there are instances where architects may undertake work that is speculative or research-oriented, these will be less frequent and generally do not create income directly. In the vast majority of cases it is the needs and aspirations of a client that the architect seeks to address and ultimately satisfy. As we have seen in Chapter 1, the relationship between architect and client has changed dramatically over time. However, the client remains a driving force in the professional activities of an architect.

Beyond the initial step of identifying a potential client there comes a series of issues that must be considered in order to ensure that both client and architect are able to work together. More than simply the issue of cost (although establishing an agreement on fees is important), there are personal as well as professional relationships that must be established and maintained in order for a project to run smoothly. This chapter explores the steps that are necessary to establish the architect–client relationship and to agree the terms under which the project will develop.

The client

Clients come from all areas of life, from individuals to corporations to governments—and everything in between. The role that the client plays varies greatly depending on the nature of the project in question. The specific requirements of the client will also vary depending on the scale of the project. While a single family residence and a large apartment building are both about living space, there is a clear difference in the way that the architect will need to address each project and its client.

Left
MAAD, Residential Remodeling, London, UK
No matter the size or type of project, the establishment of a good architect–client relationship will play a crucial role in ensuring that the project develops and progresses. For the client this relationship may be one that reassures during a complex process. For the architect, maintaining a good relationship may lead to further work in the future. In residential projects, it can be crucial for the architect in understanding the client's needs and reassuring a client who may be undertaking building work for the first time.

Left, top and bottom
Enric Miralles, Scottish Parliament, Edinburgh, UK
Clients are as varied as the architects they hire.
Whether for a small residential scheme or a large
government complex, the client defines the initial
direction that a project may take. In working with
an architect, a client is both seeking a service and
looking for new ideas.

How do architects get clients?

It is often found that the most challenging part of architectural practice, particularly for sole practitioners and small firms, is in generating or finding project opportunities. As so much of architectural practice is in the service of clients, it is the "finding" of new clients and the maintaining of relationships with current/past clients that requires careful consideration. As a young architect, perhaps having only just started a practice, finding the first client is not really the problem; in many cases, it is having the first client that instigates one to establish one's own architectural practice. For architects, it is always the *next* client or *next* project that is the challenge.

Referral—word of mouth

The vast majority of clients come to architects via word of mouth or referral. Having worked for one person, company, or other organization, an architect will often find that work of a similar type starts to be more available. As their client speaks to others and (hopefully) tells of how successfully the relationship and the project developed, they are recommending an architect's services to others. Such referrals are, for small practices, their main source of work, and maintaining relationships with past clients is vitally important in keeping that referral process active. The difficulty with referrals is that they will tend to be of similar scope and type—a residential client will generally recommend the architect to others who are interested in having residential work done. Finding ways in which these referrals can expand the type of projects that are on offer requires careful maneuvring. Offering a residential client some assistance with design or specification services related to their work environment may help that client to realize that an architect possesses skills that would be of service to them in a different context. Such things may not lead to new kinds of project immediately, but they "plant a seed" that may grow for the future.

Below, left and right
Charles and Ray Eames, Eames House, Los Angeles, USA
Architects find clients via many different routes. In some cases an architect may be their own client—potentially giving the opportunity to explore new ideas in an experimental way. In the design of their own house, built in the 1950s, Charles and Ray Eames were able to explore ideas that would later appear in a number of projects for other clients. Their home thus became a testing ground for new architectural ideas.

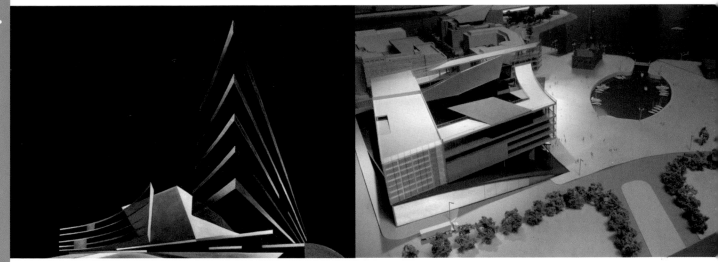

Competitions

For many young architects another way of breaking into a different market sector is through competitions. For large, established practices competitions offer another way of gaining projects of large scale that support the continued work of the practice.

Competitions can be of many different types. Choosing the right competition is important in order to recognize what can be achieved by putting time and money into the process. For small practices there is a need to balance the work on competitions, which may not lead to fee income, with other work for clients that does generate fees. Competitions can be expensive in terms of direct costs, such as printing and model-making, as well as the time that is allocated to the design and presentation process. In some cases there may also be costs associated with registering for the competition, travelling to the site for information-gathering, and shipping the competition entry to the judging panel. Despite these costs competitions remain both an exciting design exercise and a good way to generate new work for a practice.

Competitions are generally speaking of two types: open and invited. The open competition has less restriction on who may take part. While it may be that the person or teams must have a registered or qualified architect, the ability to obtain the brief and the information for the competition is open to all who register.

Having registered for an open competition, which usually involves paying a registration fee to cover the cost of the documentation, the procedure will usually go through a series of stages. Most open competitions will have a question-and-answer period, wherein competitors have time to ask questions of the organizers in relation to the documentation, rules, site, and so on. Once questions have been answered the competitors will then have a period of time in which to prepare their entries. All competitors will be required to make submissions in a specific format by a specific date. In some larger competitions this pattern may repeat with additional stages of competition. In multi-stage competitions the first round of judging will narrow the field to a small number of practices who will then be asked to undertake further work toward a final judging procedure to determine the winner. In many cases the second stage of a competition will see the practices involved receive a small fee in order to continue the development of their proposal. However, it is also the case that this fee is seldom sufficient to cover the costs of either the initial work or the second stage.

Invited competitions are those that have limited access. These types of competition are usually for very large projects where the scale of the project is such that only teams with experience of large-scale work would be suitable to take part. The scale of these large invited competitions is such that the entrants will often be a team of practices, each taking on a different part of the competition. For example, one architectural practice may act as the designer of the masterplan, within which other architects might work on the design of specific buildings, engineers might work on infrastructural aspects of the overall project, and other consultants may also be involved.

The judging of competitions can be varied as well. Most will have a panel of judges from a variety of sources. The client will usually be one of the judges, but in large projects the client may actually be represented by a team. In large, international competitions it is often the case that there are well-known architects and designers on the judging panel—and they may also have been involved in the development of the competition brief. Competitions that are related to public projects (those for local or national government, or receiving considerable funding from government) may also have judges drawn from local- or national-government agencies. There are also competitions in which the general public is involved in voting for the winning entry.

Not all competitions are related to the award of a building project. Most architects are more interested in competitions in which the winner will be awarded a contract for services, but there are also competitions that are purely about the generation of new ideas. Ideas competitions, while not resulting in built projects, can serve as opportunities for architects to explore new ideas and can, for the winning entrants, lead to positive publicity, which in turn might lead to further paid work. Ideas competitions may also lead to publication, and hence further opportunity for paid commissions.

Competitions as research

Architects may also choose to undertake competitions as a way of researching ideas and methods. They offer a practice a number of ways to combine different research methods toward design outcomes. For example, a small firm wishing to work on a large competition might develop collaborative relationships with other creative practitioners, in order to form a team to develop new ways of approaching the design brief. The team will undertake a variety of design, material, and process research in order to support

Above
Raymond Hood, Chicago Tribune Tower, Chicago, USA
Some of the most well-known buildings in our major cities are the result of architectural competitions. Through competitions a client is able to engage a number of architects to explore new visions for their project. In cases where the winning entry is built such a process can be a major step forward for an architectural practice. The importance of competitions is not always based solely on the winning entry. The competition for the Chicago Tribune Tower in the 1920s has become one of the most famous—while the winning entry by Raymond Hood has become iconic on the Chicago skyline, entries by Walter Gropius, Eliel Saarinen, and Adolf Loos continue to be recognized as landmark designs.

Left, top and bottom
Nekton, Turf City, Masterplan for Vatnsmyri
(Competition Entry), Reykjavik, Iceland
Competitions allow both designer and client to
explore the limits of what might be possible. For
the architect they allow the introduction of new
ideas and theories into their work. For the client
they provide an opportunity to find the best design
and understand the full possibilities of their project.

innovation in their competition entry. All of these will combine to support the
development of new ways of working for all participants in the team.

Competitions are also a way of exploring the boundaries of what is
possible. Whereas, when working on fee-paying projects, a practice may
need to take a more pragmatic approach to their design solutions (in order to
work within a budget or to meet a client's specific needs), a competition can
be more "open" in what would be considered an appropriate response to the
brief. Practices may choose to stretch themselves and break out of their
"normal" approach to projects, thus challenging their own (as well as others')
orthodoxies of design. This freedom is not simply a matter of "playing" with
ideas—it may lead to real benefits for the practice in terms of its approach to
design, and, if the competition is for a real project, such innovation may lead
to a winning competition entry. Some of the most prominent contemporary
architects began their practices based on winning competitions with designs
that were markedly different from those of their contemporaries.

Request for proposal

The other way in which architects sometimes gain clients is through a *request for proposal* (*RFP*) or *tender* process. This may be for a small or a very large project, but essentially this is a case in which a practice, either alone or in conjunction with other consultants, puts forward a proposal to provide services. Depending on the nature of the request for proposal, this may simply be an outline of the services that the team can offer or it may be a cost proposal for the project. If a cost proposal is to be included, the RFP will usually give some parameters within which the project should be considered. The process is often found in relation to large projects or those that are to be undertaken by a public-institution client. Within the European Union, for example, there is specific legislation that requires any project that will cost more than €148,000 or $200,000 (this varies depending on the type of work to be carried out) to be put to tender rather than directly appointing an architect.

Many of the projects that architects long to be involved in (such as schools, embassies, stadiums, etc.) are only available through a first round of requests for proposal or expressions of interest. Once a shortlist of suitable practices or teams has been selected, the process may move forward in a very similar pattern to an invited competition.

For smaller firms it can be a great challenge to be included in a shortlist based on RFP. In many cases the scale of the project may mean that larger practices with a "track record" are automatically more favoured. In order to break into this market a young practice may seek to form a working relationship with a larger, more established company. Such relationships may see the smaller or younger practice providing design services, with the more established firm providing technical and management services. Through such arrangements each participant gains a greater opportunity for success in the request for proposal process.

Above
Hampshire County Council Architects, Queens Inclosure School, Hampshire, UK
Some projects may require that architects provide information about their suitability and experience prior to being awarded a contract. This process, called tendering, is often the one adopted when public money will be used to procure the project.

Below
Herzog and de Meuron, Olympic Stadium, Beijing, China
Whether for a private residence or a major cultural building, each client will have their specific needs, which will form the basis for the architects' work. Meeting client needs is the starting point, but often architects will seek to go beyond need and address aspiration as well.

Types of client

Each client will have a specific set of needs, which the architect will try to accommodate. It is often the case that a client will suggest that they wish to hire an architect for one reason, but that—through discussion, research, and design—it will be found that the need is actually different to that which the client originally envisaged. Part of an architect's responsibility is to work with a client to ensure that the project is able to help the client achieve a better situation—whether in terms of their home, increasing business effectiveness, or creating space for lease or rent. How the architect deals with each client depends on the needs of that client. Understanding the difference between types of client can help architects to recognize the ways in which they can best work.

Private

When we speak of a "private" client we are usually referring to an individual or family. In most cases these clients will be seeking an architect to assist with some aspect of their home. Whether the design of a new residence, the

Left
Future Systems, Hauer King House, London, UK
Private individuals/families with residential projects are the type of client with which many architects start their careers. While some may progress toward larger and larger projects, many architects find great satisfaction in the close client relationship and the level of detail that they can explore in their private work.

renovation or extension of an existing home, or simply a new kitchen layout, such schemes (while small in comparison to other project types) may be one of the largest undertakings that a family could embark upon. The architect must therefore be careful to understand the needs of such clients fully, and to manage both the project and client expectations.

It is all too common to hear people talk of how the cost of a residential project spiralled out of control. Such circumstances could be caused by a variety of factors, but it should be the architect's role to ensure that the cost of a project does not exceed the client's means. This can sometimes mean saying "no" to a client who does not recognize that their decisions will increase the cost of the project. In many cases, cost overruns are related to changes that the client requests, either during the design process or after construction has begun. Because private clients may never have been involved in an architectural project before, it is an important part of an architect's role to help them understand the process as well as the pitfalls that may appear along the way.

Commercial

In considering commercial clients we are speaking of a very wide range of potential clients. These may include small companies looking to fit out a new office or store, a new restaurant wishing to create a unique environment for its customers, a clothing company looking to create a new identity for its stores, or a nightclub trying to change its image by redesigning its dance floor and bar areas. Effectively, commercial clients are interested in the use of design to enhance, support, or promote their business interests.

Left
Branson Coates Architecture, Katherine Hamnett Store, Sloane Street, London, UK
The success of a commercial project lies in the architect being able to understand the nature of their client's business and develop a design solution that supports or promotes that business. This can be a complex and challenging process, particularly with new companies or those going through changes. The right architectural design can be very important in helping a client define and support their commercial vision.

For architects to support commercial clients effectively they need to understand some basic things about commercial activity in general, and more specifically to possess an appreciation of the client's business. A commercial client will sometimes see design as a "value-added" part of their business. This means that while the design itself does not create more income directly, it can enhance the way in which customers experience the business and this can lead to indirect sales. Such issues require that the architect is able to understand the nature of the client's business, what they wish to achieve through the design, and some idea of the customer. Getting a sense of the relationship between these factors, as well as a client's budget and timescale, can be a challenge, but getting it right can have very positive results.

While every commercial client will have a different set of imperatives that drive their interest in engaging an architect, there are some things that are generic. In the majority of commercial projects the client will have a very specific budget that may be determined by external factors. In addition, most commercial clients will have a very specific timeframe within which to complete the works—and, again, this may be influenced by external factors. With these very distinct pressures it is sometimes the case that a commercial client is less concerned about quality in detail provided that the overall impact is visible, the project stays close to the budget, and is finished on time. The architect must remember that for every day that a commercial premises is not open, the client is losing money.

There are situations in which budget is not a factor. With some very prominent, high-value commercial companies (like haute-couture or designer-clothing stores) budget may be secondary. The obvious cost of a flagship store may even enhance the status that the company projects to its clientele. In such situations the quality of design and construction becomes the overriding issue, and the architect's role is to ensure that the highest standard is maintained throughout the design, specification, and finished project.

Corporate

Generally, corporate projects are office-related: either the fit-out of office space for a business, or the construction of a building that is specific to a company's needs. Such buildings might be, for example, headquarters, which contain offices for management and other executives, or a laboratory facility to support research undertaken by a pharmaceutical firm. As with commercial projects, the needs of a corporate client can be quite varied. Some, while wishing to commission a new headquarters, might seek a very cutting-edge design in order to project an image of innovation. Others, when seeking the same type of premises, will wish to have a conservative building that speaks of stability and longevity. The values of the company are, in these cases, being expressed by the architecture.

Architects are often engaged to plan the spatial layout of offices and workspaces. Although there may be no structural work related to such projects, the architect still plays an important role. Architects, owing to their

Above
Zaha Hadid Architects, BMW Plant, Central Building, Leipzig, Germany
In designing new office space for a corporate client an architect will need to address a variety of issues. There is a need to provide effective and efficient workspaces, but the client may also want the offices to act as an inspiration to both their workforce and their customers. Balancing a range of needs and aspirations is an important part of the architect's role.

Left, top and bottom
Kohn Pederson Fox, Proctor and Gamble World Headquarters, Cincinnati, Ohio, USA
Corporations are often the largest type of client for which an architect can work. As well as providing office space, the design of a corporate building may also seek to project the right image for the business. Some projects, such as the Proctor and Gamble World Headquarters, are of such a scale that they become an urban-design as well as an architectural project, reconfiguring a major part of the city around them.

education in creative problem-solving, are often able to see issues related to the way in which a company's workspace does (or does not) function effectively. Through careful spatial planning, as well as the design of those spaces, companies can increase productivity because their internal processes run more smoothly. In addition, the use of color and lighting in a considered manner, in relation to furniture and partitioning, can make the difference between an uninspiring workplace and one in which employees and management feel engaged and enjoy their work.

With the increase in the use of computers and technology, the nature of the workplace is changing rapidly. For those companies that are at the forefront of these changes the traditional office environment may be neither the correct expression of their values nor the right environment for their employees to work in. Architects, again, can be well placed to seek the integration of different (and sometimes conflicting) influences on the built environment.

As with general commercial schemes, time and money are strong forces in corporate projects. A company that is considering an office renovation will be concerned not just about the cost but also the amount of time it will take to complete the works. Each day that employees are unable to work at their desks costs money somewhere within the organization.

However, in regard to company headquarters (whether a new building or a major office-space renovation) we may see something along the lines of the commercial flagship store. In such cases a company may well wish to spend above the normal rate in order to project an image of both quality and financial health. Whether it is in the size of the building, the finish on the reception desk, or the furniture in the boardroom, the appropriate allocation of budget to those things that will provide the client with the correct "image" can help a company say the right thing to its shareholders and to new customers.

Developer

Not all clients intend to use a built project for themselves—at least, not in terms of living or working within the space that the architect is designing. Developers are individuals or companies that build speculatively. That is, they will see an opportunity (perhaps a demand for two- or three-bedroom apartments in the center of a given city) and will seek to capitalize on this by building to meet that demand. Developer-led projects can be of varying sizes—from individuals developing a house for sale or rent, to corporations developing a multi-use project that may be worth hundreds of millions of dollars.

A developer may be a single individual or a international corporation (and anything in between). The scale of the project will differ based on the nature of the developer, with some developers specializing in speculative commercial property (shopping malls, office space, etc.) and others concentrating on residential property (individual houses, apartment buildings, entire housing

estates). What is common to all, no matter what the developer's size or specialism, is that the basis of the project is the desire to generate more income than expense. When it is often the case—particularly with very large, developer-led projects—that the input funding comes from investors, it is a great imperative that the return on investment is maximized.

The relationship between an architect and a developer can take many forms. In some cases it may be a straightforward relationship like any other architect–client arrangement. However, in large developer-led projects architects may also undertake work speculatively. This is to say, they may do initial work for no fee based on the prospect that, should the project proceed beyond the initial planning or feasibility phase, then the architects will be paid a premium in line with the value of the project. While this may seem a risky venture it can lead to a large fee when the overall project value is measured in millions (or even hundreds of millions) of dollars.

The driving forces behind developer-led projects can be quite complex. As the main interest for the developer is in maximizing return on investment, there is a clear sense in which the lower the cost of the project and the higher the rent/lease/sale value the more profit the developer will make. However, this is complicated by the need to make the project attractive to buyers or tenants and to compete within a potentially highly volatile property market. As a result the challenge becomes a careful balancing act of designing a building that is attractive to the market (in terms of facilities, materials, design, etc.) while limiting the expense to the developer.

Opposite
Foster and Partners, 30 St Mary Axe, London, UK
Many large projects are undertaken by developer clients. These projects are usually speculative, in the sense that the developer undertakes the project based on a view that the sale or lease of space will recoup costs plus profit. For an architect such projects can often be exciting to design as the client will wish to have a building that is identifiable and notable in order to encourage potential buyers.

Left
Hellmuth Obata Kassabaum, Georgia Archives, Morrow, Georgia, USA
Increasingly, commercial activity within cultural institutions is an important part of the business model for such organizations. Therefore, architects working on new designs for museums, galleries, performance venues, and the like must develop strategies for integrating commercial activities within the overall program for the building.

Coop Himmelb[l]au, Urban Cabinet of Curiosities, Akron Art Museum, Akron, Ohio, USA

Entrance to new galleries.

View of existing museum with Roof Cloud.

Although most of the types of building that architects will be commissioned to design have been in existence for many years (if not centuries), there continues to be a need for rethinking the nature of these typologies.

As a building type the public museum was established in the eighteenth century (prior to this most collections were kept in so-called "wonder rooms" or "cabinets of curiosities" held by wealthy private or royal collectors). In terms of the use and facilities of a museum, the basic program of the building-type has remained relatively static until recently. While the display of collections continues to be the primary program of a museum, there is now increasing pressure to include retail, catering, and other facilities to further fund the museum.

For Austrian architects Coop Himmelb[l]au the museum has become a *new* typology, one in which the building is "an urban context." The museum has become a sign within the city, which acts as a projector of visual culture and the visual world. While still the containers of visual information, museums are now urban experiences in themselves. According to Coop Himmelb[l]au, the art should be able to extend beyond and spill out of the building and into the surroundings. This "in-between" space becomes one where boundaries are blurred—between public and private, high-art and street-art, and viewing and discourse.

In their design for the Akron Art Museum in Ohio, the architects have challenged the relationship between old and new as well as the traditional conceptions of the museum. The extension, completed in 2007, is divided into three areas— the Crystal, the Gallery Box, and the Roof Cloud— each serving as an interface between the urban experience and the gallery experience.

Each of these areas acts as a different aspect of the museum, while also working together as components of a heating and cooling scheme that aims to be both efficient and controlled, protecting the artwork on display. The Crystal acts as a new entrance, an interface between the old and the new, the museum and the city. Divided into "microclimate zones," it can be temperature-controlled in discrete areas, allowing for less energy use and a more responsive environment. The Gallery Box is a large, flexible space with few columns. By eliminating natural light in the Gallery Box the museum is able to ensure that there is no damage to artwork. The Gallery Box and Crystal use the large, cast-in-place, concrete floor slab as a heating and cooling element. The large mass of this floor, with water-filled tubes cast within, allows for a stable temperature environment to be managed without the need for mechanical ("forced air") systems.

While the new museum initially may appear jarring, with such radical difference between the new and the existing, it is an embodiment of the history and transformation of both city and museum. Just as the museum becomes an urban experience, so too the city becomes a new expression. Akron, Ohio, like many former industrial centres (Akron was considered the "rubber capital of the world," owing to the establishment of the B.F. Goodrich Rubber Company in 1869), has had to transform itself. The Akron Art Museum is a new museum typology representative of the transformation of the city— a combination of historic and contemporary, the Classical and Post-Industrial.

Interior view of the Crystal.

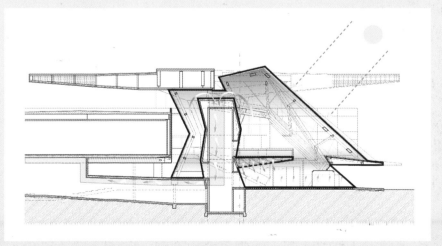

Environmental strategy diagram.

Institutional

Museums, galleries, theaters, and schools are all examples of what we may consider institutional projects. The client for these projects may be a private group, a trust, or a government-related or -funded organization. The main focus for such clients is to achieve a project that supports the aims and values of the institution while providing facilities to support or expand the operations of the organization.

Institutional clients can be very complex, owing to the way in which their funding is obtained. For example, a major art institution may receive the bulk of its funding through government support, but this will be based on application to the appropriate government department. In addition, it may need to secure further revenue through fund-raising activities with the public or other private-funding bodies. In this context the scope of the project will be constantly under review in order to ensure that the institution is able to afford it. It is not uncommon for such institutional projects to start with one set of parameters only to have this alter several times, as funding arrangements change.

When working for institutional clients, architects must take into account a wide range of issues. First, there is the need to understand the values and aims of the institution. Whether it is a contemporary art gallery or a national theater, the architectural design must reflect the way in which the institution wishes to present itself to the public. But achieving success with an institutional client will not be achieved merely by providing them with a building that meets their functional requirements and expresses their values. Increasingly, institutional organizations must engage in other activities in order to generate revenue. Thus, the gallery has a café, the museum has a store, the theater has a bar, and so on. The architect must work to balance these additional commercial activities with the aims of the institution, while also ensuring that the range of activities can be accommodated within the budget and the physical space.

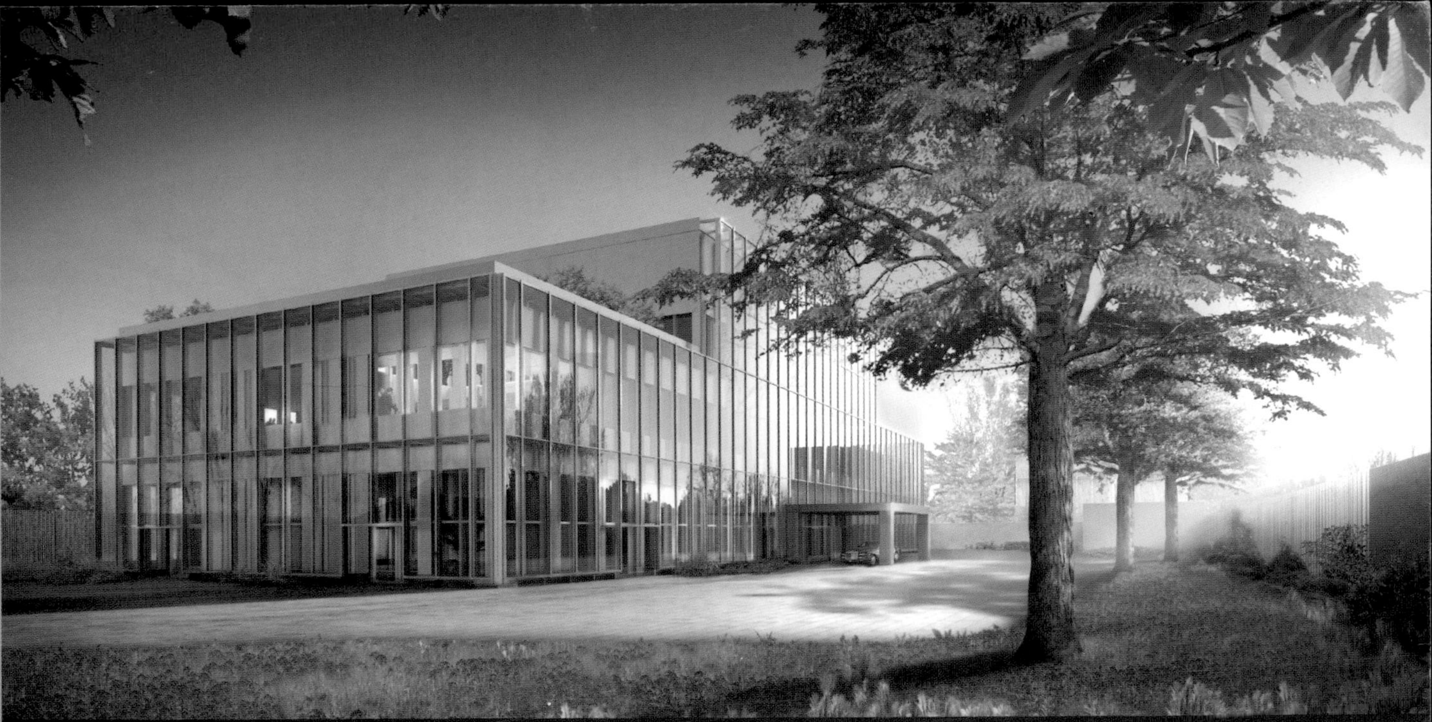

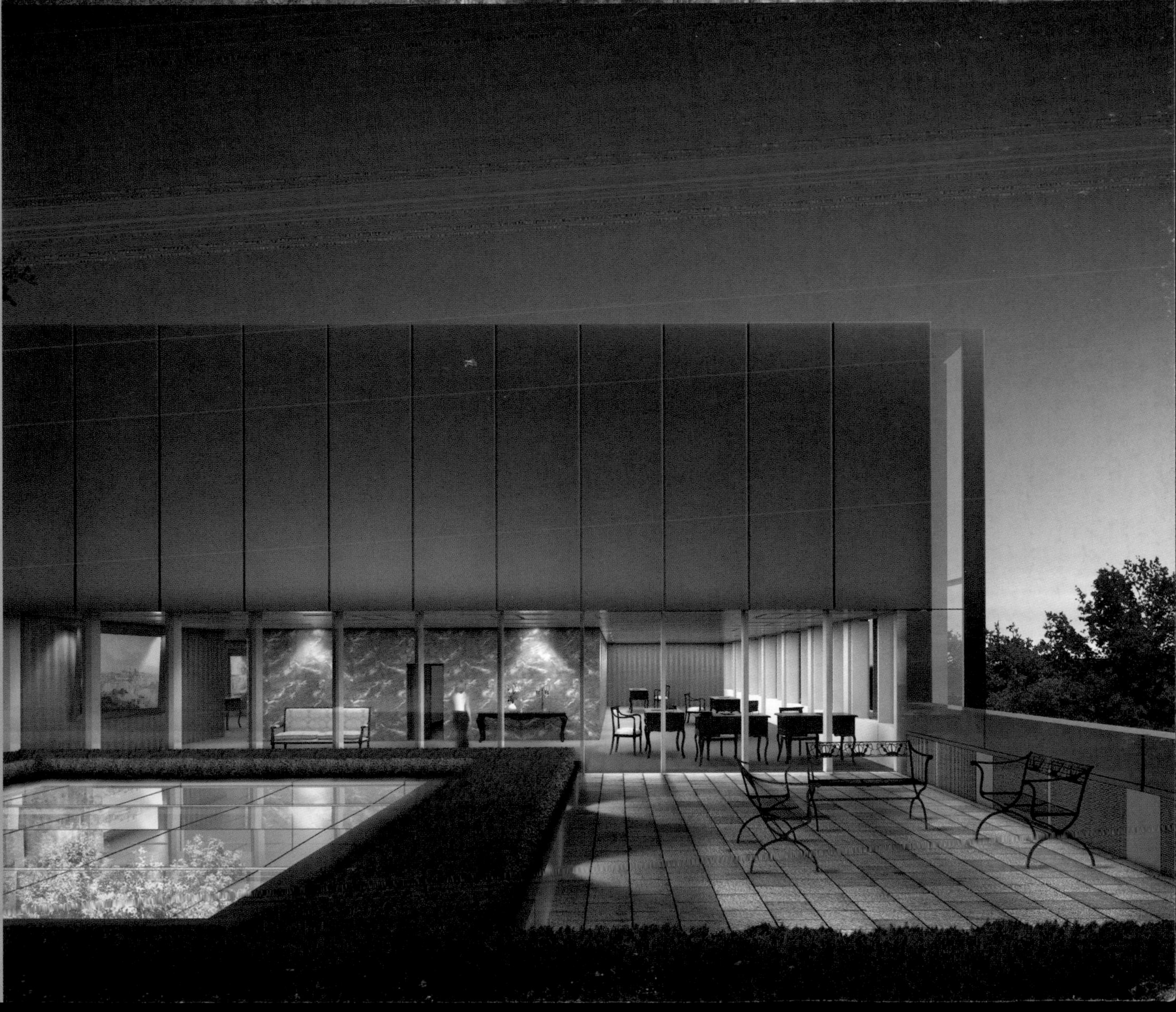

Institutional clients often select an architect via competition or requests for proposal. In some cases, as we have mentioned above, this may be specifically required by legislation (because of government funding). For the architect such clients (whether via competition or other means) are valuable, as a major institution will often be a notable project and to be associated with it can lead to further work from the same sector.

Government

As a client, local and national governments commission architects for a wide range of project types on different scales. The appointment of an architect in relation to a government client is increasingly undertaken by RFP. The types of project that a government may commission will depend upon the locality or nation in question, but might include such projects as schools, hospitals, office buildings, and embassies.

Increasingly, architects working for government clients in some parts of the world need to take into account issues related to the maintenance of security for personnel as well as property. While many older embassies, for example, have been "retrofitted" for increased security through the addition of concrete barriers around their perimeter, new embassies integrate this need for protection within the design—and in some cases have rendered the increased security provisions almost unnoticeable to the visitor.

The funding of projects in which the government is the client, as with institutional-client projects, can comprise a complex set of issues. While there is the need for accountability in the way in which public funds are spent, this is complicated by the fact that the funding may sometimes be related to specific allocations made further up the government chain. In many situations there will be specially defined contracts for the appointment of consultants, including architects, in relation to government-related work. As with

institutional projects, government clients can be very good for architects as it is often found that once a firm is on the list of "preferred suppliers" further projects will become available. Should one be privileged enough to be commissioned for a major government project this may well raise the firm's profile and awareness with the public, leading to other potential clients.

The architect–client relationship

As we have seen, there are many different types of client, each with some unique aspects as to how an architect must consider their needs. What is common to all of these types is the need for the architect to develop the proper relationship with the client. A poorly managed client relationship can lead to a less successful project and, in extreme circumstances, may lead to the loss of the client altogether.

Depending on the type of client the architect may take a very personal approach to the relationship or a very businesslike approach. With a private client who has never worked with an architect before, and who might be undertaking their first design and building project, an architect may take

Above and left
Wannemacher Jensen Architects, Coopers Point Observation Tower, Clearwater, Florida, USA
Presentation drawings and models, particularly those produced at the start of a project, seek to give a client a sense of what the project may be like. Whether produced on computer or with pencil and paper, these drawings are intended more to give a sense of the project than what might actually be built.

a more personal and friendly approach in guiding them through the process. It is sometimes the case that an architect working with such a client will spend a good deal of time with the client, trying to understand their needs and allaying their fears. In residential projects for private clients a deep understanding of the client—the way in which they live, their daily activities—can be invaluable in helping an architect to understand how to interpret that client's brief. By contrast, with a commercial client the architect may develop a more businesslike relationship reflecting the professional relationship between two companies.

Maintaining a good relationship with the client is an important part of architectural practice. For many architects it is through past clients that a good proportion of new work will be found—referral or word of mouth is a good way for architects to generate new projects. It is, however, not always an easy thing to maintain a good relationship. Even when projects go well it can be a challenge to keep the relationship positive. It can be frustrating for a client to be told that there are problems or that they cannot achieve what they wish given budget or other constraints. Similarly, the architect may feel that the client is not taking their advice or appreciating their design direction. Throughout, the architect must try to balance the many competing pressures on both themselves and the client.

Roles and responsibilities

In any relationship, particularly business relationships, each party has certain roles and responsibilities. By ensuring that these are known and adhered to the relationship has a good chance of working for the benefit of all.

The role of an architect is to provide a client with a service. The nature of that service will vary depending on the client and the agreement into which architect and client enter. In general we may say that the role of the architect is to provide design services in support of meeting the client's needs. The architect's role is not to tell the client what they should or shouldn't do—although there is clearly a need for the architect to be able to advise the client when they may be making decisions that seem to run contrary to their stated objectives. Throughout the process the architect is expected to act in the client's best interest.

During the course of most projects the architect will be expected to present design ideas to the client for discussion and review. Once a design is agreed, the architect will develop those initial ideas into a set of drawings and specifications that can be used to build the scheme. Depending on the scale of the project, the set of drawings produced may be a few in number or hundreds of sheets. Similarly, for small projects there may be no specification (this information being included in the drawings), while for substantial schemes this document may run to hundreds of pages in multiple volumes.

The architect may also be tasked with the management of the construction contract. In this process, the architect acts as the client's representative in interacting with the contractor or builder. In this phase of a project an architect will make site visits to monitor the progress of the works, discuss any changes with the client and contractor, review the contractor's requests for payment, and provide any additional drawings or specifications required to clarify the construction issues.

We will go into more detail about the phases of a building project in subsequent chapters.

Complex/multiple clients

With the range of different client types that an architect may come to work with, and the increasingly diverse way in which projects are financed (especially large, developer-led, institutional or government schemes), the relationship between client and architect, and the role of the architect itself, can become complex.

For example, in some cases a large development may have more than one client. The overall development may see the architect contracted directly to the developer to design the shell (outer structure) of the building. If the developer is able to lease the building (or a major portion of it) to a tenant before the building is completed, then the developer and the tenant may enter into an agreement that sees the building being changed slightly to accommodate the tenant's specific needs. This might, in turn, lead to the architect working for one client for the design and construction phases of the outside of the building, but having another client for the interior of the building. Alternatively, it may be that two architects end up working on the same project: one managing the shell, and one the internal works (fit-out). In this case the two architects will need to develop a good relationship in order to ensure that both of their clients' needs are met.

The brief

In order for a project to commence an architect needs some idea of what the client requires. Defining these requirements is one of the most important aspects of the initial phase of a project. While it may seem like a straightforward notion—the client says what they need, the architect gets on with it—it is often the case that a client may not be completely clear about what their requirements are, or that the needs they express do not seem to match with what they seek to resolve.

The client's brief will also form a part of the contract with the architect. Therefore it is important that both parties are clear about what is to be considered in the project and the way in which it is described. As the contract is a legal document the language used within it becomes critical. For this reason it is often advisable that the client's brief is reviewed several times before it is deemed ready to form a part of the agreement.

A residential client may recognize a problem such as "we don't have enough space in our house because we have had another child." So, their expressed need might be "we need to build an extension to our house."

Initially this might seem a fairly direct and obvious solution, but it may be worth discussing with the client the way in which they are currently using their existing spaces. It may be that there is no need to go to the expense of building a new extension if a reconfiguration of the existing house would provide a better use of space, and thereby give the client the additional accommodation they require.

If we take a commercial client as a further example, we can see that there are definite economic benefits to the client in the architect rigorously "interrogating" the initial client brief. Let us consider the owner of a small clothing store who states that they "need a new store-display system, because customers aren't spending time in the store." The suggested problem is one of a lack of customer engagement with the shop and its product because of a lack of interest in the store environment. However, what would the client think if, having spent the time and money to have a new display system built according to the architect's design, they then found that there was no change in customer spending? Before simply embarking on the design of a new display system, the architect might consider spending some time observing the way in which customers experience the store. It may be that there is more required than simply replacing the old display system with a new one. An architect, when trying to establish and clarify the client's needs, must be an observer as well as a designer. It may be the case that the layout of the store is confusing or too crowded for customers to be able to enjoy the experience of shopping. In addressing this issue, as well as the display system, the architect may achieve an even greater return on investment for the client.

In the examples above there is an amount of "decoding" that is taking place when the architect is first presented with a client's requirements. It is not uncommon for an architect to feel the need to suggest to the client that their perceived solution to a stated problem seems to be at odds with what the architect observes. Our previous examples would suggest that the outcome of the initial work would lead to a rewrite of the client brief. This is not uncommon, and the brief will continue to evolve during the course of a project. The *initial brief* may provide only a general overview of the client's needs, without any specific detail. While this will almost certainly be too vague to allow for detailed design work to be undertaken, it can provide enough guidance for the architect to be able to begin work on the *feasibility* stage of a project.

As the project develops and more information is generated, both by the architect and via feedback from the client, the brief will become more defined. This second stage of the brief is often referred to as the *project brief*. The project brief will provide the overall direction of what the architect is to do for the client, including technical and managerial services and design. Following on from the project brief, the *design brief* will seek to define and clarify all aspects of the design of the project. The design brief is crucial, as it will have great impact on the overall character of the finished project. The final

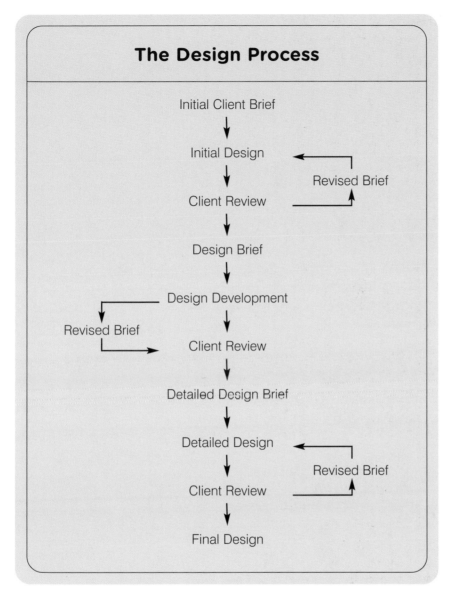

The Design Process

Initial Client Brief

↓

Initial Design

↓

Client Review → Revised Brief

↓

Design Brief

↓

Design Development

Revised Brief

↓

Client Review

↓

Detailed Design Brief

↓

Detailed Design ← Revised Brief

↓

Client Review

↓

Final Design

Left
The Design Process
Throughout the design phases of a project there is a continuous process of review and revision of the brief. Through each of the reviews and revisions, both the brief and the design become more refined and detailed, until the design is finalized and the project continues toward more information-production phases.

brief, also referred to as the *consolidated brief,* forms the grounding for the detailed design and construction information that will be required to take the project through to completion. In most cases an architect will ask a client to formally accept (usually in writing or by signing a set of drawings) the content of the consolidated brief, as this will be the document that informs the rest of the project.

What if the brief changes?

Early in a project one would expect the brief to change in any number of ways. As the project progresses, however, the changes should be fewer and fewer. Clarification, rather than change, should be the direction in which the brief moves. If, for some reason, the client makes substantive changes to the brief

Left
Carlo Scarpa, Brion-Vega Cemetery, Treviso, Italy
Throughout the course of a design project the brief
is constantly evolving based on the development
of the architect's ideas in response to client
direction. When this process of feedback and
development is structured well, and both architect
and client are communicating effectively, the
results can be both functional and poetic.

after the consolidated/final brief has been agreed, then it is likely that some of
the previous design work will have to be abandoned. Returning to this work,
to revise or redesign, will incur additional time for the architect and further cost
to the client.

Managing client expectation about the ability to make changes to a project
is often a challenging part of the relationship. While on the one hand the
architect is working for the client, it is also the case that this is a business
relationship and there is a need to ensure that the client does not see it as
their right to change their mind at will. Of course in some cases changes must
be made, but these should be minimized (as far as possible) so that neither
party will feel that they are being unduly burdened. The way in which such
situations can be best managed is by reference to the contract.

The appointment

When initial discussions with the client have reached the point at which
the architect feels prepared to put a fee proposal to the client, a letter of
appointment is issued. For very large projects, or complex clients, the form
of agreement will be written on a case-by-case basis and may well involve
the use of legal experts to ensure that all parties are fully protected by the
terms of the agreement.

Types of agreement (contracts)

In order to manage the architect–client relationship effectively and ensure
that there is a clear understanding of what is expected from both parties, a
contract is required. A contract is a legally binding agreement between parties
that sets out an offer, acceptance, and consideration.

Contracts need not be written. However, no matter how good the
relationship between architect and client it is in both parties' best interest
to have a written contract in order to ensure that there is no ambiguity or

Opposite
Sample letter confirming appointment.

NoName Architects

NoName

96 some avenue
new york ny10345
t: (212) 234-5678
e: query@noname.arch

30 August 2009

J. Doe
32 West 44th Street
New York NY 87609

Dear J. Doe,

Thank you for inviting us to act as your Architects in connection with:

- The design of a new home located at 456 Another Avenue, New York, NY 10023

This *Project Description* records your requirements as made known to me, and the information, which you have or will provide, to enable me to perform the Services.

I confirm my terms in this letter.

As per our discussions, the Services offered shall include:
- initial survey and drawing of existing conditions
- initial design proposals
- design development
- preparation and submission of planning permit (as required)
- preparation and submission of building permit (as required)
- preparation of construction drawings and associated schedules
- bidding and appointment of a general contractor
- administration of the construction phase

Based on this amount of work, the proposed fee shall be:

$15,000.00 (Fifteen thousand dollars)

Fees are exclusive of expenses, which normally cover statutory application fees (planning and building control), printing costs, and material/sample costs. Fees will be invoiced monthly, with the amount calculated to be in accordance with the stage of work that we have undertaken up to the date of invoice. All invoices are due for payment within 30 days of receipt.

I would recommend that a Structural Engineer be appointed as early as possible to assist you in obtaining Building Control approvals as necessary. If there are structural engineering firms that you have worked with or would prefer to engage I would be happy to work with them. However, if you wish, there are several engineering firms that I have worked with in the past and can recommend. If it becomes necessary to seek other appointments for the completion of our services I will advise you at the appropriate time about such appointments and the fees entailed.

In the unlikely event of a dispute or difference arising under this Agreement, without prejudice to any right of adjudication, it shall be referred to Arbitration. The appointment of an adjudicator or arbitrator shall be in accordance with guidance set out by the American Institute of Architects and the American Arbitration Association.

I confirm that the Effective Date of the Agreement (that is the date on which I will commence performance of the Services) will be 24 September 2009.

If these arrangements are acceptable to you, please sign the Agreement below and return one copy to our offices. We will forward a signed copy to you upon receipt.

Kindest regards,
N. Bloggs
Principal

MVRDV, WoZoCo Housing Estate, Amsterdam, The Netherlands

North façade detail.

Sometimes the client, who pays for the project, may not actually be the user or resident. In such projects an architect may be challenged to design in such a way that the finished project is able to meet the needs of both the commissioning client, who may have strict financial requirements, and the users, with their own specific functional needs.

Like many European countries, the Netherlands is facing a rapid increase in the number of elderly people within its population: a "grey wave," which puts increased pressure on local and national governments to provide health care and housing. Commissioned by the Het Oosten Housing Association, WoZoCo (1997) is a complex of 100 housing units for people over 55 years of age. The site itself was limited in a number of ways, which led to the innovative design of the project.

Amsterdam-Osdorp, the location of the project, is a garden suburb to the west of the Dutch capital. Initially built between 1950 and 1960 the development has continued to grow, and its density is now putting extreme pressure on the amount of green space available in the area.

The first challenge that MVRDV faced was the fact that the client-requested target of 100 dwellings was not possible, since the urban-development plan (established in the 1920s) restricted the number of units in a block to 87. Rather than reduce the number of dwellings, the architects took the radical step of proposing that the "leftover" 13 units be suspended from the north façade of the building, thus ensuring the required total without violating height and built-footprint restrictions.

The dramatic effect of these cantilevered housing units does, without doubt, make WoZoCo one of the most striking housing projects of recent times. The result is both unique and challenging, as there is no visible structure to suggest how such long cantilevers are achieved. In fact, the structure is hidden within the timber cladding and main body of the housing block. Such effects do not come about without additional cost.

The challenge of providing the full 100 units meant that the project would inevitably move beyond the client's budget. To address this MVRDV looked at the rest of the project in order to identify areas in which additional cost savings could offset the increased cost of structural innovation. Through the use of basic and standardized elements—such as windows, doors, and balconies—

View of north façade.

combined with simple plan layouts, the overall costs were kept within budget. This does not, however, mean that the project became simplistic apart from those cantilevered 13 units. On the contrary, by varying the placement and colour of balconies and windows in the south façade the project retains a dynamism that is rarely found in many comparable developments.

Through careful rethinking of their way of working with local planning guidelines, MVRDV were able to provide housing for the elderly users of the building while staying within the client's stated budget and unit numbers, and without reducing further the highly valued green spaces of the locale. A considered evaluation of the different pressures upon the project brief allowed the architects to design something both innovative and necessary.

View of south façade during construction.

misunderstanding of their rights and responsibilities. The more detailed the contract, the more it will serve as a good document to protect both architect and client. Should disputes arise, a well-written contract can help to alleviate much of the difficulty.

Tailoring contracts to projects

In most localities there are standard forms of agreement that can act as the template or framework within which contracts may be drawn up. Such standard forms clearly set out a range of services that an architect may offer a client, as well as some "additional" services, which may not be part of a typical project but that are likely to be encountered. In addition, there will be space in which to set out the client's requirements. Such standard forms of contract between client and architect will only be applicable to those projects that follow the traditional course: that is, typically, design, tender/bid (the process of getting builders to quote for the work), and build. With certain types of project (private residential, for example) this will account for the vast majority of cases, and the standard form of agreement will be more than sufficient.

However, where the nature of the client or the type of project deviates from the standard, it is necessary to consider other forms of contract. Again there are usually framework agreements to help set out the details of alternative arrangements, and these will give the architect and client a way to quantify and clarify the terms of their agreement.

The *design-build* contract is a form of contract that sees the architect having a different relationship with the owner of the building. Typically, the design-build system will see an organization—or, in the case of very large projects, a consortium—acting as a single entity in the overall process of delivering a project. In one configuration the architect may be commissioned by the contractor; this is referred to as *contractor-led design-build*. In such a case, while the architect will still work to the needs of the owner, the client (in terms of architectural services) is the contractor. The other form of design-build is one in which a design firm heads up the organization/consortium, and this is referred to as *design-led design-build*. In this arrangement the contractor will be employed by the architect/designer to undertake the construction phase of the project.

In practice design-build arrangements are chosen for situations in which the project is of such a scale that the owner wishes to streamline the communication processes among what may be a large number of consultants. In order for this streamlining to be effective it is often the case that a number of different stages of a project may be happening simultaneously. For example, while the architect may be working on very early design ideas, a planning application will be submitted (based on *outline* information), and initial cost estimates will be developing. All of these will progress simultaneously, and as elements of the design are agreed and *fixed* the contractor may actually start on site. Thus, information will be developed

Opposite
Sauerbruch Hutton Architects, GSW Headquarters, Berlin, Germany
Regardless of the size of the project, there will always be some form of agreement between the architect and the client. This contract will serve to ensure that both parties are clear about the scope, nature, and timeframe for the project. For a project such as the GSW Headquarters, which involved both new building and renovation alongside urban planning, the nature of the architect–client contract had to take into account a range of different types of service that the architects were providing.

in *contract packages*, which follow the construction process. So once the overall form of the building is defined foundations might begin, while the detailed design of the upper structure is still being developed, and so on.

There are some potential drawbacks of the design-build process. Cost estimating can be difficult because there is only partial information available. It can be the case that decisions made early in the process can lead to unforeseen costs later on, or that changes are difficult to accommodate owing to the fixed nature of the earlier packages. Because of these challenges the owner puts a high level of trust in the consortium to deliver a project to specification and cost. While the single point of accountability can make this process easier to manage, it does not ensure success.

In some instances the architect may be asked to take the role of the leader of a large team of other consultants on behalf of a client. Such *project management* contracts may see the architect not as designer, but as coordinator of the design and consultancy work of other architects. The *project manager* is charged with ensuring that the client's requirements are being met by the different parties involved in a project. This duty may include the development of the client's brief, the appointment of a design architect and other consultants, management of the design process, and construction management.

Above
Wilkinson Eyre Architects, Gateshead Millennium Bridge, Tyneside, UK
Architects do not only design buildings: they are unique in their professional capacity to engage in a wide range of services for clients. Whether it is in the design of a building, a bridge, or a new range of cutlery, an architect's education prepares them to take on many different roles. In addition there are times when architects do not design, but manage the overall project process. In such cases it is their understanding of both the design and construction processes that allows them to have an overview of what can be an extremely complex operation.

As mentioned previously, in order for there to be a valid contract there must be several things present. We can now put specific names to these parts of the agreement:

- The offer will be set out as a combination of the initial brief and those services that the architect may be offering. If using one of the standard forms, the services will usually be listed in the contract template.
- The acceptance will, as usual, be the client's signature, confirming that they have accepted the terms of the agreement. The architect will also sign the contract, confirming that they agree to provide the services offered in return for the consideration.
- The consideration will be the fee that the architect is charging for the services (we will look at fee calculations shortly).

A client may wish to include some scheduling information within the agreement. This may take the form of an estimate of time allowed to reach specified phases of the project, or an overall project time-period. While it is perfectly reasonable for the client to wish to have some sense of how much time the project may take, it must be made clear that any schedule offered is dependent upon a timely flow of information from the client and other consultants.

In providing estimates of time it is necessary to ensure that the dates offered are realistic and achievable. There is nothing to be gained by suggesting to a client that something can be done in a short period of time if that is unlikely to happen. Similarly, where there are statutory requirements (planning permission, building regulations approvals, etc.) it may be the case that a considerable "buffer" needs to be included to allow for delays caused by the statutory bodies. The architect must make clear to the client those issues and obstacles that may arise during the course of the project. There is nothing so frustrating to a client as discovering that things are taking longer than suggested and not having been forewarned about potential delays.

Fees

Of course one of the things that both the architect and the client will wish to have specified in the agreement is fees. This can be one of the most difficult parts of an agreement. On the one hand the client will wish to keep the overall costs of the project low, and professional fees can often be an area where they hope to make savings. On the other hand, the architect will naturally wish to be paid fairly for services rendered. The reconciling of these divergent positions can be difficult.

The fee is one of the elements that makes the agreement between architect and client a binding contract. Therefore it is vitally important that the fees are included in the agreement and are set out clearly.

Depending on the services being provided by the architect, the fees will need to be considered carefully to ensure that they are both fair to the client and reflect the amount of work to be undertaken by the architect.

Some professional organizations offer architects and clients guidelines as to how fees may be calculated. The usual method for establishing the architect's fees in relation to the project is by using a percentage of the estimated construction cost. This method, which has been developed over time, sees the amount of work that the architect must do in relation to the size of the project and sets the fee percentage accordingly. Generally, these percentages are for a standard set of services. When limited services, or special services, are being provided the fee will need to be adjusted.

What may be surprising is that the smaller the project the higher the percentage. This is intended to reflect the fact that there is not that much difference between the amount of work that is required for a small project and a larger project. Many of the requirements—such as planning applications, building regulations approvals, design meetings, and so on—will still be necessary regardless of project size. Thus, for smaller schemes the percentage fee is higher in relation to the overall project cost.

With very large projects the fee percentage of the overall construction cost will be much lower. This reflects the fact that with a large project a small percentage fee may actually be a considerable amount of money. It also reflects that there is likely to be an amount of repetitive information in the project. For example, in a large multi-story building it is typical to have a standard building "core" (usually the area that will include elevators, fire stairs, service areas, etc.) that will be repeated on each floor. Thus, once the building core is designed it does not need to be redrawn or detailed for each level. Similarly, many of the details associated with the doors, windows, fixtures, fittings, etc. will be standardized, and only need to be designed and drawn once. In this way we can see that there is an economy of scale that comes into play with large buildings.

Another way of calculating fees is on an hourly basis. It is typical for an architect's office to have an *hourly fee* scale that is used for special situations. In many projects, even when using the percentage method of calculating fees, hourly rates will be quoted as well to give the client some indication of the fees that may be necessary to cover non-standard work. The kind of non-standard work that might be encountered includes changes to the design after approval has been agreed, protracted negotiations in regard to planning applications, or additional services not included in the original agreement.

In setting out hourly rates it is also important to define the types of work and the rates that will apply. It is usual for a schedule of rates to be offered by a practice. At a minimum it will usually be the case that there will be three hourly fee levels to cover work carried out by the architect, the drafting team (these may be junior or assistant architects who are not yet fully qualified), and the administrative team (those who manage the company and carry out office/clerical work). In large practices, with staff at many different levels of experience and responsibility, the range of hourly rates may be more finely allocated and diverse.

While less common it is possible to structure the fee agreement for a project around hourly rates. There are several reasons why this can be a difficult way to agree fees. First, it is likely that the client will wish to have some sense of the overall costs for professional fees. Therefore, the architect will need to know quite closely how many hours the project will require. Secondly, there will need to be some way of ensuring that the number of hours quoted will be enough to cover the necessary work or else there will be the thorny issue of requesting that the client pay additional fees.

If the project is of a specific type, and the architect is very familiar with what might be required, then quoting a *flat fee* may be an attractive option for the client. A flat fee simply means that the client is provided with a quote for a specific amount related to a defined set of services. For the client this is a way of ensuring that they know exactly how much their architect's professional fees will be. However, for the architect it can be a challenging endeavour. If the estimate of the amount of time that has led to the flat fee is wrong, then there may be little profit in the project. Some examples of work that might be considered for flat fee would be basic design services (such as initial concept sketches), feasibility studies (the early phase of a project where the focus is on determining the parameters of the project), space planning (working out a set of options for how to arrange internal spaces within a building), drawing services (to draw basic plans for a planning application), or similar activities in which the scope of the service can be discretely quantified.

Choosing the right type of fee can be an important part of the agreement with the client, and can mean financial success or failure for the architect. The architect must balance the desire of the client to minimize their costs with ensuring that the fee provides fair remuneration for the amount of work to be undertaken. In finalizing the agreement between architect and client, the fee will often be a point over which negotiation is required. Clients are often in the position of having discussions with several architects, and it may not be solely on the quality of the architect's design work that a client will make their decision. Architects must maintain a competitive position with regard to their competitors, but must also ensure that they are not putting themselves (and the profession) in a difficult position by undervaluing the service they offer.

Having achieved a signed agreement with the client—which includes information about the brief, the services that the architect will offer and how much those services will cost—the architect will now be in a position to begin the main part of the project. The brief will act as the guide to the client's needs, while the agreement will form the legal framework within which architectural services will be provided.

Above
Ábalos & Herreros, Tour de la Chappelle, Paris, France
With projects that are won via competition, there will often be complex fee structures in order to accommodate the fact that the architects will have undertaken considerable work prior to the contract being awarded. However, architects will also recognize the value of getting competition-winning designs built for their longer-term benefits of promotion and publicity.

4.

Having secured a client and agreed the brief and the terms of appointment, the architect can then begin work on the project itself. Every designer will approach the beginning of a project by implementing a different strategy, based on their particular experience, their training, and the type of client. However, there are a number of stages that will be followed in order to ensure that the project is developing in response to the client's needs and requirements.

In different countries, and in relation to the different professional organizations, the name of these "stages" of a project will vary. In the UK the RIBA Work Stages help provide a good breakdown of the different phases that may form part of the project. In addition, these RIBA Work Stages establish a framework in which the architect may plan the project timeline, explain the process to the client, and also identify specific points for fee payments and other milestones. Within the USA, the AIA provides guidance on five stages of design, which help to define the broad project phases. Wherever the project, using an established set of defined work phases can help make the overall process more defined and clear for all parties involved.

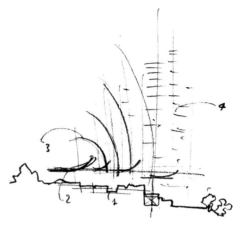

Above
Renzo Piano Building Workshop, Sketch for the Jean-Marie Tjibaou Cultural Center, Nouméa, New Caledonia
The start of a project will find the architect seeking to define its character. Through research, sketches, models, and discussion, the architect will then begin to establish a response to the client's brief.

Left
The Stages of Architectural Projects.

AIA "Five Phases of Design"	RIBA Work Stages
Originate	A – Appraisal
Focus	B – Design Brief
Design	C – Concept
	D – Design Development
	E – Technical Design
	F – Production Information
	G – Tender Documentation
	H – Tender Action
Build	J – Mobilization
	K – Construction to Practical Completion
Occupy	L – Post Practical Completion

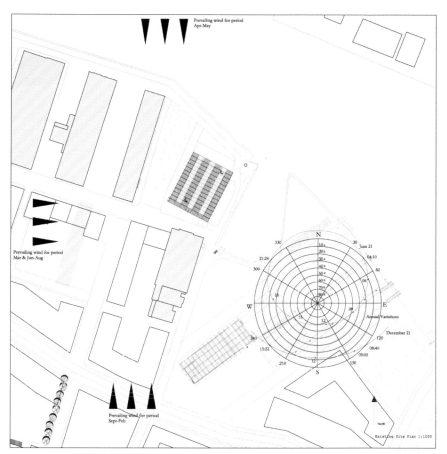

Left
Magdalena Prus, Site Analysis: Sun and
Wind Study, Gdansk, Poland
Establishing the feasibility of a project will require
a variety of research and analysis processes.
In some cases the establishing of outline costs
will be the main determinant (can the project be
completed within the client's budget?), while in
other cases it may be a question of environmental
impact (can the project be completed without
undue damage to the local environment?). The
feasibility process may see the project go through
fundamental changes, but the aim is to ensure
that what the client wishes to achieve can actually
be provided.

Inception and feasibility

The first part of any project, as we discussed in the previous chapter, is to
define the client brief. This is often referred to as *inception*. Once the brief is
agreed it is necessary to establish whether the project is actually feasible.

Inception usually involves a series of steps that will help to get the project
off the ground. Some of these are professional activities that are necessary to
avoid problems later, while others are about establishing the clear parameters
of the project. Together these phases will determine the overall aims of the
project for both client and architect, and will set in motion the rest of the
project structure and timeframe.

It will come as no surprise that one of the first steps is for the site to be
fully documented in order to understand the starting basis for the project.
Whether the site is an empty lot within a city, an open space in the
countryside, or an existing building/house, having accurate information
will be vital as the project moves forward.

The site-survey information can come from a number of different sources.
Obtaining drawings from the client may be the first stage in starting the
process of exploring and understanding the site. If the project is large the
client may have had a professional survey undertaken by a firm of specialists

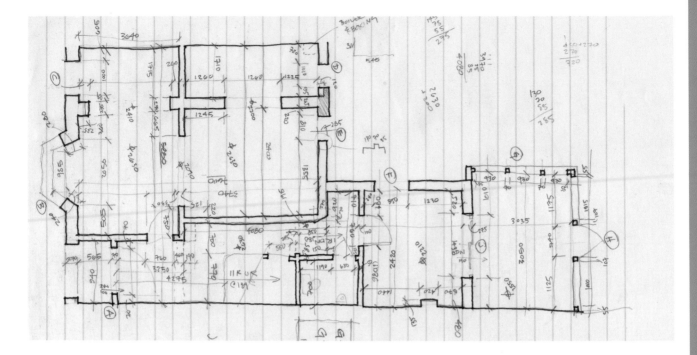

who can provide accurate information about the site in terms of levels, boundaries, and existing features (trees, buildings, etc.). It is also possible to obtain some of this information from commercial mapping services—an architect can specify the site location and the service will provide information for a set fee.

With smaller projects, and when working on existing buildings, it is often the architect who will take up the task of measuring and drawing-up existing conditions. For those members of a firm who have only recently completed university, or may be on their "year out" for work experience, this can be an excellent way to learn about buildings and to develop good drawing skills as well.

The accuracy of this initial information can be of paramount importance. Incorrect information at the outset, in terms of the size of the site or the position of existing features, can have an impact on both the design and the cost of the project. For this reason it is often necessary to spend a good amount of time verifying that site measurements are correct. In those cases where the client may supply drawings or survey information it is advisable for the architect to check this information with further measurements in order to ensure accuracy.

It is not just the measurements of the site that must be considered. There will also be information that, while not necessarily immediately required, may become vital at a later stage. It is best to try to gather as much of this information as possible at the outset. Such information may include:

- Orientation of the site—this will provide information about the amount of sunlight the site receives at different times throughout the year and may be important in developing the design.

Above
MAAD, Site Measurements, London, UK
For smaller projects the architect may undertake the initial survey—taking measurements to establish the existing conditions. For large projects a specialist surveying firm may be employed to provide detailed information about the existing site, soil conditions, and services.

Below
Bennetts Associates, Site Explorations, Basinghall Street, London, UK
The initial exploration of a site may lead to a number of issues for the feasibility study. In areas where there is the possibility of important historical material underground, an archaeological survey may be required by the local authorities. Should such historical finds be made there will need to be consideration of how to preserve or remove those finds before further work can begin.

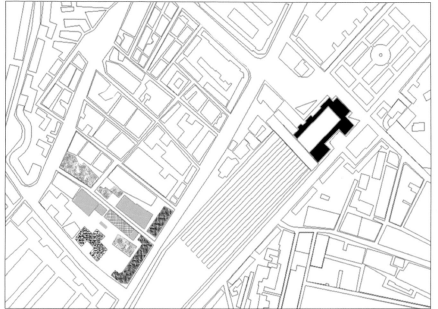

■ Gara de Nord station

▦ Proposed site

▓ 10-story residential block

░ 2- to 3-story residential blocks

▨ Commercial activities

▓ 7-story residential block

Above
Matteo Mantovani, Site Survey, Bucharest,
Romania
In exploring a site an architect may need to
consider a wider context than just the site itself.
Where the movement of pedestrians and traffic
may be important, the architect will explore a
larger area to establish the factors that affect how
people, vehicles, and goods move around the site.

- Height and location of surrounding buildings—this may be important in terms of the amount of shadow that falls on the site, but might also be relevant in terms of the restrictions that may be placed on the proposed design in terms of not restricting sunlight or views from the existing buildings.

- Height and location of existing trees—as above, this may be important in order to determine the amount of shading that is offered by the trees. In addition, if these are long-established and mature trees it may well be desirable (or even a requirement) to retain them.

- Traffic patterns—the movement of vehicles and pedestrians around and on the site may be important in terms of maintaining clear movement, and may also be valuable in determining how goods will be delivered to the site during construction.

- Soil conditions—whether the project is for a small addition or a new tower block, the existing soil conditions will be important in determining structural solutions for the subsurface works (foundations, basements, etc.). This will also provide information about the height of the water-table (the natural level of subsurface water), which will determine the type of damp proofing required to protect the building.

It is not uncommon for the initial stages of a project to be carried out under a separate agreement with the client. This is owing to the fact that the outcome of this phase may mean that the project goes no further—that it is not feasible, for whatever reason. As the inception and feasibility may be under a separate agreement it is important to establish the scope of the works to be undertaken in this initial stage of the project.

David Adjaye, IdeaStore, Tower Hamlets, London, UK

Whitechapel Road façade.

Entrance view with overhanging atrium.

The process of developing a brief may lead an architect to consider that the client's aims are not going to be met by their initial idea. In some cases the early phases of a project may lead the architect to suggest a different type of scheme to that originally considered by the client.

It has long been accepted that the public library provides a range of services that are very specific to a local community. However, it is also the case that this institution is increasingly under threat from reduced public spending as well as shifts in public attitudes toward reading and entertainment.

When Tower Hamlets, in London, decided to build seven new libraries across the borough they knew that they needed to take a fresh approach. Working closely with the client, architect David Adjaye sought to redefine the experience of the library and, more fundamentally, the range of services a library offers. This rethinking of the brief, while not necessarily what the borough had in mind, allowed the architect to show the client a new way of meeting their needs and the needs of their users.

While still a public library, the IdeaStore redefined the nature of the institution to include a range of services that encourages the community back into the library. As well as the usual functions the IdeaStore also integrates retail outlets, a café, and classrooms—with the aim of becoming a central focus in the lives of the local residents.

The design goes further to enhance the visitors' experience and to integrate with the community. Each floor is designed as a promenade, from where the visitor is able to see quickly the range of services offered and that also provides extensive views over the area. Along the Whitechapel Road, the main thoroughfare in this part of East London, the building's atrium overhangs the pavement and provides a sheltered location for the escalator. At the top of the building the café provides food and drink as well as stunning vistas across London— all features that serve to entice members of the community into their new library since 2005.

Internet workstations.

Where the inception phase looks to establish the basic information about the project and the needs of the client, the feasibility phase will consider whether the project is possible. Such an investigation will need to look at:

- Cost—can the type of project envisaged be achieved within the initial budget that the client proposes? This will, in turn, be based on a range of issues, from site conditions to changes in the economy and professional fees.

- Statutory obligations—are there issues in relation to planning or the environment that may adversely affect the ability of the project to meet the needs of the client?

- Procurement—under what form of contract will the project be completed? There may be both cost and time considerations to be explored in undertaking the project through different forms of contract.

In some cases looking at feasibility may be a simple process of considering the amount of work that the client has defined in the brief in relation to the amount of money that the client suggests they are willing to spend. It can often be the case that a client, particularly one who has not undertaken architectural projects previously, will have a distorted view of the cost of building, and it is best to identify such problems early. Similarly, on a large scheme there are a great many variables that can affect its overall cost. For a project that may take years to reach completion, fluctuations in the local/national economy can increase costs considerably as it will affect land values, material-supply costs, labor costs, and so on. In either of these situations, the client will need to decide very early on how they wish to proceed. Either they will need to adjust their ambitions for the project (e.g. reduce the size, scope, or specification) or increase the amount of money they are willing to spend. This can be a very difficult phase of the project, and the architect will need to work closely with the client and other consultants in order to ensure that the best balance can be found in the relationship between costs, scope, and specification.

Another part of the feasibility of a project is the consideration of whether the scheme will provide the client with a solution to their perceived problem (as defined through the brief). It is possible that the assumptions that were used during the setting of the brief will need to be tested in more detail. For a commercial client this may require some work to explore the potential return on investment. For example, can the size of store that may be within budget allow for the requisite amount of merchandise to be on display, which, in turn, would allow for the amount of potential sales required to offset the building costs? Similarly, for a developer, given the size of a site and planning restrictions, would the proposed new building be able to accommodate the number of units (flats, houses, etc.) that could be sold or rented at a market rate to make the building affordable?

For projects located in specific areas this feasibility study may also include issues that are related to the environment. Architecture has a

significant impact on the environment, both in terms of its use of materials
and the way in which the design of a particular project can affect the local
environment. With projects located in environmentally sensitive areas there
will often be a requirement by the statutory authorities for an *environmental
assessment* or *environmental impact study* to be completed. Such studies
can be lengthy, intensive, and costly, but are important as they will help the

authorities to gauge what effect the proposed project will have on the environment and will help the designer and client to consider ways in which the impact can be minimized—or, in some cases, the project might even be designed to help or enhance the environment.

Scheme design/schematic design

Once the feasibility of the project has been established it is possible to start a more developed design process. At this stage, designs will still lack detail but the team will be looking toward developing ideas in response to the issues raised during feasibility. Where the feasibility stage will have defined certain parameters for the project, the initial design phase will explore what can be achieved within those parameters.

Typically, the outcomes of the initial design phase will be drawings and models that set out both the overall form and scale of the proposal. There may be detail given in relation to aspects of the design, but this will remain flexible in order that changes can be accommodated as the design continues to develop.

As part of this phase of the project there will be a good deal of research and conceptual development. This stage will be crucial in defining the character of the design as well as the physical parameters of the project. Site research will provide the design team with a range of different types of information that may help to define the nature of the design proposal. Some elements of this research will be physical—in terms of size, orientation, elevation, sunlight, wind direction, etc.—while others may be more transitory or ephemeral. Together these will provide the design team with a "macro" view of the site and related issues.

Understanding the site is an important aspect of the design process, as the way in which the proposal responds to its location can have a great effect on the way in which the building form is derived and how people will understand the project. The most typical site research is the physical information that will inform the architect about the plot: its location, size, slope/elevation, existing conditions, and so on. This will be recorded in photographs, surveys, sketches, etc. At the most basic level this information will allow the design team to start considering how the proposal will be situated on the site and what restrictions there might be (in terms of land features, wildlife habitats, or existing trees to be retained). This type of physical information is sometimes referred to as "mapping," but there are other types of mapping that are often explored when considering a site.

It is often the non-physical or transitory aspects of a site that offer the most interesting possibilities for design development. Research into the history of a site can often been a rich source of design inspiration. At times this may be a literal attempt to rebuild some aspect of the locale that is no longer visible—while in other cases the site's history may be a driver for some aspect of the design without being directly visible.

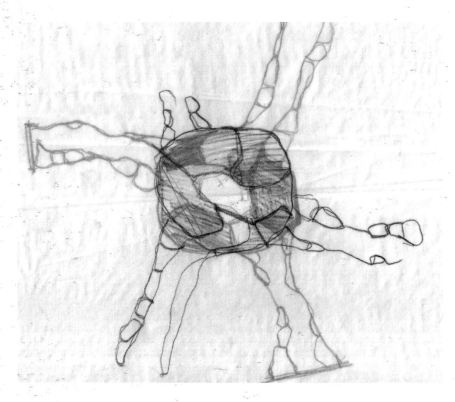

Left
Lewis Scott, Concept Sketch, Women's Institute,
London, UK
The initial development of the design for a
project will combine site analysis, research, and
conceptual thinking. Sketching (through drawing
and modeling), while not necessarily for
presentation to the client, will help the architect to
establish parameters for future design development.

Opposite
Bennetts Associates, Basinghall Street,
London, UK
The existing conditions of a site will inform and
influence the way in which a design develops
and, later, the way that construction is undertaken.
The relationship, both physical and conceptual,
between new and existing will affect all aspects
of a project.

Another aspect of the site that the architect will need to explore is any existing use of the site that may affect the way a new structure is placed on it. If there is an existing building, clearly there are issues as to whether this is retained and integrated into a new design or demolished. However, particularly in urban situations, there may be pedestrian and traffic movement that needs to be considered. If the site is currently empty but is used by pedestrians to move through the area, the architect may wish to explore the possibility that such movement is allowed to remain in some fashion. This will require careful study of the way in which people move through and use the site. Do pedestrians tend to walk through the middle of the space or around the perimeter? Do they use the site at specific times of day? In the summer, do people stop and sit in the space? All of these questions could have a bearing on the design response to the brief.

The movement of vehicles will also need to be considered for many types of projects. At one level this simply may be about recognizing the most appropriate point at which to provide vehicular access to the site. In other cases it may involve a more complex traffic system, which needs to be analyzed or developed. For example, when planning a large development it will be necessary to consider the traffic patterns in relation to an area larger than the site locale alone. The introduction of a large number of new vehicles (for a housing development, large factory, shopping mall, etc.) can have a great impact on existing traffic patterns. Therefore, understanding the way in which the existing traffic flows to and around the site will be important, so that decisions about the design do not cause problems in the future.

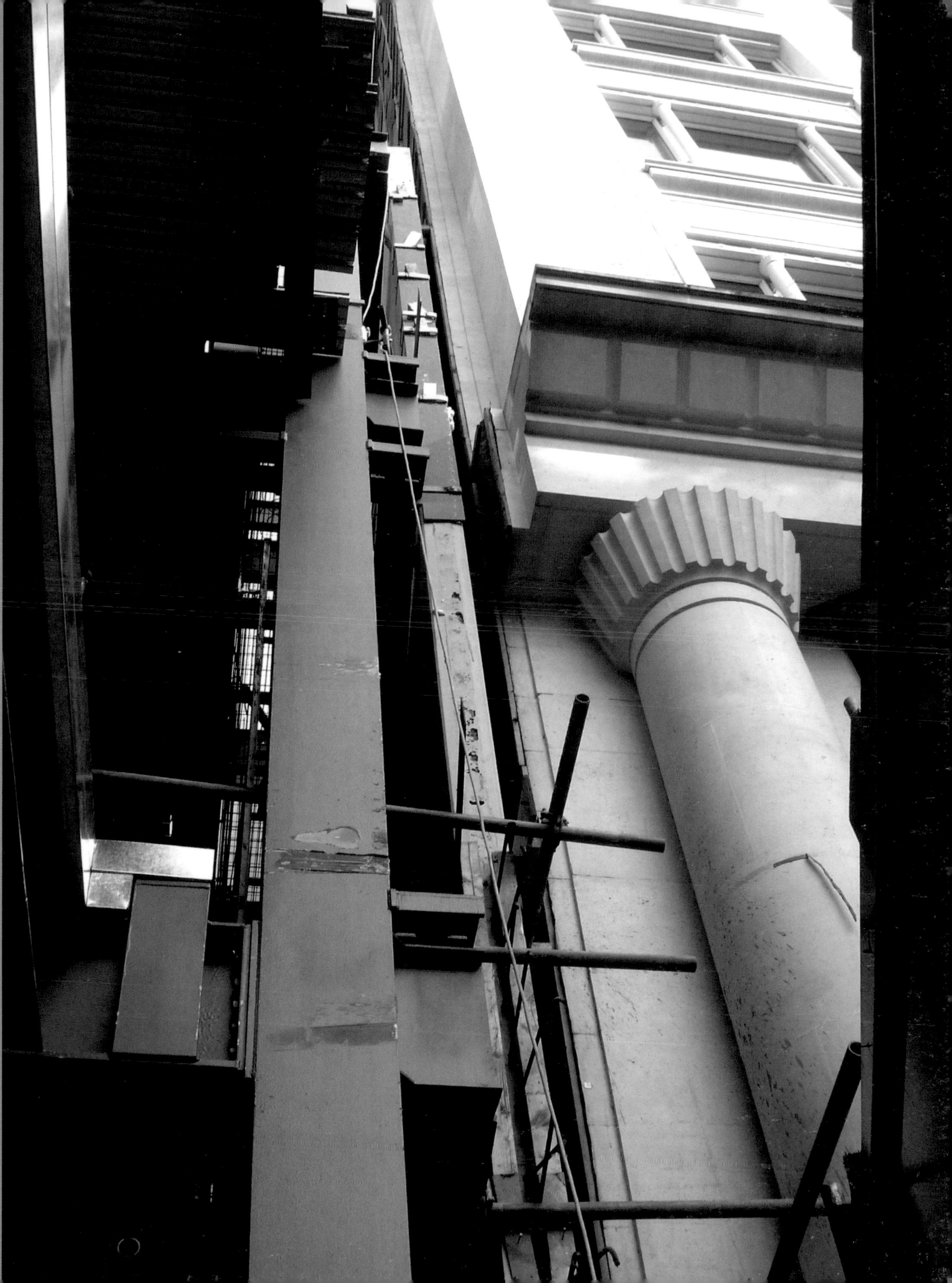

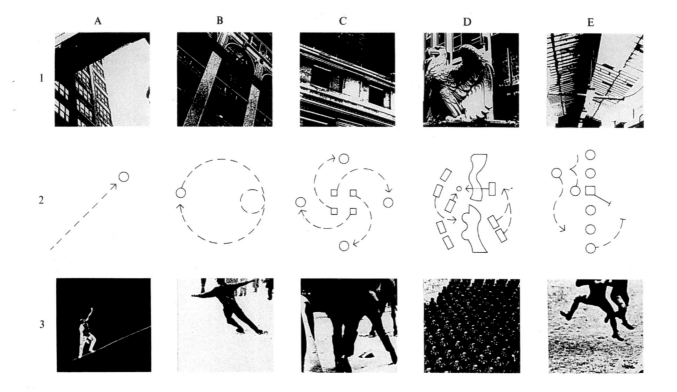

Above
Bernard Tschumi, *The Manhattan Transcripts*
Movement is not only something to be analyzed
in a site, it may also be a conceptual starting point
for design ideas. Through mapping of movement
and event within film, Tschumi developed a new
formal language for his architecture.

Along with the movement of people on and around the site, the mapping
of the area may extend to consider the activities and events that are taking
place. This may lead to some consideration of whether the proposal should
seek to maintain support for these activities or to "embody" them in some
way. Again the mapping of these elements can take the form of photographs,
sketches, video, etc. Whichever medium is chosen the designers will be trying
to find ways of recording the activity/event as it takes place. The aim is both to
understand the nature of the activity and to seek ways in which it may come
to inform the design.

In Bernard Tschumi's *The Manhattan Transcripts*, we see one way in which
the mapping of events might lead to ideas of architectural form. Tschumi
started with a series of photographs of events, from which a language of
mapping was derived that sought to record event, actions, and the nature
of the event within space and time. According to his firm's website, "The
Transcripts' explicit purpose was to transcribe things normally removed from
conventional architectural representation, namely the complex relationship
between spaces and their use, between the set and the script, between 'type'
and 'program,' between objects and events." While this remains a theoretical
project and publication, the methodology that Tschumi developed would later
be echoed in his design for the Parc de la Villette in Paris (1987).

Where Tschumi sought inspiration from an exploration of the relationship
between event and space, other architects are influenced by a wide range of

different disciplines and processes. It would be safe to say that architects may draw inspiration from just about anything.

When discussing the design of a project, architects will often refer to the *concept*. This is a term that comes from cognitive science and it refers to an abstract idea, which is, in turn, associated with a representation of the idea. In essence, the concept is the underlying idea of why the proposal takes the form that is represented. As concepts are the bearers of meaning (rather than the instigator or "agent") they are used in design to drive the decision-making process. If the design is to maintain its relationship with the concept, then the design decisions must make logical sense in relation to that concept.

Concepts are often not readily visible within the finished project. Unless the concept is made explicit, which can be difficult, there is little that can be done (short of a plaque on the building that states: "The concept of this building is ... ") to ensure that everyone will be able to recognize the concept. However, this is not the reason that concepts play a part in design. Architects use concepts in order to attempt to bring other disciplines, influences, or methodologies into their design process. For example, when designing a building for dance performances an architect might explore Labanotation (a system of notation, developed by Rudolph Laban, used in choreography). This may then lead to different ways of conceiving of the mapping of

Above and below
Harry Cassell, Concept Model, Collective
Eco-housing
When architects refer to "concept" they mean the underlying idea behind their design. Whether expressed through drawing or model, a concept can become the central idea upon which the entire design is built.

movement within the proposed building, and subsequently to design decisions that embody these ideas. The concept, in this example, would be related to the recording and choreography of movement (effectively seeking to make the building an embodiment of a process of dance), but would not be visible within the building unless the visitor is familiar with Labanotation.

The concepts that are found in architecture are hugely varied. In order to explore the way in which concepts inform architectural design, we will consider a few further examples. These are by no means intended to cover all possible types of concept that might be found in architecture (as this would be impossible). Rather, with these examples we will explore some of the different ways in which specific architects have used concepts to inform their work.

Inspiration and concept development can come from the very process of exploring a particular site. For the Port Authority Triple Bridge Gateway Competition, New York, in 1994, Greg Lynn used computer simulations to model the flow of pedestrian, automobile, and bus traffic across the site. Each of these different modes of transportation, with different speeds and intensities, when mapped using the simulations, created a "field of forces." This simulation was then animated with particles that were affected by the

Opposite, top and bottom
Greg Lynn, Port Authority Triple Bridge Gateway Competition, New York, USA
Site analysis, in itself, may be a conceptual starting point for a project. In this competition entry Lynn uses an analysis of pedestrian, automobile, and bus movement in the area of the site to develop an architectural language for the project.

Below
Louis Kahn, The Salk Institute, La Jolla, California, USA
Concepts can sometimes be apparent in a design, or may not be directly visible. This difference will be based on how an architect approaches the project. For some the concept is purely a part of their process—a way of internally making decisions about the design. For others the concept may be expressed very strongly in the way the design presents itself, as here.

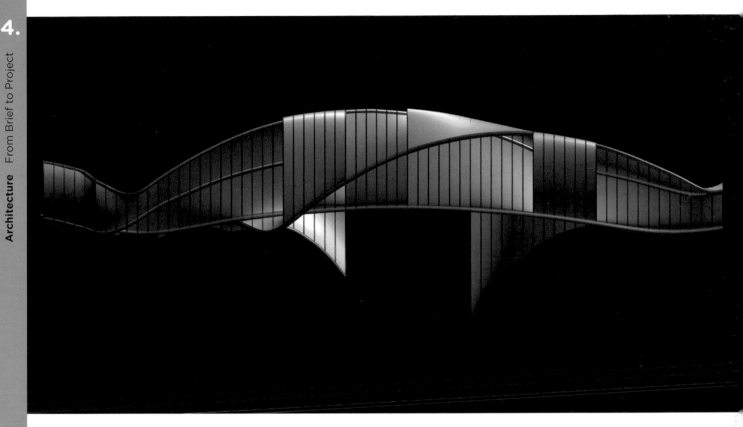

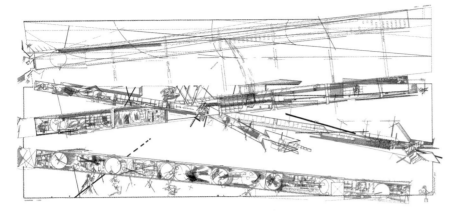

Left, top and bottom
Daniel Libeskind, City Edge Competition, Berlin,
Germany
Literature can also be the driver or conceptual
influence for a design. From a passage by Walter
Benjamin, Libeskind developed a project that
challenged the division of the city of Berlin.
Here the concept is not readily visible but
influences the way in which the project is
developed within the architect's design process.

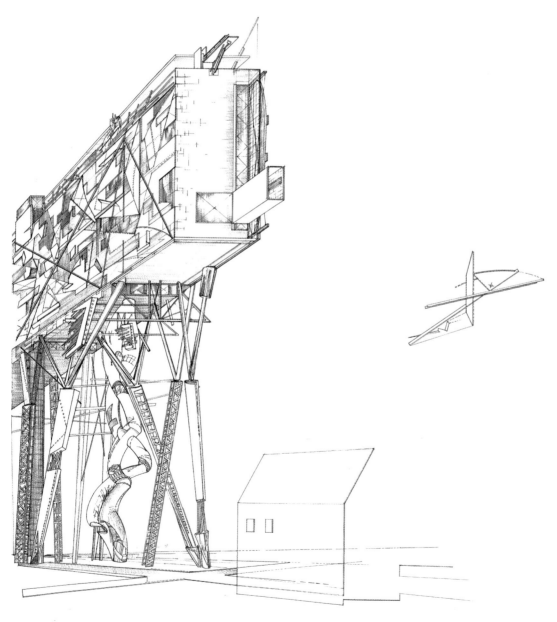

intensity of those forces—their size and position changing accordingly. The animated particle mappings then led to the development of form and structure. This project illustrates how a concept might be derived directly from the design process: in this case, a digital simulation process leads to an architectural form and structural solution.

Concepts and inspiration can come from other fields as well. In his winning entry for the Berlin City Edge Competition, Daniel Libeskind made use of history and literature to develop his proposal. A challenging building project for urban regeneration in Berlin (part of the 1987 International Building Exhibition program), Libeskind's entry saw a fragmentation and exploding of the Berlin Wall, reflecting both the history of a divided city and a vision of the city united. Within the design process there was a use of literary reference, exploring a passage from Walter Benjamin. While the literary aspect was not overtly apparent within the design proposal, without some foreknowledge of the Benjamin passage and its connection to the specific site one could not fully appreciate the decision to raise one end of a long building ten storys above the ground looking over the existing Berlin Wall. Thus, a story about a missed train (the event that forms the core of the Benjamin passage) becomes a vehicle by which Libeskind's proposal subverts and disrupts the then-divided city of Berlin.

Nature, too, can be a strong inspiration or conceptual driver for architecture. Eero Saarinen's TWA Terminal Building of 1962 at New York's JFK Airport is a symbol of flight. Saarinen's design for the terminal, with soaring wings, presents the visitor with a vision of the grandeur and

Below
Eero Saarinen, TWA Terminal, JFK Airport, New York, USA
With its soaring wings, this terminal embodied the spirit of air travel for visitors in the 1950s and 1960s. Such abstractions of nature provide a way in which an architect may refer to something without being overt.

Oppenheim Architecture + Design, COR, Miami, Florida, USA

Urban context view.

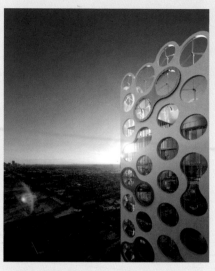

View of façade at roof level.

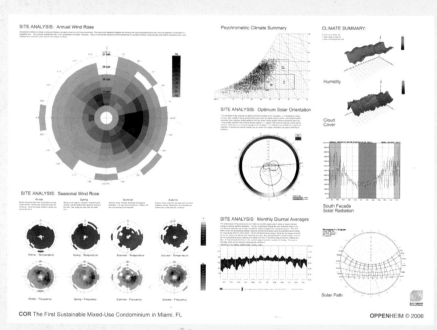

Energy-efficiency data.

Street-level view.

Alternative energy need not be an "add on" to a building. Architects are beginning to explore ways in which the structure itself can start to integrate new methods of generating electricity, as well as conserving power.

Oppenheim Architecture + Design, in conjunction with Buro Happold Consulting Engineers, have developed a building that employs urban, construction, and individual-dwelling strategies in order to minimize the carbon footprint of a building and its inhabitants.

COR integrates wind turbines, photovoltaics, solar hot-water heating, green roofs, and adequate shading—as well as a variety of material specifications for environmentally friendly products. As a package, these support a new vision of how buildings can bring technologies together to serve both the residents and a wider community.

Sustainability and environmental performance are vital for architects. With the building industry representing one of the highest producers of carbon-dioxide emissions, architects have an important role to play in helping to conserve and improve our environment.

View of roof terrace.

excitement that air travel represented for people in the 1950s and 1960s. Nature as an inspiration or conceptual device can be found in the derivation of form, or may provide a less obvious source if it is a natural process that is the starting point. Nature, with its breadth of form and process, can provide a wide range of opportunities for architects.

In the design of the Jean-Marie Tjibaou Cultural Center (Nouméa, New Caledonia) architect Renzo Piano sought inspiration from the indigenous or *vernacular* architecture of the South Pacific island. Based on the design of traditional Kanak villages of the region, this center (dedicated to Tjibaou, who died in 1989 leading his country in the fight for independence from France) brings together ideas of traditional local design with modern construction and environmental considerations. Taking principles of hierarchy from the Kanak village organization, Piano has used a similar hierarchical system to allocate space related to the building functions. The soaring "huts," divided into three groups and connected by a sinuous path, create smaller "villages" or functional groupings—exhibition spaces, library, auditorium, etc. The construction of these traditionally inspired huts makes use of the prevailing winds to naturally ventilate the building, with the double skin of the structures acting as a chimney to draw warm air out of their interiors. The use of vernacular or indigenous design as the starting point for architectural projects requires careful consideration of the outcome. It is all too easy for the new to be seen as mimicking the original without respecting the relationship between form and culture. However, where they are successful, such designs become valued for both the new image of an existing culture and for their respect for the primary origin.

Above
Renzo Piano Building Workshop, Jean-Marie Tjibaou Cultural Center, Nouméa, New Caledonia
Vernacular architecture can often be an inspiration for an architect. Basing a design on the types of buildings associated with a culture and its traditions must be handled carefully. With sympathy and understanding, such projects can provide a link to the local community while bringing new ideas and technologies to bear in the creation of a new building.

FAT (Fashion Architecture Taste), Islington Square Housing, Manchester, UK

View of existing resident's sitting room.

Detail of new staircase.

Just as the vernacular architecture of a particular region or culture can lead to the concept of a project, so too can the broader cultural milieu. Practices such as Fashion Architecture Taste (FAT) draw upon aspects of the contemporary urban cultures that they encounter in order to give both meaning and visual stimulation to their projects.

In their Islington Square project from 2006, this young practice combined a modern layout and plan for a series of 23 new low-cost housing units with traditional, iconic, cultural images of "house." The aim of the design was to "unify the residents' desire for traditional homes with the New Islington masterplan commitment to innovative and world-class architecture."

Working closely with the residents of the area, FAT sought to understand the variety and character of their end-user clients. Rather than see the tastes of the residents as "kitsch," or without value, the architects explored ways in which their design might allow people to make the housing their own. The resulting design reflects new ideas, traditional values, and individual desires.

View of new façade.

Façade detail.

The Environment

A growing area of design inspiration is the environment. There has long been a tradition of architects designing buildings in direct response to the landscape that surrounds them, whether they seek to integrate into that landscape or to use it as a "canvas" on which to set the building. However, the environment is also becoming a design inspiration and driver in terms of its protection.

The building industry is one of the world's largest energy consumers and producers of carbon-dioxide (CO_2) emissions. With the amount of material and transportation involved in the construction industry there is a great need for the industry to consider the impact that it has on the environment. Architects play a key role in ensuring that the design, building process, operating, and maintenance of building stock can be carried out with environmental awareness. As the architect is one of the only professionals who will be involved in a project throughout the construction process, they are key to finding design solutions that meet the client's needs while having as little impact on the environment as possible.

Architects should consider it their responsibility to design with the environment in mind. It is the architect who specifies the materials and procedures that will be employed in the building process, so it is during the design stage that decisions can be made that allow the project to be environmentally sound. This is by no means easy to achieve in all cases. We are still in a period in which, within the building-materials industry, there are many companies who are not yet providing key building components that are environmentally responsible. This poses challenges to architects who wish to develop projects responsibly.

The most direct way in which architects are able to develop designs that are environmentally conscious is through their selection of materials. The specification of materials within a project is both a primary way in which the character of the project is defined and has a direct bearing on the way that the project addresses the environment. Through the careful selection of material types and sources (manufacturers) the design team may limit the amount of environmental impact that their proposals will have.

The specification of recycled materials is one, very direct, way in which architects can minimize the environmental impact of their designs. For example, when laying a sub-floor or erecting building partitioning, rather than specifying plywood an architect might explore alternative renewable sources. Strawboard, as an example, comes from a renewable source (agricultural waste). 100 percent natural (straw produces its own binding resin), it can reduce the amount of timber required (when used to build partitions), is 10 percent lighter than traditional particle board, contains no formaldehyde, and is recyclable. Products such as strawboard are used in a very small percentage of projects (compared to traditional board materials such as plywood or particleboard). If architects continue to specify such products instead of their more environmentally damaging alternatives, then the industry will begin to shift toward greater production of sustainable materials.

When considering materials for use in a project it is not simply the environmental quality of the material itself—whether it is renewable, recyclable, etc.—that is of importance. Architects must also take into account the method of production, the source of the raw materials (in relation to the location of assembly or production), and the distance that the material will be transported in order to reach the building site. At each stage in the production and movement of a material an amount of CO_2 is produced. The aim is to minimize the quantity of CO_2 released into the atmosphere in the production, transportation, or use of a material. We refer to this as the *embodied energy* of the material. It may be that a material is 100 percent recycled but that its production is intensive and uses a good deal of energy (producing CO_2), or that it must be transported long distances to get to the building site. Thus, a seemingly environmentally friendly product may actually be quite damaging to the environment owing to its embodied energy.

Increasingly there are more and more "green" alternatives available to the traditional building materials. In many cases these environmentally friendly materials are often more expensive than the traditional materials. However, as more architects and designers specify the green alternatives, costs should come down.

Above
Plastics awaiting recycling
The most straightforward way for architects to engage with environmental issues is to specify materials that can be recycled or that are based on recycled components. This strategy can help to keep usable material out of landfill sites. As more architects specify such materials, their cost will start to drop as demand increases production.

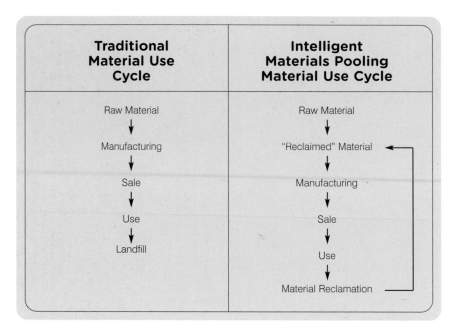

Traditional Material Use Cycle	Intelligent Materials Pooling Material Use Cycle
Raw Material	Raw Material
↓	↓
Manufacturing	"Reclaimed" Material
↓	↓
Sale	Manufacturing
↓	↓
Use	Sale
↓	↓
Landfill	Use
	↓
	Material Reclamation

"Cradle-to-cradle" design and Intelligent Materials Pooling

One of the difficulties with an approach to materials that relies on recycling
is that, generally speaking, the recycled material is of a lower quality than the
original one. Where materials may go through multiple recycling processes
there is a lowering of their *use value* over time. Ultimately they cannot be
recycled again, and thereafter become waste.

Take, for example, structural steel. In most cases any recycled structural
steel loses some of its structural-application possibilities in each round of
recycling that it may go through. The reason for this is that most recycling
systems do not take into account the different grades of structural steel.
Thus, a high-strength steel may be melted down with a lower-strength steel—
resulting in a loss of use value for the high-strength material. If this process
continues there comes a point when the steel can no longer be used
structurally at all. In order for recycling to be an effective method of
maintaining the quality of material output, a different approach is necessary.

One way to address this problem is through a process known as Intelligent
Materials Pooling (IMP). Intelligent materials pooling is an approach to the
production, use, and recycling of specific materials, and is linked to the
quality of the material. In essence, a group of material users (say, architects in
their capacity as specifiers) identify a shared set of values around which to
combine their efforts in sourcing a specific material. In doing so they make
an agreement with a supplier/manufacturer wherein the manufacturer agrees
to take the material back when it has finished its use cycle. Through such
a process a manufacturer may be able to bring a material back into the
manufacturing cycle, thus saving money on the production of new materials.
In addition, the recycled material does not fall victim to the lowering of its use
value by dilution with lower-grade material. By agreeing the return cycle of the

Left, all

William McDonough + Partners, Ford Rouge Dearborn Truck Plant, Dearborn, Michigan, USA
As the centerpiece of a large factory regeneration this building uses a range of environmental strategies in order to minimize its impact on the environment. Most notably the large, 10-acre (4-hectare) roof is a living mat of vegetation, which manages the stormwater that collects on a roof of this scale while also creating a new ecosystem not seen in this area for many years. Already, species of bird and insect are returning to an area that was previously dominated by heavy industry.

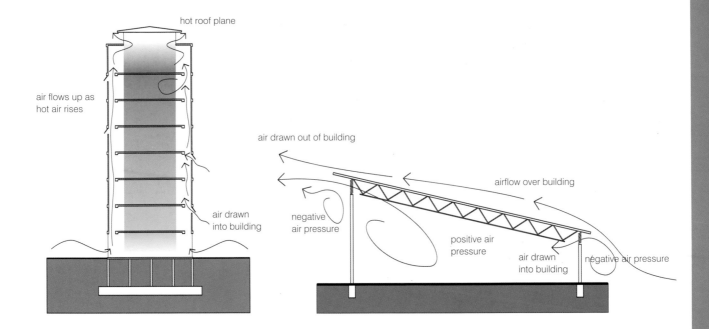

hot roof plane

air flows up as
hot air rises

air drawn
into building

air drawn out of building

airflow over building

negative
air pressure

positive air
pressure

air drawn
into building

negative air pressure

material, the manufacturer/supplier is able to be assured of the input quality
and therefore manage the output quality.

Intelligent materials pooling is one aspect of a larger environmental
strategy known as "cradle-to-cradle" design. The Cradle to Cradle[SM] design
protocol, developed by chemist Dr Michael Braungart and architect William
McDonough, sees materials as nutrients in either a biological or a technical
metabolism. Materials that form a part of the biological metabolism are those
that will biodegrade within the environment with no detrimental effect. The
technical metabolism, which mirrors the operation of the biological, is a
closed-loop system of high-quality, high-value materials and resources in
a continuous cycle of production, use, and recovery. As McDonough and
Braungart point out in their book *Cradle to Cradle: Remaking the Way We
Make Things*, in using this approach "companies are creating products and
materials designed as biological or technical nutrients, which either safely
biodegrade or provide high-quality resources for subsequent generations
of products. While nature manages the cycles of the biological metabolism,
IMP is a *nutrient management system* for the technical metabolism."

It is not only through the use of materials, however, that architects can
have an impact on the environment. Through the design of the building it
is possible to limit the need for some mechanical systems. Typically the
ventilation and air-conditioning of buildings is achieved through the use of
a costly and environmentally damaging set of mechanical systems. The
amount of energy required to power such systems creates a tremendous
drain on the electrical supply grid of a locality, thus increasing the amount of
carbon emissions from electricity production. Furthermore, air-conditioning
systems, particularly older installations, often release harmful gases into the
atmosphere that can deplete the ozone layer and add to the greenhouse

Above left
The Stack Effect
Above right
Wind Flow
The design of a building's form can also
encourage a more environmental approach.
Through the careful consideration of heat
differences or air pressures, a building can be
ventilated using natural processes rather than
expensive and power-consuming mechanical
systems. Through such designs an architect is
able to limit the ongoing building cost and level
of CO_2 emissions.

effect. However, it is possible to reduce such power consumption dramatically through the use of natural ventilation.

The "stack effect" is a simple process whereby airflow within a building is driven by a temperature difference. In essence, by allowing warm air to escape from the building at high level (since hot air rises) and drawing cooler air into the lower part of the building, airflow can be created. This will, when managed, allow the building to be cooler than the ambient outside temperature. In more sophisticated systems the airflow can be further increased by the addition of vertical "chimneys," which are designed to enhance the temperature differential between the bottom and top of the resulting "stack."

A similar effect can be created by locating vent positions where there will be a naturally lower air pressure caused by the wind flow over or around the building. As air passes over a building it may create negative pressure in certain areas. As these will have a lower air pressure than the air around them, a pulling effect will be created. As with the stack effect, this can be used to draw air through a building, increasing the amount of air movement within that building and thus cooling it. Furthermore, the design of the building may actually increase the negative-pressure areas by channelling the airflow to such an extent that the negative pressure is actually higher than that which the normal wind speed would produce.

In both of these cases it is interesting to note that we are not talking about "high-tech" solutions. In fact, such methods have been used throughout the world for centuries. In hot climates the stack effect can be found in many traditional dwellings. Just as architects may look to vernacular or traditional forms for visual-design sources, so may we also find many solutions to enhance the environmental conditions within our buildings by looking at the past and at regional designs.

Since buildings are a large user of power, architects can play a role in reducing CO_2 emissions by seeking to design with alternative energy supplies in mind. Designs that seek to use *renewable energy* can also support a shift toward more sustainable cities and towns. Solar energy has long been recognized as one of the most promising sources of energy. For many regions of the world there is ample sunlight to provide both passive and active forms of energy.

Passive solar energy systems are those that do not require the use of additional technologies to convert the sun's energy into a usable form. Instead they rely on the sun's capacity to provide heat energy that can be used in a variety of ways. The most obvious is by using the windows of a building to allow sunlight in—this provides both light and heat. Moreover, this heat can be stored in a variety of ways for release when the building cools. For example, a stone floor that receives direct sunlight throughout the day will become warm with the heat stored in the mass of the stone. After the sun sets the heat in that floor will be released back into the space, thus limiting the amount of additional heating needed from mechanical systems.

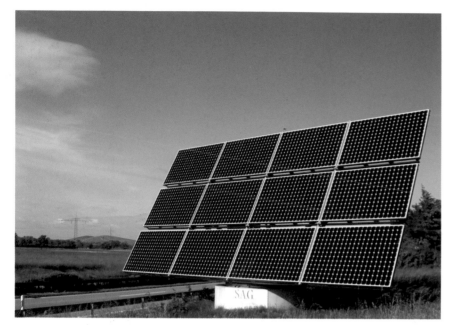

One of the most common forms of passive solar application is in the provision of hot water for heating systems. Water inside a coiled pipe set on a black surface that receives direct sunlight will heat up naturally, and can then be pumped into a standard radiator network to provide heating. Adding a hot-water-storage tank to the system will allow for continued use of the hot water even on days when the solar gain may be limited. This is a form of system that requires very little technology, and which can be made with very simple materials. The reduction in the need for gas or electric hot-water heating can considerably reduce the building's use of fossil fuels and its emissions.

Active solar power systems are those that make use of an intermediate technology to convert the sun's energy into another form of power. In most cases this involves a shift from radiant energy to electrical power. Photovoltaic (PV) cells have been in existence for many years; however, the widespread use of PVs for energy generation has not yet been achieved, primarily owing to cost of the production of the cells. Currently about 0.05 percent of the world's electrical power comes from photovoltaic installations. Furthermore, the efficiency of PV technology is still such that the period of time before the system will pay for itself is considerable. However, PV technology is improving rapidly, and its cost is falling as well. It may soon be the case that active solar-energy systems are affordable and efficient enough to permit their widespread use.

The large-scale production of electricity by wind power constitutes an increasing source of energy around the world. Whether you are among those who find beauty in the slow spinning of a series of large windmills or are concerned about their visual impact in rural areas, it is difficult to dispute the benefit that such clean sources of energy are bringing in order to reduce our reliance on damaging fossil fuels.

4.

Simone Giostra & Partners Architects, Greenpix, Zero Energy Media Wall, Beijing, China

Daytime view.

Detail of façade panels.

Behaving as an organic system, GreenPix (2008) absorbs light during the day through photovoltaic cells built into the panels of its façade. At night this electrical energy is used to drive 2292 colored LEDs (light-emitting diodes). Thus the façade becomes a 23,700-square-foot (2200-square-meter) digital monitor, able to project moving images and other digital data.

As China's first venue dedicated to the presentation of digital art, GreenPix explores both new forms of art and new ways of bringing alternative energy technologies into the design of buildings. Through the collaboration of architects, engineers, manufacturers, and programmers, this new façade goes beyond creating a self-powering media wall. By laminating the PV cells into the

façade elements, which are themselves adjustable, the amount of solar gain in the building can be reduced. This further improves the performance of the overall building, and reduces its need for systems such as air-conditioning.

Night view with digital screens active.

In 2007 about one percent of the world's power was generated by wind. While this is a small amount overall, it is a rapidly growing source. It is predicted that by 2010 the amount of electricity generated by wind will have more than doubled and will continue to rise at an increasing rate. Furthermore, the related technologies—batteries for the storage of generated electricity, and inverters for converting direct current to alternating current—continue to improve and to make wind-power generation more efficient.

Technological advancements have also meant that the scale of viable wind-power generators has decreased. Where once it was simply uneconomic to have a small windmill, it is now increasingly the case that small (sometimes referred to as "micro") generators can produce enough electricity to be viable. This has opened up opportunities for architects to consider ways in which the inclusion of wind-power generation can be integrated into the fabric of a building. As these solutions, and the technology that supports them, continue to improve, there will be more and more ways in which architects can integrate "green" power solutions into their projects.

From concept to proposal

Once the initial design has been established, in the sense that basic design ideas have been fixed, then the result can begin to be developed toward a detailed proposal. This phase may be a fairly long process depending on the needs of the project, the flow of information between consultants, and the pace of decision-making by the client. This is also the phase in which the design team will be seeking to ensure that the overall project is meeting the ambitions and aspirations of the client while remaining in budget and within the scope of the timeframe for the project. As with the initial design phase, this is an iterative process in which designs will be developed and presented to the client and then revised and re-presented, and so on.

In each iteration of the design-development process the project will move toward a more definitive design proposal. This will involve the architect and consultants in meetings and the relaying of information on a regular basis. This flow of information will be very important in order to ensure that all members of the design team are up-to-date with any modifications that are taking place. If information, such as drawings and specification, are "out of sync" between different members of the project team then it can become difficult to manage the design process. As the lead consultant, the architect will be expected to manage this information flow and ensure that any design changes are relayed to the necessary consultants. Regular meetings will ensure that information and progress are in step with each other.

It is important to remember that this phase of the project is not about developing information for construction or manufacture. While the work done in this phase of the project may, later, be used to develop construction information, what we are aiming to do is to develop the design to a point where as many issues as possible have been addressed.

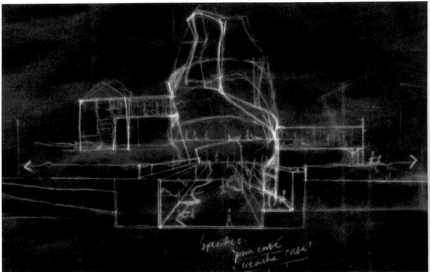
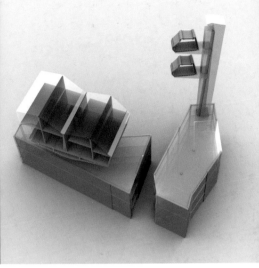

Above, left and right
Lewis Scott, Women's Institute, London, UK
As a design develops from sketch to more refined
and defined ideas, architects will often shift from
the sketchbook to the computer. Increasingly the
use of computers earlier in the design process
allows for rapid development of form and structure
in three dimensions. This information, if kept up-to-
date as the design develops, can form part of a
more complete information package as the project
moves further toward a fixed design and into the
production of construction information.

The drawings and models that are produced during the design-
development stage of a project may take many different forms. However, they
will be drawings and models "in-progress," which is to say that they are not
intended to show the fine detail of the design or how it is to be constructed.
Instead they may be more refined sketches and working models. The specific
character of these will change as the project moves toward a finalized design.
Where in the early part of the design development the drawings may be very
loose and sketchy and the models may be meant primarily to illustrate the
massing of the overall design, they will now take on more and more detail as
parts of the design become more fixed and determined.

Design drawings/models are some of the earliest work that will be
undertaken in this process. These will start as sketches that aim to establish
the basic idea of the project. There will usually be many iterations to this type
of work, each step taking the design a little closer to being a more clear and
defined proposition in response to the brief. If there are models to be made in
this phase of a project they will tend to be rough mock-ups made in card or
foam board. This allows them to be made rapidly and modified quite readily.
The aim of work during this phase is to define the way in which the ideas
(concepts) will be expressed. There is less concern, at this stage, with the
detail of the proposal. When the design is felt to have achieved a level at
which it can be more specifically defined, in terms of scale and proportion,
the drawings and models will likely be moved to a more "finished" state.

Drawings and models may now be worked-up further on the computer.
Again the aim is not yet to consider closely the details of the proposal, but to
begin to be able to quantify the overall design in terms of volume, proportion,
allocation of space, etc. While it is not necessary to move the design drawings
and models into the computer, the use of digital technologies allows for
the design to be further defined while maintaining the ability to make large
changes relatively quickly. It is likely that during this stage of the drawing and

modeling process the team will begin to produce the sort of drawings that will remain a part of the information as the project moves forward. Where early in the design phase a sketch may have been simply an idea, and not necessarily indicative of the building design, the drawings will now include plans, sections, and elevations—and may also begin to consider (particularly with the use of computer models) the way that the proposal will appear from different vantage points.

These more refined drawings, while still being concerned with design rather than detail, will become the basis for the material that may be used to present the proposal to the client and to other interested parties (planning authorities, developers, etc). Presentation drawings are those that are specifically produced for use in explaining the design proposal to others. In most cases the drawings and models produced for presentation will be about giving a sense of the project rather than giving detailed information. They may include views of the proposal in context (with other buildings around it) in order to show how it might appear in reality, and colored elevations and plans to show the layout of spaces. The aim of such presentations is to give the audience (whether the client or a local authority) an understanding of the proposal without going into fine detail or technical information.

Above, all
Preconstruct, East St George Street, London, UK
The use of high-powered computing in the creation of CAD models with realistic materials and lighting has allowed architects to provide clients with photorealistic imagery during the design process. Such visualizations can help a client, and other stakeholders, understand the design within its context.

Left
Massing Model on Google SketchUp
Computer modeling software has become
more and more intuitive and easy to use. This
allows architects to use 3D modeling as part
of the design process. The ability of tools, such
as Google SketchUp, to support rapid modeling
of buildings for massing studies means that
the design process can include a better
understanding of the building form and
its relationship to its surroundings.

It is now often the case that presentations can also include a range of
photorealistic images and even animated "walk-thru" and "fly-over" views.
The use of computer modeling, rendering, and animation software (often all
three of these functions are provided in a single piece of software) allows the
design team to create computer models that can be used to generate a range
of different types of presentation. Rendered views are a good way of allowing
viewers to see what the proposal will be like, as these can be made to show
material properties, natural sunlight, and shadows, etc. Such a rendering,
when collaged into a photograph, can appear almost real.

Increasingly computers are being used in the earlier phases of the design
process. While it is still more common for initial ideas to be sketched by hand,
there are now tools that allow architects to move rapidly into the digital realm
in order to progress their designs. Tools such as Google SketchUp have
reduced significantly the learning curve and time required to develop fast
models, particularly in exploring massing and basic form. If developed
correctly, such basic massing models can be transferred to more high-end
modeling and drafting software in order to form the basis of more detailed
models and information documents.

However, it can still be valuable to create *real* models. Using cardboard,
paper, wood, and plastic allows architects to model quickly and easily. Whether
the results are intended to be simply sketches or presentation material, the use
of easily manipulated, low-cost materials means such efforts can be treated as
working models. There is no need for specialist software or for members of the
team to be conversant with computer modeling. Perhaps most importantly, it
can be something worked on by many hands (including a client's).

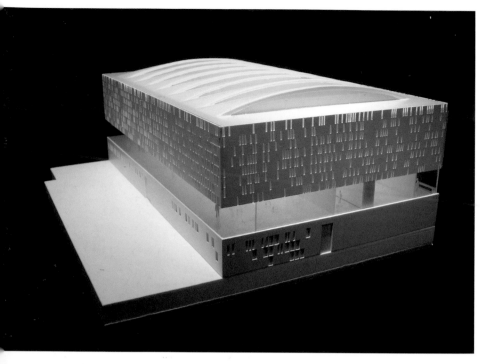

Left
Brisac Gonzalez, Pajol Recreation Center, France
Below
Magdelena Prus, Sketch Models, Gdansk
Performance Space, Poland
While computer models can be valuable in certain
circumstances, it is often the case that architects
will continue to make "real" physical models.
Whether these are basic sketch models of
card and wood or rapid prototypes, the physical
presence of the model can be an excellent way
of getting a different view of the project.

For some practices, such as that of US architect Frank Gehry, the relationship between physical and computer modeling is integral to the design process. For many of their projects Gehry's practice will start with a very rough physical model that is then digitally scanned (using special 3D scanning technology) so that the model may be further manipulated by highly specialized software. Then a new physical model will be made and further manipulated by hand. This is subsequently re-scanned, and the iterative process continues. This way of working has resulted in some of the most innovative buildings and construction methods of recent years.

What computer models can provide, beyond the potential rapidity (given a skilled software user) of changes that can be implemented, is the ability to "inhabit" the model. While physical models can be used to understand the overall view of a project, it is difficult to "get inside" the spaces in the way that a computer model allows. By the positioning of the camera (point of view) within a computer model, the viewer can be placed at any position within the virtual building or landscape. From such positions even the most basic model can give a sense of the scale and scope of a project. As these models

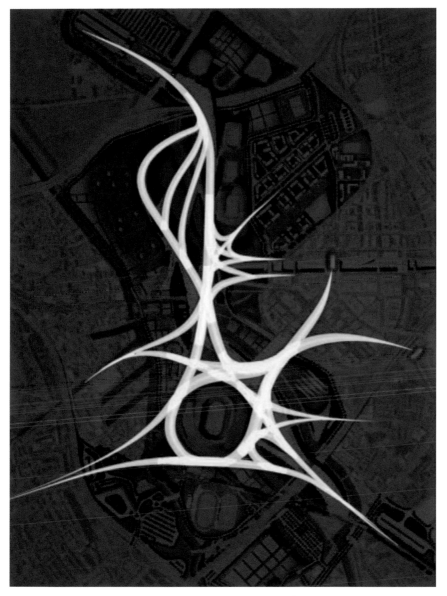

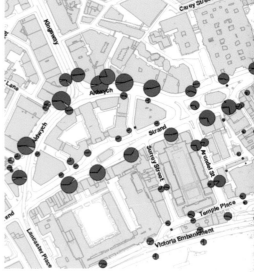

Above
Space Syntax, Victoria Embankment, London, UK
Left
Space Syntax, Aquatic Centre, London, UK
The use of computers can also help to understand
the way in which people move and interact with a
site or building. The use of computer simulations
can allow architects to design with human
behavior in mind, thus easing pedestrian
congestion across a site or within a building.
For practices such as Space Syntax the use
of computer simulation has allowed a theory of
space use and human behavior to inform their
design process.

develop greater detail this sense of being within the project will increase.
With the addition of realistic materials and lighting, computer renderings
can become photorealistic, and by animating the viewer through the model
(commonly termed a "walk-thru") it is possible to create very realistic
experiences of the intended project.

Computers do not only allow us to see what the project might look like.
During the design-development phase, when many pragmatic issues must
also be addressed, simulation software allows designers to verify that their
proposals will meet safety standards. Through the use of *agent-based
simulations* (in which human behavior is programmed into virtual agents),
we are able to study the way people will move through and around buildings.
By programming crowd behaviors simulations can determine what may

happen in the event of a fire when many people attempt to escape from the building. Similarly, designers may use such systems to explore the manner in which numbers of people may use an elevator, lobby, or public space.

As we have discussed, the aim of the outline-design or design-development phase is to move the project from initial design ideas toward a more fixed state, so that further detailed development can take place. It is also the aim to ensure that the project is meeting the needs of the client as it progresses. By integrating the work of other consultants--engineers, quantity surveyors, other designers—the architect is able to ensure that the design of the project is moving toward a more realizable state.

Through meetings with client and consultants the architect will have defined the parameters of the project and reached a point at which the design is agreed. It is usual that, at this point, the client will be asked to "sign off" on the design. This means that the client agrees that this is the finalized design, and that it meets their requirements. By literally signing a copy of the drawings, the client agrees (if this has been made clear in the contract) that if any significant changes occur owing to a change requested by the client, then additional time and fees may be charged. The reason for this is that the next phase of the project will start to place specific obligations (both legal and functional) on the project, and any changes will then have potentially dramatic effects on the overall scheme.

This is not to say that there will be no changes. As the project continues to develop there will, inevitably, be minor changes that will be made, either through client requests or by the design team, in order to enhance the project, manage costs and structural requirements, or for any of a number of other reasons. An architectural project is evolutionary—a constant process of development, revision, and evaluation.

5.

Every architectural project is unique. Regardless of type of project, scale, fee, or client, each new project brings with it a different set of challenges. Even those projects that might be repeated, such as designs for a chain of stores or restaurants, will have unique characteristics owing to their having a new site, new location, new client directions, etc. However, most projects—after achieving an agreed design—will follow a similar pattern from start to finish.

In this chapter we will explore the stages a project goes through after the design has been agreed. We will consider the different needs that a project will have in relation to statutory requirements, such as planning permission and building regulations, as well as the steps that are usually followed in preparing a project to begin construction. Finally, we will look at the process of works during construction and the architect's role in this phase of a project.

Outline proposals and scheme design

Once a project has developed to the point at which a design has been agreed, and no (or few) further changes are likely to be made, the project will move into a phase in which more detailed information is produced. This information, while still necessary to meet the client's needs, will be directed toward a series of professionals other than the client. These will be statutory authorities, contractors, engineers, quantity surveyors, and others. In part this information is prepared in order to meet specific responsibilities in relation to planning and building regulations, and in part to form the basis for the information that will be used for the tender process and then construction.

Planning and building regulations

In order to manage the process of development of a city, town, or district, most places have some form of planning regulations in place. These are a series of policy guidelines that are intended to provide for managed growth and the alteration of the fabric of the built environment. In addition, planning regulations provide for some control over the visual aspect of the locality.

Depending on the project's location, planning or *zoning* regulations will be either local (based on the specific city), regional, or national. Whatever the scale, planning or zoning refers to a system of land-use regulation that will determine what sort of use may be undertaken in specific locations. Some large cities will have their own set of specific planning regulations, while others may be determined at national level but implemented locally. At local level there can be further detailed planning regulations in order to address the particular needs of a city or even a neighborhood. Such detailed planning regulations may be intended to ensure that the historic character of an area is maintained, or to promote regeneration in areas that have been in decline.

Planning and zoning regulations are under constant review because they have both physical and economic implications. For example, zoning that promotes business development may help to increase the tax revenue for

Below
New York City Zoning Map, USA
Zoning or planning regulations exist in almost every major metropolitan center. As a system of land-use management, zoning aims to ensure that there is effective distribution of building types, scales, and uses across a city.

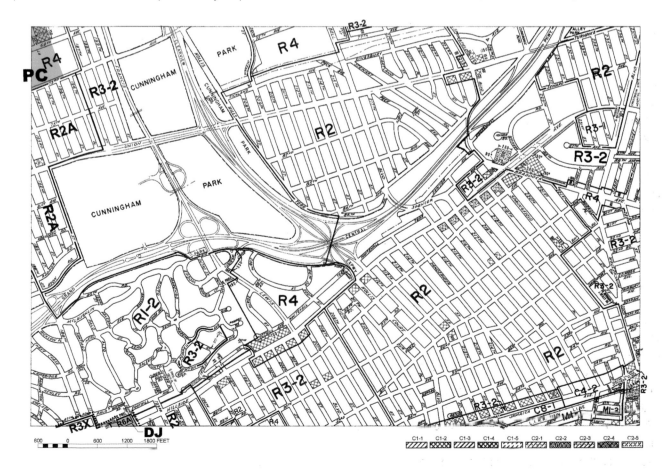

Architecture and Regeneration:
Santiago Calatrava, City of Arts and Sciences, Valencia, Spain

View toward Planetarium and Opera House.

Park area above the Parking Structure.

A flood in 1957 led to the diversion of the River Turia to the south of the city of Valencia, Spain. The dry river bed that this created became a promenade through the city, but in the intervening years had become an area of decreasing activity and a divide within the city.

In 1991 Santiago Calatrava (himself a native of Valencia) won the competition to design a new communications tower for Valencia located in the area of the river-bed promenade. Later that year he was awarded the commission for the entire complex. While Calatrava had been very successful since his architecture and engineering practice began, this was a unique opportunity for him. The majority of his previous work had been individual buildings—this project afforded Calatrava the opportunity to design a complex of buildings, effectively establishing his own context.

Like a number of other high-profile projects around the world (most notably Frank Gehry's Guggenheim Museum in Bilbao and Herzog and de Meuron's Tate Modern in London), the City of Arts and Sciences was viewed by the government of Valencia as a way of reinvigorating a part of the city in need of regeneration.

The 86-acre (350,000-square-meter) development, completed in 2005, includes L'Hemisfèric (Planetarium), Museu de les Ciènces Prìncipe Felipe (Science Museum), L'Umbarcle (Parking Structure), Palau de la Música (Opera House), and Palau de les Artes Reina Sofia (Art Museum), as well as L'Oceanogràfic (an underwater village designed by Felix Candela).

Like many of Calatrava's projects the complex abounds with visual metaphors and some of his "signature" elements. L'Hemisfèric appears as an eye, with the reflection in the surrounding pool completing the shape. Further, the "eye" is able to open. The Museu de les Ciènces, with its white concrete struts and spikes, recalls the bleached bones of a dinosaur. This glass-and-concrete structure provides a powerful centerpiece for the entire complex. The Palau de la Música appears to be an egg frozen in the process of shattering, with a physics-defying concrete cantilevered roof shade. The parking structure (L'Umbarcle) is a series of lightweight ribs housing both the parking and an enclosed garden. These main buildings are connected by a raised walkway that provides access to the buildings and views toward the sea.

To integrate these new buildings into the existing community the design allows access to all ground-floor levels, with their stores and cafes, without the need to pay entrance fees to the museums or performance spaces. Such a design decision means that the project does not simply exist as an oasis within the city, but becomes a link between different parts of the city and the approach to the coast. But it is not only the local community that is linked into the project. Through the use of materials such as broken tiles (pieced together in mosaic to be used as a surface treatment) that are popular and widely used across the region, the project has both a modern and traditional aspect. Similarly, the uniqueness of Calatrava's forms and details, with their natural but distorted character, finds some reference to the work of Antoni Gaudí and Salvador Dalí.

In the parched atmosphere of Valencia these pure white structures sitting in their shallow, reflecting pools offer an exuberant yet peaceful environment. As one of the largest art and science developments in Europe, the project is bringing needed tourism to the area through a redefinition of the underused river basin. The future will determine to what degree the City of Arts and Sciences (or the Guggenheim, Bilbao, or Tate Modern in London) are forces for regeneration, but already Calatrava's development has become a destination for people who simply wish to see the excitement and daring of the architecture.

Interior view of Science Museum.

View toward Science Museum.

a specific area. Alternatively, planning regulations that encourage the renovation or construction of residential property may help to bring people back to an area, and this in turn will help to drive forward economic developments elsewhere. In addition, most locales will have systems in place to allow for *variances* from the established zoning, so that new uses may be introduced into an area without the need for a complete review of the land use of that area.

Many architects can feel frustrated by the planning process, arguing that it is a limit on their ability to provide creative, contemporary solutions to their client's needs—or that the planning authority is obstructive to change. However, just as an architect is working to meet the needs of their client, planning officers are working to meet the requirements set out in legislation for the protection of the built environment and those that might be affected by development. How planning regulations are interpreted (by both architect and planning officer) can be an area of dispute, but it is important to remember that both sides are ultimately working to ensure that what is built meets the needs of all parties that may be affected.

Planning is not always required for all types of project, and regulations will set out guidelines as to when planning permission is needed. In general planning permission will be required in situations where *development* may have impact on others or where a change of use is proposed (for instance changing from a commercial use to a residential use for a site or building). In the context of planning, development is seen as any change to the built fabric of an area, large or small. There are exemptions to the requirement for planning permission, and such projects are considered to be *permitted development*. In the majority of cases such permitted development will only be applicable to small projects—usually residential—in which the amount of new work will be limited (such as small extensions). However, even with small projects there will be situations in which, even though the amount of change is minimal, planning permission may still be required owing to the

Opposite top
São Paolo, Brazil
Opposite bottom
New York City, USA
Planning regulations seek to manage density as well as visual aspects of an area. While in developing countries the rapid expansion of urban centers has led to social as well as spatial conflicts, in the more established cities density remains relatively constant.

Left
Olson Sundberg Kundig Allen Architects, Rolling Huts, Mazama, Washington State, USA
Not all buildings require planning applications. Where structures may be temporary or movable they may not be classed as "buildings" at all.

proximity of the new work to any neighboring properties or to the proposed height of the new work. An architect should be familiar with the planning regulations that are relevant to their locality and should always check to make sure that they are advising the client correctly about the requirements for planning permission.

Some building proposals may be approved without the need for a full planning procedure. If the proposed works fall within the stated zoning use and comply with the various restrictions of use, density, height, etc., for the site, then the proposal may be deemed to be in compliance and can proceed. Where there is a change of use (variance), or where the proposal contravenes the published zoning regulations, then a process of consultation may need to take place, which might include public hearings and require additional work to be carried out by the architects and other consultants.

In general the planning regulations or zoning are intended to allow for most development unless there is good reason for refusal. Where there are challenges for an architect is in those situations where both client and architect feel that the project sits successfully within the planning guidelines, or that there are good reasons for allowing some variance from the guidelines, but the planning officer does not agree. The planning phase of a project can, in some cases, become lengthy and require a considerable amount of negotiation and discussion between a wide range of individuals and groups: architect, client, planning authority, neighbors, community groups, environmental groups, etc.

The planning process is relatively straightforward. In most countries the process is "plan-led." This means that the process is based on the submission of drawings and information that set out the intention of the client team. The information that is provided will be the basic parameters of the project (size, location, basic layout), not detailed designs. Detailed information is not generally required for planning, as it is only the overall volume and character of the proposed design with which planning will be concerned. In special cases, such as when historic buildings are involved, there may be a requirement for more detailed information at planning stage, but these are exceptions. The types of information normally required for submission of a planning application are:

- Existing Site Plan—a plan that shows the overall site (and adjacencies) as it exists.
- Section(s)—drawing(s) that cut through the site and proposed works, showing the existing and new levels of the landscaping and buildings.
- Plan(s) —floor plan(s) of each level of the proposed works.
- Elevations—views of each face of the proposed building.
- Proposed Site Plan—the site plan with new works indicated.
- Planning Application Form—each locality will have a specific form that must accompany drawings.
- Planning Fee—all planning applications are subject to a fee.

Depending on the specific location and legislation, the application fee may be a standard amount (no matter the size of the project) or it may vary depending on the type and scope of the proposed works.

Once an application is submitted there may be a set time period within which decisions must be made by the planning authority. Where an application is complex or there is a need for further consultations, it may be necessary to agree with the planning authority an extended period of time. In some locales there is no set time limit within which planning decisions must be made. The amount of time required to reach approval is determined by the Department of Buildings (or similar office within the local authority), based on the scale and complexity of the proposal. It is important that an architect makes the client aware of the statutory responsibility of the planning authority to act within the legislation that sets out the process. All such systems of development control will allow for an appeals procedure, and an architect should (if necessary) make the client aware of their rights in such cases.

Planning approval alone does not allow construction to begin. The planning process only considers if the proposal is allowable under the regulations of the local area. It does not take into account any issues related to the safety of the proposed works. Building Regulations or Building Codes are a set of agreed standards by which a city, state, or country can specify the performance of construction works. For a project to begin construction and subsequently be occupied, the building must comply with the relevant codes. These regulations are intended to ensure that the proposed works meet requirements for:

- Structural integrity.
- Fire safety.
- Health (with regard to air circulation and quality, washroom provision, water supplies, noise mitigation, etc.).
- Accessibility (ensuring that all users of the building, including those who may have limited mobility, are able to gain access and move around freely).
- Energy conservation (both in terms of the operation of the building and of the materials that are used in its construction).

In some countries, the UK among them, the planning and the building regulations processes are separate. Planning is usually achieved first, with building-regulation approvals sought when the project has moved forward in more detail. In the USA, however, the two processes are generally taken together and are often referred to as the process of obtaining a *Building Permit*. Since the US process is a combined planning and building-regulations application it is generally made later than a UK planning application would be, since more detailed information is required for the approval under building regulations.

As both the planning and building-regulations processes are plan-led, the production of information for these submissions is an important part of the project process. In addition, information produced for submission to the local authorities will almost certainly form some part of the information that is subsequently required for construction.

Left
Left
Troppo Architects, Rozak House, Lake Bennett, Northern Territory, Australia
In most countries, the planning process is "plan-led," meaning that drawings form the basis upon which planning applications are made. While each locality will have its own requirements for the types of drawing necessary for submission, the overall aim for the architect is to ensure that the relevant information is presented—even though the design may continue to develop. Typically, the drawings submitted for planning applications will provide general information. Floor plans will show the layout of spaces, while sections and elevations will indicate levels, heights, and form. The aim of planning drawings is to give the local authority sufficient information to understand the scale and character of the proposal.

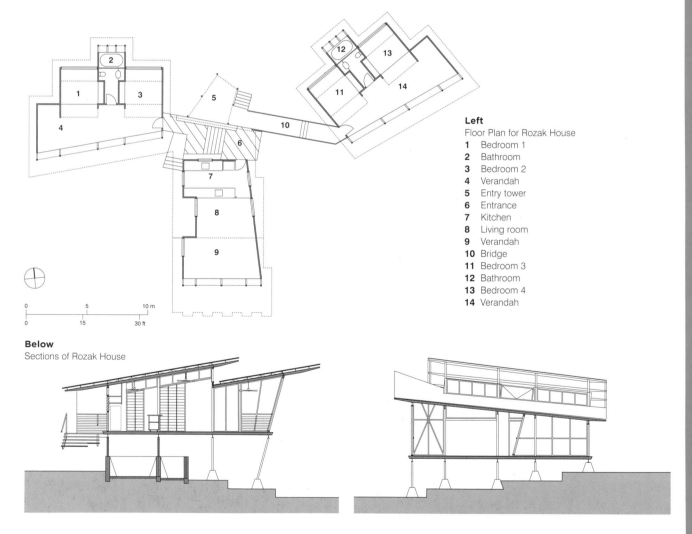

Left
Floor Plan for Rozak House
1 Bedroom 1
2 Bathroom
3 Bedroom 2
4 Verandah
5 Entry tower
6 Entrance
7 Kitchen
8 Living room
9 Verandah
10 Bridge
11 Bedroom 3
12 Bathroom
13 Bedroom 4
14 Verandah

0   5   10 m
0   15   30 ft

Below
Sections of Rozak House

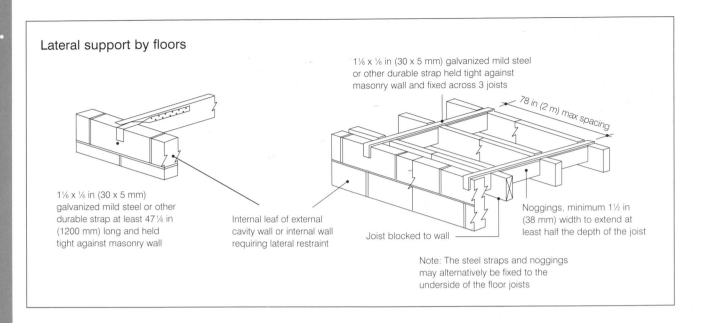

Lateral support by floors

1⅛ x ⅛ in (30 x 5 mm) galvanized mild steel or other durable strap held tight against masonry wall and fixed across 3 joists

78 in (2 m) max spacing

1⅛ x ⅛ in (30 x 5 mm) galvanized mild steel or other durable strap at least 47⅛ in (1200 mm) long and held tight against masonry wall

Internal leaf of external cavity wall or internal wall requiring lateral restraint

Joist blocked to wall

Noggings, minimum 1½ in (38 mm) width to extend at least half the depth of the joist

Note: The steel straps and noggings may alternatively be fixed to the underside of the floor joists

Design and production information

The generation of forms of information that will support the process of a design becoming a finished project is often the most time-intensive stage of a project. In large projects this may involve many people working on discrete parts of the proposal, producing specific types of information. As mentioned, some of this information will be used to support applications such as planning and building regulations, but the project will continue to develop after those applications are made. The aim of this phase of the scheme is no longer to design the overall project, but to work out the fine details and to produce the information that will allow the proposed costs to be established and the project to be built.

The most obvious part of the information required is the drawings package. Whether referred to as *working drawings* or *construction drawings*, these are the drawings that provide an overall understanding of the project as well as a detailed description of it at many different levels. A full set of construction drawings may run to hundreds of sheets, and even a small project can have many drawings in the set.

There are many specific types of drawing that can be included within a set of construction drawings, but they fall into two broad categories: general drawings and detail drawings. General drawings give an overall view of a project, either in plan, section, or elevation. Detail drawings, as the name suggests, provide detailed information and are usually drawings that focus on specific aspects of a project.

The aim of plans, sections, and elevations is to provide both an overall understanding of how the project looks and the information that locates the building on the site, indicating its overall size and the dimensions and

Above
Example of Building Regulations
Where planning seeks to manage the land use and distribution of building types in a city or area, building regulations or building codes are intended to ensure that the design meets the safety and performance standards necessary to protect the public. This is achieved through the articulation of guidelines that govern the materials, performance, and construction of different aspects of the building.

All

Shuhei Endo, Springtecture B, Biwa-cho, Shigo Prefecture, Japan

In terms of construction information, drawings will form the most important part of the information provided to contractors or builders. The nature of such drawings is complex, as they are intended to show detailed information on how something should be built while also giving some understanding of what the overall project should look like. The "drawing package" may include hundreds of sheets, each one referring to a specific aspect of the project. While plans, sections, and elevations provide information about the project from an overall perspective, the detail drawings provide information about specific items. Wall details will often show the materials and their assembly in order to facilitate construction.

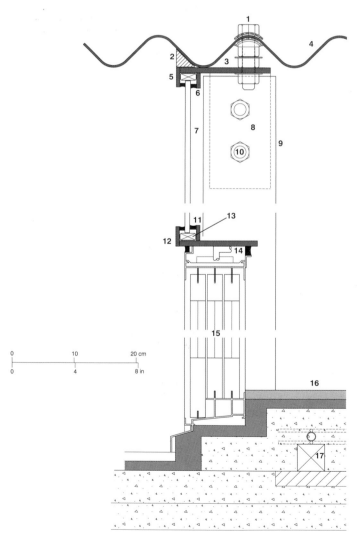

Left

Wall/window detail for Springtecture B

1   Bolt and washer fixing to corrugated sheet roofing
2   Timber packing
3   6 x ⅓ in (150 x 9 mm) flat steel bar
4   Corrugated sheet steel with hot dip galvanized finish
5   1¼ x ⅓ in (32 x 6 mm) flat steel bar
6   1 x ⅓ in (25 x 6 mm) flat steel bar
7   Fixed glass
8   Gusset steel plate
9   Japanese cypress mullion
10 Bolt fixing to mullion
11 1 x ⅓ in (25 x 6 mm) flat steel bar
12 1¼ x ⅓ in (32 x 6 mm) flat steel bar
13 Timber packing
14 5 x ⅓ in (125 x 9 mm) flat steel bar
15 Double sliding window assembly
16 Marble floor on setting mortar and insulation over reinforced concrete slab
17 Sub-floor structure

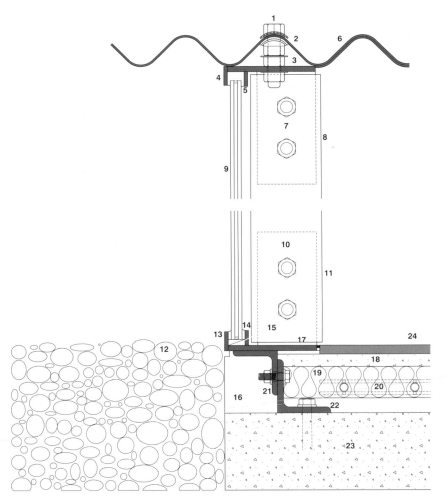

Left

Glass wall detail for Springtecture B

1　Bolt and washer fixing to corrugated sheet roofing
2　Corrugated steel sheet with hot dip galvanized finish
3　Flat steel bar
4　Flat steel bar with hot dip galvanized finish
5　Flat steel bar with hot dip galvanized finish
6　Heat insulating coated film
7　Gusset steel plate with hot dip galvanized finish
8　Japanese cypress mullion
9　Insulating glass
10　Gusset steel plate with hot dip galvanized finish
11　Japanese cypress mullion
12　Gravel courtyard
13　Flat steel bar with hot dip galvanized finish
14　Flat steel bar with hot dip galvanized finish
15　Timber packing
16　Resin mortar
17　Flat steel bar with hot dip galvanized finish
18　Setting mortar
19　Cinder concrete
20　Insulation
21　3 x 3 in (75 x 75 mm) pre-formed steel angle
22　3½ x 3½ in (90 x 90 mm) pre-formed steel angle
23　Reinforced concrete
24　Marble flooring

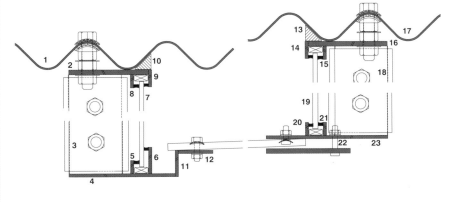

Left

Roof details for Springtecture B

1　Corrugated steel sheet
2　Flat steel bar
3　Japanese cypress mullion
4　Flat steel bar
5　Flat steel bar
6　Flat steel bar
7　Polycarbonate sheeting
8　Flat steel bar
9　Flat steel bar
10　Timber packing
11　Flat steel bar
12　Flat steel bar
13　Timber packing
14　Flat steel bar
15　Flat steel bar
16　Flat steel bar
17　Corrugated steel sheet
18　Japanese cypress mullion
19　Polycarbonate sheeting
20　Flat steel bar
21　Flat steel bar
22　Flat steel bar
23　Flat steel bar

Building Information Modeling (BIM):
Perkins+Will, Bank of America, Charlotte, North Carolina, USA

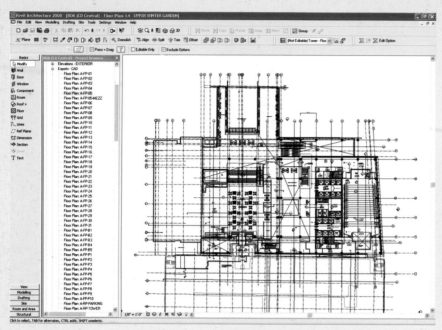

Plan view.

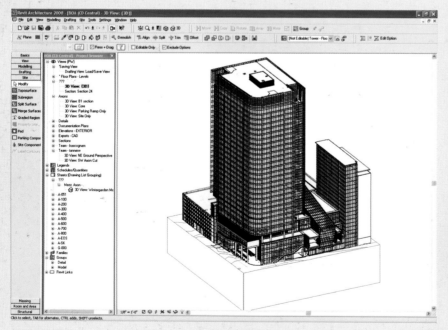

Overall axonometric.

There is growing use of a form of computer technology that brings CAD and 3D modeling together, called "Building Information Modeling" (BIM). BIM software is a shift from the use of the computer to replace and enhance the traditional drawing process in the production of construction information. Instead it starts from the point of view that the best way to design and to produce information is from the same source—the model. BIM software allows architects to create an "intelligent model" where each element within the model has properties that can be extracted in different ways depending on the type of information needed. Essentially, in using BIM the architect builds a virtual building (the model) and then tells the software where to cut the model in order to extract information for drawings.

BIM has some additional benefits, beyond the further acceleration of the process of producing information. Because many of the industry-standard BIM applications have versions developed specifically for engineering, it is possible for structural and mechanical engineers to work from the same model when developing their parts of a project. Further, with the architect and consultants working from the same model, it is also possible to ensure that there are fewer conflicts within the building (e.g. a wall that cannot be supported because there is no structure below, a heating or cooling duct that intersects a structural member, a beam that cuts across a staircase at a level that would cause people to hit their head, etc.) Such "clash detection" is built into some BIM applications, or is available through additional software that scans the model specifically for such problems. This can further streamline the process of the project and avoid problems on site that might cause delays and cost overruns if changes are required once the building is under construction.

Because the BIM model can be started early in a project, many of the software applications allow designers to create a model based only on the overall mass of the building and add detail information to this. In this way it is possible to use a single model throughout the design and documentation phases of a project. The model can also be used to create client presentations (either within the BIM application or by exporting the model to a specific modeling/rendering application) with the confidence that the image that the client sees is accurate.

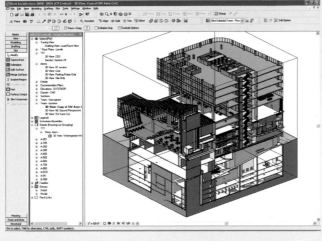

Cut-away axonometric.

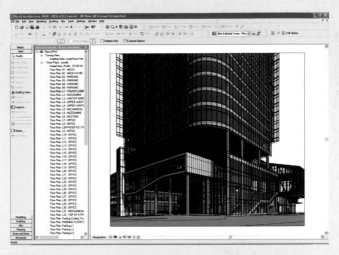

Ground-level render study.

For their design of a new building for Bank of America Corporation, Perkins+Will have used Building Information Modeling for the entire project process. The 30-story, 750,000-square-foot (70,000-square-meter), glass-and-steel tower incorporates advanced sustainable features as well as new technology. The building will be constructed largely from recycled and recyclable materials. Daylight harvesting, automatic light dimming, and LED lighting will reduce the energy consumption. On every third floor of the building is a "Sky Garden" that provides interior-landscaped spaces for relaxation and informal meeting spaces. Such features not only help make the proposal environmentally efficient, but create a better atmosphere and sense of well-being for employees.

To achieve such a complex building program and design requires considerable coordination throughout the design, production, and building process. By using BIM, Perkins+Will are able to manage the entire project through the model, ensuring that the ambition of the design is achieved.

Shaded rendering of entrance lobby.

arrangement of the large elements of the building (rooms, column spacing, floor-to-floor heights, etc.) They will also provide the basic identification of rooms and areas, from which detail can later be developed. Typically, such general drawings will include:

- Site Plan (locating the building on the plot and locating access points to the site).
- Floor Plans (at least one for each level of the building).
- Elevations (showing the overall building from all sides).
- Building Sections (cut through the building, showing the heights and the make-up of the floor, wall, and roof construction).

Detail drawings are intended to provide a considerable amount of information about how the building is made, the materials that are used, and the size of smaller elements of the building. Again, depending on the size of the element to be detailed, the scale of the detail drawing will vary. In some cases where a very small element of the building is being detailed, the drawing may be full (1:1) scale.

Construction drawings use a very specialized system of pattern and symbol in order to indicate materials and building components. There are some accepted standards, but there is also a fair amount of uniqueness to each practice's drawing conventions. It is not necessary that a national or international standard for drawing symbols and material representation is used (although it can make things easier), provided there is a consistency throughout the drawing set. The aim is not to draw things as they would appear in reality. Rather, the goal of construction drawings is to indicate

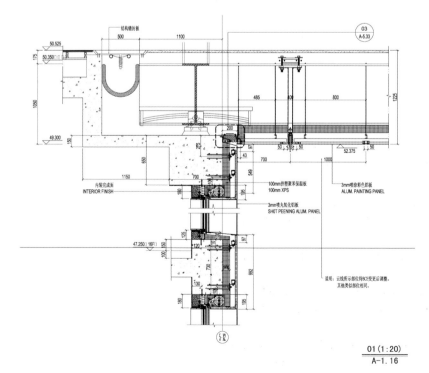

Left

Bennetts Associates, Construction Details, Basinghall Street, London, UK
The information in construction drawings is communicated through a highly specialized language of symbols and patterns. With detailed construction drawings the use of standard symbols for materials and structural items, as well as drawing conventions, ensures that those tasked with building are able to understand the properties of the building they are to construct.

Left
Skidmore, Owings & Merrill, New York Office
The use of CAD for the production of construction
information is now, by far, the most prevalent form
of drawing in architects' offices. Drawing boards
have been replaced by computer workstations.
When used by trained operators, CAD systems
help architects to maintain a consistency in their
drawings, speed up the time needed to make
changes to designs and construction information,
and help to ensure that the information is clear
and precise. However, to be effective in the use
of CAD systems one must still understand the
principles of construction and the conventions
of drawing.

Below
Matteo Mantovani, Lea Mouth Project,
London, UK
Computers have become a central feature in
many architects' offices, as well as a primary
tool in their design and production processes.
Computer modeling is now very commonly used
to explore forms and materials at an early stage
in the design process.

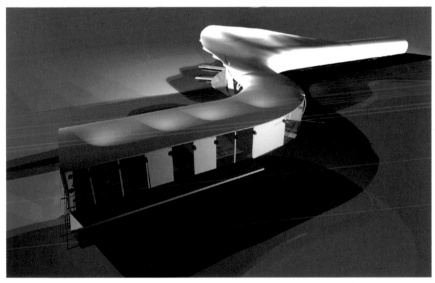

clearly materials and construction methods so that the contractor is able
to build what has been designed, and so that it will look as the architect
intended (and the client expects).

In a relatively short period of time the use of computers has become the
more commonplace tool for the creation of construction drawings. Within the
space of around 25 years we have seen a shift from pencils and drawing
boards being the most common objects in an architect's office to a point
where we may be hard-pressed to find a drawing board at all. The increasing
power of low-cost computers and the continued growth in sophistication of
computer-aided design (CAD) software has meant that the use of computers
has become widespread.

The use of computers and CAD for drawing has a number of advantages.
When used by a trained operator the amount of time needed to develop

drawings can be reduced, thus allowing the time between scheme design and preparations for work on site to be minimized. Because the computer allows for rapid changes there can be more design work going on throughout the project—it is less onerous to make changes in CAD than on traditional pencil-and-paper drawings. When used properly CAD provides a level of consistency across a set of drawings, even though there may have been many people working on different parts of the drawing set. Finally, with modern CAD systems it is possible to have many people working on parts of a single drawing—as the drawings can be digitally shared and updated from each CAD operator's workstation.

There has also been a rise in the use of the computer as a 3D modeling tool for architects. These models can be used in a number of different ways. One of the most common methods is for the design team to build computer models in order to show the client what the project will look like. (These models may not be very useful in the production of construction information, as they will have been constructed for aesthetic reasons rather than with precision in mind.) The other type of model is one that is used in order to understand complex geometries or arrangements. These will be carried out with more accuracy, and may be used by the CAD team to procure information that can be used in the production of construction information. However, in both of these cases the computer model is really just a substitute for a "real," physical model.

Specifications

Drawings are generally not enough to get a building costed and built. There is some information that is very awkward to include on drawings (unless the project is extremely small and very basic). Generally speaking, it is difficult to include information about manufacturers, suppliers, and quality of workmanship on a drawing. However, this information can be very important in allowing the contractor to understand the specific nature of what the architect and the client have worked to design. Therefore, it is often the case that a set of *specifications* are written to accompany the drawings.

A specification, by definition, is a set of requirements that are to be satisfied by a product, material, or service. For the purposes of an architectural project the specification is intended to set out the requirements for the completed scheme. Specifications, combined with the drawings, should provide a fully detailed building proposal, from which costs can be very closely estimated.

There are two types of specification used in construction. The *performance specification* does not seek to prescribe the material or manufacturer that can be used, but sets out the performance parameters that a particular item must meet. The other form of specification is the *prescriptive specification*, in which the item may be specified as coming from a certain manufacturer or being made in a certain way—or even giving the catalog number of the product. There are reasons why one form of specification might be used over another.

The performance specification allows for flexibility by the contractor to cost for a low-priced material provided it meets the performance requirement. This may lead to a lower overall building cost, if the savings are passed on to the client. However, if not managed carefully it can mean that lower-quality materials or products are used. The prescriptive model ensures that the contractor will use a material from a specific supplier or a product that has been specifically chosen, but these may not be the most economical choices. The prescriptive method also requires more time to undertake the research necessary to locate the products to be specified.

The writing of specifications can be a very complex task, and it requires a high level of understanding of the type of building contract that is to be used, as well as of products, manufacturing, and the building process. Specification writing is a specialization in itself, and there are professional designations for such "spec writers" in some countries.

For small projects the specification can be relatively simple: a basic listing of products, materials, and suppliers. However, for larger projects a specification should usually be based on a standard template that has been developed specifically for the size of project being undertaken. There are a variety of standard specification formats used in different countries. While each will reflect the character of the building and design processes unique to the locale, they all seek to formalize the language and structure of the specification. Most will be based on a breakdown of the materials and process of construction into a series of a categories. Within these, there are then sub-sections that allow for further detail to be added.

Above, left and right
Jean Nouvel, Institut du Monde Arabe (Institute of the Arab World), Paris, France
With projects such as Nouvel's Institut du Monde Arabe, for which materials came from around the world and the technical sophistication of the façade required many elements to be assembled carefully, a well-written specification is paramount.

When preparing a specification the writer is also assisted by the fact that many manufacturers publish standard clauses for the specification of their products. Thus, the spec writer does not always have to create the text necessary for the product, but can simply "cut and paste" this into their standard format.

As with CAD, computers have had a considerable impact on the writing of specifications—and not just in the sense that we can now use a word processor for the task. Often the publishers of the standard formats also offer software applications that help to manage the creation of specifications. Following the on-screen prompts the specification writer can very quickly add the relevant information without having to sift through the full template. In addition, some on-line information services (which provide further specification information and also act as "libraries" of product data and specification clauses) can be accessed directly from within the specification-writing software.

Schedules

Along with specifications, *schedules* play an important part in clearly quantifying the elements within a project. Schedules are, in their simplest form, lists of information. We use schedules as a way of allowing the architect, client, contractor, suppliers, and others a way to very quickly ascertain basic information about parts of the building. Schedules may appear on drawings, in specifications or in both locations.

Schedules will always correspond to a system of numbering or lettering on a drawing, such that it is possible to locate the particular door, window, room, etc., on a drawing when considering its specifics as listed in the schedule. For example, on a plan, section, or elevation a door will be noted with a number or letter, which will then be referenced in the schedule. With doors and windows there may also be a set of small elevation drawings that help to clarify the type of unit to be used—and, again, these will use the same referencing as the main drawing and the schedule.

There are a number of different types of schedule that can be found in a project. The most obvious are:
- Door Schedules.
- Window Schedules.
- Hardware Schedules (listing the type of hinges, handles, etc., on doors and windows).
- Room Schedules (providing information about area, use, etc.).
- Finish Schedules (the materials and colors used to finish a space).

A more complex form of schedule is the *bill of quantities*. This will usually be prepared in conjunction with a quantity surveyor, and will be a listing of all the materials and products to be used in the scheme, as well as the cost of those items. This is prepared so that the client, the architect, and the contractor are able to reach an agreement on the cost of materials for the project. The contractor will then base their cost for building on the amount

2.02 CONCRETE DESIGN MIXES

A. Footings: Compressive Strength: 2500 psi, 56-day ultimate strength, no entrainment; Slabs on. Grade: Compressive Strength of 4000 psi, 56-day ultimate strength, 6% air entrainment.

B. Portland Cement: ASTM C 150, Type I/II.

C. Ground Granulated Blast Furnace Slag: ASTM C 989, Grade 100 or 120.

D. A. and B. above or Blended Hydraulic Cement: ASTM C 595M, Type IS, Portland Blast Furnace Slag Cement, or ASTM C 1157.

E. Normal-Weight Aggregate: ASTM C 33, uniformly graded as follows:
   a. Class: Moderate weathering region, but not less than 3M.
   b. Nominal Maximum Aggregated Size: 1 inch (25 mm).

F. Combined Aggregate Gradation: Well graded from coarsest to finest with not more than 18% and not less than 8% may be retained on coarsest sieve and on No. 50 (0.3-mm) sieve, and less than 8% may be retained on sieves finer than No. 50 (0.3 mm).

G. Formwork: Reusable metal panel formwork or approved equal sufficient for structural and requirements.
   1. Form release agents:
      a. Form release agents shall be delivered in manufacturer's sealed and trademarked containers.
      b. Form release agents: Vegetable-based form release only. Do not use petroleum solvents such as creosote or diesel oil. Paraffin and waxes shall not be used when a concrete finish is required.

H. Subslab Materials:
   1. 3/4-inch gravel, 4 inches deep.
   2. Rigid insulation: 2-inch EPS.
   3. Sub-slab ventilation stack stub: 3-inch PVC "T" set in upper surface of gravel bed, 4-foot lengths of perforated pipe attached to "T". 3-inch pipe stub extends up through the slab pour. See Drawings for locations. (Reference: *Builder's Guide: Cold Climate*, 5th ed., 2001, Fig.4.5, p.39.)

I. Finishes:
   1. Interior Concrete—smooth steel troweled. Alternative finish—give unit price, pigmented surface treatment on slab-on-grade units and basements. (For example, see Davis Colors; Los Angeles, CA; PH: 800/356-4848; www.daviscolors.com.)
   2. Exterior Concrete—Broom finish.

PART 3: EXECUTION

3.01 INSTALLATION

A. Refer to Drawing detail for sub-slab insulation, sub-slab ventilation, and sub-slab drainage (Reference: *Builder's Guide: Cold Climate,* 5th edition, 2001, Fig.4.9, p.45).

B. Continuous damp-proofing or flexible membrane shall be installed over the top of the footings per the Drawings (Reference: *Builder's Guide: Cold Climates*, 5th ed., 2001, Fig.4.10, p.44).

of labor and time that is required to construct the building using the agreed materials budget.

On smaller projects a *schedule of works* may be prepared. This is a listing of the various materials and actions that a contractor is expected to undertake in the course of a project. On large schemes there may be too many actions taking place to be able to identify clearly a step-by-step process; therefore, a schedule of works may be more generalized rather than detailed. In some cases, when the project is relatively simple, the schedule of works may be used in lieu of a full set of specifications. In such an instance the information provided in the schedule of works will be more detailed than usual.

The tender/bidding process

Once planning permission has been granted, building regulations compliance has been confirmed, and construction documents prepared, the project should be ready to start construction on site. The first thing that will allow this to take place is the appointment of a contractor or builder. The selection of the contractor is a vital stage in the process of the project, as it is they who will work to make the design become a reality based on the information provided.

There are, generally, two ways in which the selection of a contractor may take place: by bid/tender or by negotiation. Each method has benefits and challenges, but the choice of approach will be based on cost, time, and security.

If the client or architect is familiar with a specific contractor, say because of a recommendation or by previous experience, they may choose to enter into negotiations to reach an agreed price for the works. If this method is known about early enough in the course of the project it is possible to start the negotiations prior to the completion of a full set of construction information. Involving the contractor in negotiations at an early stage may allow the project to develop to the strengths of the contractor's working practices, offering cost and time savings. However, as this is not a competitive situation there is less incentive for the contractor to provide a price that responds to competition, particularly since they may have been involved in the project from an early stage and wish to recoup any expense they may have incurred prior to the awarding of a contract. However, in knowing the contractor and having had them involved through the project there may be a greater sense of security that they fully understand the scheme and will perform as expected.

The tender (or bidding) process is the more common approach to the awarding of a building contract. As with the appointment of architects, for some projects it may be a statutory requirement for the project to be tendered in order to award a building contract. This is a competitive process in which a group of potential contractors submit their estimated costs for the scheme. These bids are then reviewed by the client team and architect in order to consider which bid offers the best price, service, and schedule for the project.

In order for a tender process to be effective there are a number of issues that must be addressed:

- All bidders should have access to the same information.
- All bidders should be allowed access to the site, so that they may make a first-hand survey of the existing conditions.
- All bidders must submit tenders by the same date; no one can be allowed more time.
- The bidders should know that it is a competitive tender, but should not know who the other tenderers are.

If the above matters are not handled correctly there can be issues about the validity of the tenders and the subsequent selection of a contractor. If one contractor has access to more information than the others, then those others will not be basing their tenders on similar parameters. If bidders know who they are in competition with they may change their tender in order to compete directly—based on knowledge of the other company. It is in the client's interest that all tenders are as compatible as possible, so that when a decision is made it is both fair and justifiable.

It is not the case that the lowest bid is always the one that should be awarded the contract. While the lower cost may be a positive aspect, it is important to compare other issues to ensure that the low cost is not due to some lack of understanding of the project, failure to include some cost items, or a lowering of the material quality of the project. In addition, for some clients a lower cost with a longer construction period may actually mean that any cost savings are lost due to not being able to occupy the building for continued business operations, or (in residential projects) that the cost of rented accommodation makes construction-cost savings a false economy.

It is also important that the architect and client are confident in the builder's ability to complete the project according to the design and construction information. This confidence should be based on both the tender, in terms of the thoroughness of the bid, and on the track record of the contractor. It is advisable that a number of background checks are carried out in order to verify the position of the contractor. If the contractor is a registered company the client and architect will have access to the annual accounts for that company. This will give some indication of the overall solvency of the firm, how well their business is doing, and whether they are in a financial position to undertake the project. It is important to remember that during the course of a construction project the contractor will at times be required to make large outlays of money for materials and services. If the cash-flow position of the contractor is not healthy this could be problematic and lead to delays. It is also advisable to confirm whether there are any outstanding legal actions against the contractor. If there was a problem in a previous project there may be ongoing legal matters associated with the contractor. Finally, all contractors will be required to have certain types of insurance. The architect should check to see that the contractor has the necessary policies in place and that they are up-to-date.

Project: Erpingham Road
Project No: 02-001

Item	Description	Quantity	Unit	Rate	$
	Scope of Works				
	The following work to re-arrange the layout of the First Floor				
	Notes General specification received 6 September 2009 Drawing No 001-02/051 and 102				
	First Floor				
	Demolitions and Alterations— Soft Strip of First Floor				
A	Strip out bathroom and fittings		Item		440.00
B	General strip-out of plumbing installations in bathroom, including capping off		Item		225.00
C	Strip out existing partitions and piers as detailed; including base boards and door trim throughout	441	sq.ft.	1.38	610.00
D	Strip out existing chimney breast; provide new steel support at high level		Item		1,500.00
E	Demolish existing one-brick-thick wall; dispose; new beam over		Item		1,000.00
F	Remove doors	3	No.	20.00	60.00
G	Take down plaster ceiling and de-nail joists	1127	sq.ft.	1.38	1,555.00
H	Hack off wall tile finishes		Item		250.00
J	Strip out as necessary electrical and plumbing installations		Item		200.00
K	Strip out as necessary electrical and plumbing installations		Item		500.00
L	Strip up existing floor finishings	1127	sq.ft.	0.55	620.00
M	Timber studwork and plasterboard partitions; sound insulation; decorations	140	sq.ft.	10.07	1,410.00
				Carried to Collection $	**8,370.00**

Once a contractor has been selected it will be necessary for the client and contractor to enter into a formal contract for the construction of the project. As with the architect's appointment, there are standard forms of contract that can be used between client and contractor, and these may also be fine-tuned specifically for different types and sizes of projects. For very large and complex projects it may be necessary to involve a legal team to set out the contract.

It should be noted that the contract is now between the client and the contractor—the architect is *not* a signatory to this contract. Instead, the architect will be named within the contract as the individual (or company) that will act in the client's interest to administer the contract. Thus, the architect is, in effect, the client's representative in the construction process. In this role the architect is tasked with making sure that what is being built is what was designed and specified. To this end the architect will review the work of the contractor and certify whether it is acceptable. The architect (sometimes with the support of other practitioners, such as the quantity surveyor) will also manage the flow of payments from the client to the contractor. The architect will only approve payment for those parts of the work that have been completed satisfactorily.

In most cases the client is expected to have little or no direct contact with the builder. This is intended to avoid the possibility of changes being requested by the client and undertaken by the builder without recourse to the contract. If such things happen they can be very detrimental to both the construction process and the financial management of the project. For this reason it is usual to make sure that any visits that the client makes to the site are done in the company of the architect.

Project planning and works on site

Once the contract has been signed and a starting date agreed on a small project, the architect will arrange a schedule of visits with the contractor. These will be regular visits, during which the architect can review progress and answer any questions that may arise. On larger projects the architect may have members of staff permanently on site. These "site architects" will be working very closely with the contractor in order to address any issues that arise during the course of the building process. Whether it is a small project or a very large one, it is vital that the architect and contractor are able to form a good working relationship—one that recognizes the roles and responsibilities that each party has, but also one in which there is an ability to work together to achieve the best results.

It is also important that there are clear lines of communication: that the contractor knows who to contact in the architect's team, and vice versa. Even in a small project there can be many different things happening on site (and off site) at any given time, and being able to manage and monitor these requires that all parties are in communication and are able to make decisions

Opposite
Schedule of Works
A schedule of works aims to list the various steps in the construction process. Such schedules can be used in the pricing of projects as well as a way of checking that the necessary work has been completed. More commonly used on smaller projects, for which it is much easier to quantify the stages, these schedules can become extremely important documents as the project moves through construction.

Brisac Gonzalez Architects, Multipurpose Hall, Aurillac, France

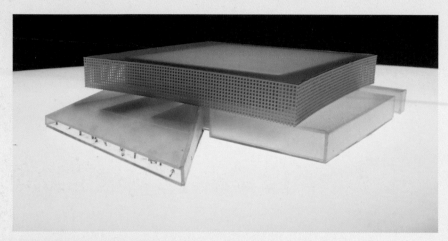

Model of Multipurpose Hall, Aurillac.

A close relationship between the architect and the contractor can lead to possibilities that might not otherwise be achievable.

Essentially a blank box, the large hall of this project in Aurillac posed a challenge for Brisac Gonzalez: how do you give character to something that is effectively "non-descript"? Their solution was to create a second skin around the solid form. With subtle curves and changing colors depending on the time of day or activity within, this new skin called for a type of glass block that did not exist. Wanting to avoid "hot spots" in the lighting, the blocks had to be designed to be diffusing and prismatic.

The problem was that no one made this type of block. Unless the quantity of blocks that would be manufactured was extremely high or there was a new market available, large manufacturing companies were unlikely to spend the time and money to develop a new product. For a large manufacturer the cost associated with "re-tooling" a factory to make a new product can be prohibitive. For Brisac Gonzalez none of the large manufacturers were able to accommodate the new design.

In such situations, where custom solutions are required, architects will be called upon to work closely with manufacturers. It is necessary that the architect be able to communicate the needs of the project to the manufacturer and develop an understanding of materials and processes used in manufacture. There will be a cyclical process of discussion, prototyping, testing, and revision. At each stage the architect, contractor, and manufacturer will be exploring whether the prototype meets the needs of the project.

Working with the contractor, Brisac Gonzalez was able to find a firm that could make such custom items. Over the course of many weeks the manufacturer made sets of glass blocks according to guidance from the architects and these were examined and tested to see if they performed as needed. Ultimately the team was able to develop a new glass block that was integrated into the façade. Through close work between architects, contractor, and manufacturer, the design for the Aurillac Multipurpose Hall (2008) presents visitors with a dynamic and ever-changing experience.

Façade detail showing custom-glass blocks.

Night view of the façade.

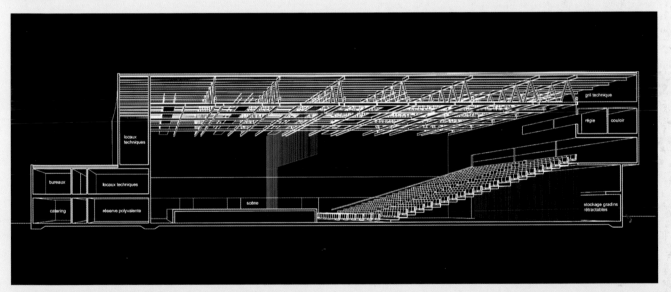

Perspective section of the main hall.

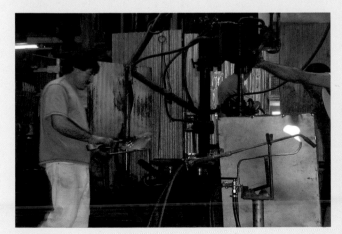

Glass workshop.

Glass blocks cooling.

Left, all

Snøhetta, Alexandria Library, Egypt

The procurement of a project (the way in which a contractor is appointed)—whether through tender, negotiation, or direct appointment—will often be related to the type of project, amount of time to construct, or overall budget. Whatever the case, the aim of the contractor is to build the project according to the design and construction information provided. For complex, large projects such as the Alexandria Library there will often be several contractors engaged on different parts of the overall scheme. Selection of the right contractors is absolutely crucial, and the architect will play an important role in the choice made at this stage of a project.

Sequencing: Bennetts Associates, Basinghall Street, London, UK

Archaeological excavations.

Pre-cast building-core installation.

Curtain-wall installation.

The sequencing of construction, particularly on large projects, is one of the most crucial aspects of a project. Ensuring that things happen in the correct order may seem fairly obvious, but getting it wrong on a large building could mean considerable delays and additional costs.

At Basinghall Street, Bennetts Associates met with a challenge at the very start of the project. Initial archaeological explorations revealed a series of important Roman sites. In order to allow the archaeological team to complete their work the construction process had to be revised and delays occurred.

However, time was regained through the use of building elements that were built off-site and then rapidly installed. The building core was formed of a series of modular pre-cast sections that could be lifted into place. This allowed construction to move ahead quickly as there was no need to wait for the concrete core to set—it was ready to use as soon as it was secured in place.

The installation of curtain-wall panels may also seem like a simple thing: put them in place until you have filled up the façade. But it must be remembered that once the façade is fixed in place, the only way to bring things into the building is through the front door and up elevator shafts or stairwells. Therefore, it is often the case that a section of the façade will be left out until all the heavy goods required inside the building have been lifted up and in by crane. Successful sequencing of the different points in a building process can make all the difference between "on time and at cost" and "overdue and expensive."

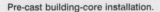

Completed building.

quickly when necessary. Every project will have a single individual from the contractor's side who is responsible for the activities taking place on site (the site foreman), and from the architect's side an individual who is responsible for the overall contract administration (site architect or site administrator). On large projects each of these individuals may have a team of people working under them.

Just as the client is expected to communicate to the contractor through the architect, so the architect should not have direct, unmediated contact with subcontractors. A subcontractor is an individual or company hired by the main contractor to undertake some specific aspect of the construction. Whether this is a company that specializes in the erection of structural-steel framing or a partition installer, the architect should not be giving instructions to these subcontractors. Rather, all communication should be through the site foreman (or a member of their team). Strictly speaking the architect (as client representative) has no contractual relationship with the subcontractor. Therefore, any direct communication or instructions are outside of the agreement and can cause problems with regard to changes that are made through such instructions.

It is inevitable that there will be changes made to the project during the course of the construction phase. Whether these are at the request of the client or are in response to issues that arise during site works, it is important that such changes are documented and are agreed by all parties. Any

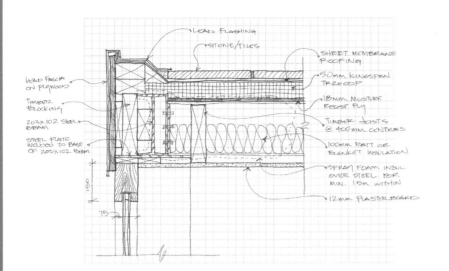

Labels on sketch:
LEAD FLASHING
STONE/TILES
LEAD FASCIA ON PLYWOOD
TIMBER BLOCKING
203X102 STEEL BEAM
STEEL PLATE WELDED TO BASE OF 203X102 BEAM
SHEET MEMBRANE ROOFING
50mm KINGSPAN TR26 ODP
18mm MOISTURE RESIST PLY
TIMBER JOISTS @ 400mm CENTRES
100mm BATT OR BLANKET INSULATION
SPRAY FOAM INSUL OVER STEEL FOR MIN. 1.5m WITHIN
12mm PLASTER BOARD

Left

MAAD, Detail Sketch, Roof Fascia, London, UK
Changes are a natural part of the construction
process. As new information comes to light, or
difficulties arise, the architect may be called upon
to make changes at short notice (in order to keep
the project moving forward on time). Recording
such changes is important, as they can have cost
implications and must be managed carefully.

change during the course of construction may well have cost and time
implications for the overall project. Many offices will have "change order"
procedures, which seek to manage the process of making amendments.
It is usually the case that the change is discussed on site, and any additional
information will be generated by the architect and a change order issued.
The change order will be sent to the contractor, with a request for the
contractor to notify of any additional cost associated with the change.
While this may seem like a complicated process it is important that such
procedures are followed so that there is a controlled manner in which
additional costs are agreed. There is nothing worse than an argument at
the end of a project over changes that were requested, and undertaken,
without prices being agreed.

One of the most important, and often the most taxing, aspects of the
role of contract administrator is the approval of works for payment. On small
schemes there may be a payment schedule that is straightforward and simply
calls for instalments of the overall cost to be made at specific points
in the course of the project. However, on larger projects the contract will
require that the contractor prepares a request for payment (a *valuation*)
based on the amount of work that has been completed and any expenditure
related to materials on site and works being undertaken off site. This is
submitted to the architect (or in some cases to both the quantity surveyor
and the architect), who then reviews the claim against what is visible on
site, and may make visits to see work off site. If the architect is in agreement
that the valuation is accurate, they may approve the request for payment
and issue a certificate to the contractor (copied to the client)—at this point
the contractor can then invoice for the certified amount. However, if the
architect is not in agreement with the valuation there will be a reduction
in the amount certified.

Steven Holl, Linked Hybrid, Beijing, China

Lit model.

Initial design sketch.

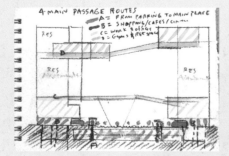

Development sketches.

With a large scheme the time period from start to finish can be many years. The process of developing the brief, exploring feasibility, and carrying out design development, through construction drawings and specifications and then on to the various stages of construction, means that an architect may spend a good deal of time involved on one project.

For a large office this may mean a single team of architects, technicians, specifiers, and others working solely on that project for a number of years. Alternatively, depending on the structure of the office, the project may move from one team of specialists to another during its life cycle. Whatever the case, large projects mean a large commitment of people and resources to manage them over what may be many years.

Projects that may last a number of years are a challenge for many reasons. They may need a large team in order to manage the sheer amount of information needed throughout the design, development, and construction phases. Above all the challenge is to keep momentum and enthusiasm high so that everyone involved continues to feel that they are a part of an exciting and interesting project.

A well-thought-out and articulated concept for a large scheme can be crucial in elevating the enthusiasm of the team, the client, and others. For Steven Holl the initial phases of a project are often a time of intense theorizing about the nature of the site, the project, and the client. When starting the competition for what would become one of the largest projects in a rapidly growing Beijing, Holl considered what it was about the site that made it unique. The scale of the project meant that this was not to be simply a housing development, it was a "city within the city." With 622 dwelling units, cinemas, a gallery, a 60-room hotel, a school, and retail space, the experience of being within the site would be immersive—stepping out of Beijing and into a new place.

Where mass housing in China has, traditionally, relied upon uniformity, repetition, and standardization, Holl saw an opportunity to offer an experience that celebrated the particular aspects of urban living while offering a range of choice and variation.

Over the last decade much of Beijing's new architecture has been of the "iconic" variety—at the expense of its surrounding context. In the Linked Hybrid (2008), Holl has sought to create a series of towers that act together: a new kind of collective housing. Linked at two levels by "loops" (the Sky Loop and the Base Loop), residents and visitors are invited to wander and experience, creating opportunities for random meetings and relationships to develop.

5.

The Linked Hybrid is also a highly technical development. The exterior structure of the eight towers is made of digitally driven prefabricated elements. This permits the internal spaces to be "beamless," while also allowing for a more rapid construction process.

Creative thinking has meant that the development is unique on an environmental level as well. Much of the material excavated has been reused to create new landscapes. The "Garden of Mounds" offers a series of landscapes, each of which supports different activities. From the "Mound of Childhood," with its playgrounds and sandboxes, to the meditation spaces of the "Mound of Infinity," the creation of these landscapes has meant that the carbon footprint of the development is reduced since there is less material to be transported off site.

What happens below ground is often overlooked. We all know that buildings have foundations, footings, and perhaps basement levels. The Linked Hybrid has 660 geothermal wells. At 330 feet (100 meters) deep, these draw upon the heat energy stored within the earth's crust to produce 5000 kilowatts of energy for use in the building. Again, this means that the building uses less energy from CO_2-producing fossil fuels and its carbon footprint is reduced.

To realize a scheme of such scale and complexity the team of consultants is often very large. In the case of the Linked Hybrid there were, alongside Holl's office, local architects (to deal with the specifics of working in Beijing), structural engineers, consulting structural engineers (to develop and manage the on-site installation of structural elements), mechanical engineers, lighting consultants, and curtain-wall designers, as well as the main contractor and a range of subcontractors and suppliers. Dealing with this array of different teams, spread around the world, was a considerable management effort, but all part of the architect's responsibility. Holl's office had design architects, a "partner in charge," project architect, project manager, technical advisor, and project designer, as well as a broader project team.

Large projects are complex and challenging from a management point of view but, as with the smallest project, they begin with a concept. The real challenge is to ensure that the project moves forward, develops, and meets deadlines while maintaining a close link with this initial idea. There can be little else as professionally rewarding as seeing an idea made real.

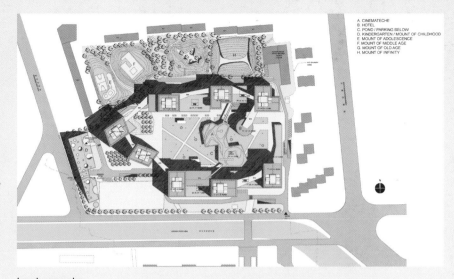

A. CINEMATECHE
B. HOTEL
C. POND / PARKING BELOW
D. KINDERGARTEN / MOUNT OF CHILDHOOD
E. MOUNT OF ADOLESCENCE
F. MOUNT OF MIDDLE AGE
G. MOUNT OF OLD AGE
H. MOUNT OF INFINITY

Landscape plan.

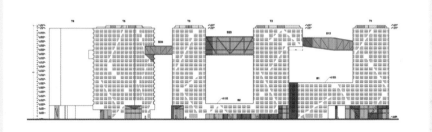

Elevation.

Design model detail.

Construction photos.

Completion

Work being completed on a building site does not mean that the project is complete. There are normally a series of tests and approvals by local authorities that are required before an architect can certify that a project is complete. These tests will include those intended to ensure the safety and functionality of:

- Electrical systems.
- Emergency systems (fire suppression, water supply for fire, evacuation systems, emergency lighting, etc.).
- Plumbing and drainage.

If these tests are passed, then the authorities will issue certification that the building can be occupied for its intended use. This completes the process of compliance with local building regulations. However, there may still be small amounts of work to be completed. These remaining items will be collected in a *snagging list* or *punch list*. The items on the snagging or punch list are usually not of a magnitude that keeps the building from being occupied, but are sufficiently large or numerous enough to mean that final payment to the contractor will be withheld. On large or complex projects the punch list may extend to hundreds of items and may constitute a considerable amount of work that, while comprising small work elements, can add up to a costly set of tasks to complete.

Once the snagging/punch list items have been completed the architect will issue a final certificate, which will allow for the remaining monies owed to the contractor to be released. In some cases the amount of money released will still not be the final amount as some *retention* may still be held. The remaining amount will be released after any defects are repaired. This is normally after six months. Defects are considered to be any items that have failed in some way owing to manufacture, installation, or workmanship—not to wear and tear. The client and the architect will prepare a list of defects that need to be corrected. Once these have been completed the final amount of the contract sum will be released to the contractor.

Post-construction and feedback

The relationship between a client and an architect does not end when construction is complete. Owing to the *defect liability period*, an architect will continue to be involved in a project for months after work on site has been completed and the client has occupied the building.

There are a number of other activities that should take place after construction has been completed. Some of these are required; others are good practice for maintaining friendly relations with the client.

One of the most important things is that a set of drawings is prepared that shows how the building actually is upon completion. This should not be an onerous task, as drawn information will continue to have been added and updated throughout the life of the project. However, it is best to review and

Opposite
Hellmuth Obata Kassenbaum, Georgia Archives, Morrow, Georgia, USA
The completion of a project will not really be reached until the items on the snagging or "punch" list have been completed. This list of items, to be drawn up at the end of a project, is often the most difficult point in the whole construction process. The contractor wishes to leave site (and thereby stop spending time and money on the project) and the client wants everything done "just so." Where projects have complex geometries and difficult details, the snagging will be even more crucial in making sure that the character of the project is maintained down to the smallest detail. The architect's role is to ensure that the work is completed according to the contract.

update drawings as necessary. For some types of project this will be a requirement under legislation, and the drawings will become a part of a body of information that is delivered to the client for future use when work may be needed on the building.

The other important thing to do is to seek some feedback from the client as to how they viewed the performance of the architect and the practice during the course of the project. It is hoped that the client will have had a positive experience of working with the architect, and it will be valuable to know if there were things that the practice was particularly good at handling. Equally, it is important to understand where a client might have had a problem with the way that the practice operates. This feedback will be invaluable in helping to ensure that future projects run as smoothly as possible.

Clients will often call upon their architect as they settle into a building. They may have issues with the way that something is working in practice, or they may not understand whom to call when something is not working and they need advice. In general, provided that such requests do not become too time-consuming it is advisable to continue to support the client whether there are fees involved or not. This "after-service" help will ensure that the client remembers the practice, and will hopefully lead to more work in the future.

Above

David Adjaye, IdeaStore, Tower Hamlets, London, UK

For the architect the end of a project is not the end of their work. Maintaining a good and ongoing relationship with the client takes time and energy, but may ultimately lead to more work. Architects will often ask for some feedback from the client at the end of a project. For projects such as the IdeaStore, where there will be public use of the building, the architect will need to be able to understand the way the building has stood up to use and whether the design has met the functional needs of both client and user. This post-project feedback is a way for the architect to understand how the project was viewed by the client: what were the triumphs and pitfalls? An architect will always wish to know how well they have done, but it is equally important to understand where there is room for improvement.

6.

This chapter will look at the day-to-day practice of architecture: what an architect needs to consider in their daily, professional life. As a profession architecture requires design creativity and high-level management skills. These management skills relate to both the management of the design and construction process and also the management of people (design teams, consultants, construction teams). In large practices—in which there may be hundreds of employees, many qualified architects, and a host of other professionals—the management structures will need to be both robust and effective in delivering the design quality that the client expects.

Types of practice

Architects practice in a number of different ways. Often the specific form a company takes will be related directly to either the type or scale of project that is normally undertaken or to the age of the practice. There are specific legal aspects related to the different forms that a practice may take, and these must be considered very carefully when deciding how one might wish to practice. It is important that the firm is organized both to provide the most effective structure to meet the needs of its projects and to be able to manage itself.

As a s*ole practitioner* an architect may either be working alone (a "one-person firm") or may have others working for them, either as employees or as self-employed individuals. The term "sole practitioner" does not necessarily

Below
Jørn Utzon, National Assembly Building, Kuwait Whether as a sole practitioner or a large corporation, the type of company will often reflect the sort of project that an architect undertakes. Typically, larger and more complex projects will be undertaken by larger practices that have well-established business methods as well as strong design direction.

refer to an individual working on their own. Rather it is a definition of a form of company in which there is no legal difference between the owner of the company and the company itself. In this form of practice the architect "wears many hats" in order to provide the client with a service. As well as acting as the designer, they will produce the construction drawings, liaise with the consultants, type the letters, and so on. Clearly, in such a practice the size of project will be limited to how much a single person or a small team can achieve.

There can be challenges to being a sole practitioner. First, there will be difficulty in undertaking work on a large scale. If the office is a one-person firm then some clients may not be comfortable in engaging the practice for a project that may be intensive in terms of time and resources. A client may also have concerns about the status of their project should the architect be unable to continue to work on the project (due to illness or personal issues). For this reason some sole practitioners make arrangements with other companies in order to ensure support for their projects should they be unable to continue. In addition, if the practice is currently engaged in a scheme it may not have the human resources available to take on another project. Similarly, the challenge to maintain such a practice can be difficult as while working on one project it may be difficult to seek out new projects for the future. Thus the profile of such practices may be one in which there is a great deal of activity followed by a lull while a new project is sought, and then back into an intense working period.

Another of the challenges faced by the sole practitioner is one of liability. As a sole practitioner the individual is financially liable for their architectural practice. Therefore, any debts accrued in the process of acting as a sole practitioner are the personal liabilities of the architect themselves. In a worst case scenario, if a client fails to pay an invoice and there are outstanding debts related to the project (say, for printing costs or material samples), the supplier (of prints or materials) will seek payment from the individual—and any of the architect's personal assets become at risk in order to pay those debts. Should the debts be such that the sole practitioner cannot pay them, then the creditors (those who are owed money) can make claims against the architect's personal assets. There are, therefore, financial issues related to acting as a sole practitioner that may make it less attractive than other arrangements—although there may, equally, be greater personal profits.

A *partnership* is an arrangement between two or more parties to act together. In the case of an architectural practice, this can be two or more architects or an architect and other professionals who bring other skills to the practice. The role of the partnership is to share both the liability and the profit. The amount of liability as well as the amount of profit allocated to the individuals within the partnership will be set out in the agreement that established the partnership. Often, such allocations will be related to the amount of capital that the individuals put into the establishment of the partnership. Typically, those who put the most into the establishment of

Reiser + Umemoto,
Sagaponac House, Long Island, New York, USA

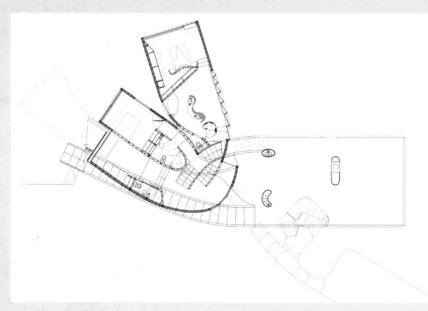

Upper-level plan.

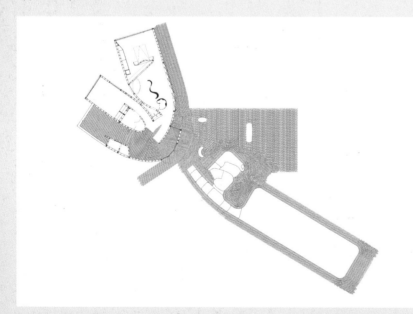

Ground-level plan.

Partnerships build on the strengths of combined effort and combined talent. For some partnerships, such as that of Jesse Reiser and Nanako Umemoto, a strong belief in giving each project a focus and particular attention leads to both a strong design response and also a commitment to the quality rather than the quantity of their projects.

Their Sagaponac House explores the notions of inside and outside, not from the Modernist position of a "universal" space but by exploring the folding-together of inside and outside to the point at which such distinctions become blurred by the formal manipulations of space and structure.

In this project, Reiser + Umemoto started from a reinterpretation of another Modernist touchstone: the idea of the dwelling as a free-standing pavilion. Feeling that this notion of "house" had achieved its highest expression in the work of Mies van der Rohe between 1930 and 1950, they felt that the challenge became one of the elaboration of the idea rather than the formulation of the idea itself. Therefore, we see in the project some of the Modernist principles of the pavilion/house (the lifting of the ground floor, continuous interior space, glass walls), but these have been twisted, bent, and folded to become something similar and (at times) identifiable, but nevertheless new.

There is little doubt when looking at the Sagaponac House that this is a complex conception of space and architecture. To sustain such a project requires a relationship between partners that is able to support the pressures such an intense intellectual position can bring. By limiting the number of projects that they feel they, as partners, are able to give adequate attention and consideration to, they allow the opportunity for their partnership to work in support both of their clients and of their own beliefs about architecture.

The office of Reiser + Umemoto, as their website suggests, has been conceived of as "an innovative laboratory in which significant social, cultural, and structural ideas are synthesized into a tangible, dynamic architecture." Thus they approach their projects not simply as specific responses to each client, but also as part of an ongoing exploration of ideas and theories.

Model view, side.

Model view, entrance.

the firm will receive the greater portion of the profit, but may also carry more
liability. One might think of a partnership as being a group of sole practitioners
working together—insofar as the partners are personally liable for the debts of
the company. However, as the liability is shared among the partners there is
less individual exposure.

In addition, a partnership means that larger projects may become
a possibility for the practice, as there are more human resources and
experience available for such projects. Similarly, the profile of the practice
will be more stable as there is greater opportunity for new business to be
developed while carrying out existing work.

Forming a partnership can be a very good way in which to develop a
practice. Many architects who start out as sole practitioners will move into
partnerships in order to expand their practice. Selecting the individuals who
will be partners is often crucial to the future success of the firm. It is a good
idea to have partners who complement each others' abilities rather than
those who replicate the same skills. So, rather than have two people who
are designers, it may be better to have one designer and one person who
is more technically proficient or who is trained in business practices. The
important thing is that the partners are able to work together toward a
common objective.

While the sole practitioner and the partnership are very common forms
of practice for architects, they have the drawback of making the individual
personally liable for the financial position of the company. For some
architects, because of their personal financial position or the small size of
their projects, this may not be particularly problematic. But where larger
projects are undertaken the financial exposure of the individual may become
considerable. Therefore it is very common for architectural firms to be

Left
Álvaro Siza, Fundação Iberê Camargo, Porto
Alegre, Brazil
While an architectural practice may be a
corporation or limited company, it might still
be associated with a single person or group of
people. Where that individual has established a
reputation for design flair and is recognized as
the driving force behind a practice, it seems only
logical that the firm continue to be promoted
under the individual's name.

formed as *corporations* or *limited liability companies*. These are legally formed
entities wherein, generally speaking, the company is liable rather than the
individuals within it.

A company can be formed by an individual or a group. There will be at
least one director and a company secretary who is tasked with ensuring that
the legal responsibilities of the company are met. Such responsibilities include
the filing of corporation-tax returns and the preparation and submission of
end-of-year accounts. Companies are publicly recognized entities and,
therefore, the financial health of the company must be available for public
scrutiny. This information is set out in the end-of-year accounts, which include
a statement by the company directors.

Companies also have shares, which are portions of the firm owned by
individuals or groups. Typically, at the formation of a company the shares will
be split between those who formed the company. Shares determine the level
to which one has control within the company structure and may also reflect
the level to which each shareholder has committed personal assets to the
formation of the business. The individual (or group) who holds the majority
of the shares will have a controlling interest in the company. Shareholders do
not need to be involved directly in the operation of the firm.

Shares may also be used to allocate profits at the end of a financial year.
This payout is called a dividend. With small companies there may be little or
no profit and the shareholders may not choose to take dividend payments.
However, in a large and highly profitable practice the dividend payment
may be considerable. In many large practices the allocation of shares may
be linked to an individual's level of achievement within the firm. Thus, an
associate may be given more shares than an assistant architect, but in turn
may not have as many shares as a principal.

Roles within a practice

Within any practice larger than a single person there will need to be defined roles in order for the firm to function successfully. As with any business, an architectural practice relies upon the input of individuals who are able to work together to achieve a common goal. Architectural practices, in many ways, are unique in their reliance upon team activities at all levels in order to complete their work. For this reason the formation of a practice relies on finding the right people for a range of positions who are able to work together in support of each other and the overall aims of the company.

The *principal* is the qualified architect at the head of the firm. In some firms there may be more than one; in large firms there may be many principals. For some practices the principal will be the individual or individuals named in the title of the practice—as with: Richard Rogers Partnership (now Rogers Stirk Harbour + Partners), Renzo Piano Building Workshop, Tod Williams Billie Tsien, Gehry Partners, LLP, etc.

As a practice becomes more successful it may be the identity of the principals that draws clients to the firm. This is not to suggest that it is always the principal who deals with every client or who generates new projects. Rather, the profile of the principal can be the deciding factor in whether a client appoints one practice over another. With firms such as Gehry Partners, LLP, Eisenman Architects, Studio Daniel Libeskind, Foster + Parters, Rafael Viñoly Architects, or Ateliers Jean Nouvel, a potential client may know little about the practice but will be aware who the principal of the practice is and may wish to engage with the high profile that they hold. With other practices, such as Gensler, SOM (Skidmore, Owings and Merrill), or HOK

Left
Rafael Moneo, Kursaal Culture Center, San Sebastián, Spain
The principal in an architectural practice is the person, or persons, who has legal responsibility as the "architect of record." This is to say that they are recognized, legally, as having been in charge of that company's projects. While some principals may have very little day-to-day contact with every scheme in the office, their role as the head of the firm will mean that they must maintain an overview and ensure that projects are proceeding as required.

(Hellmuth, Obata + Kassabaum), a client is more likely to be interested in the practice and not necessarily know who the principals are within the firm.

Associates are usually qualified architects who work at one level below the principal. They may have more day-to-day contact with projects, and may be the primary lead on a number of schemes or a single large project. They will often have a team working with them. In many practices the associates are those members of the firm who have been with the company for a period of time and have established themselves as key members of the practice. In some large firms there may be a great many associates.

It may take considerable time to become an associate in a large firm. In some cases the position of associate is a considerable step up in the hierarchy of a firm, leading to an increase in pay, possibly a number of shares within the company, and other perks. However, to match these benefits there is an increase in the burden of responsibility that associates are expected to take on. Some practices will set targets for associates in terms of the amount of income they generate by bringing in new clients and managing projects through to completion.

Below the associate there is a role that does not have a clear title. Those in this position may be designated *junior architects*, *staff architects*, *assistant architects*, or some other title. They may or may not be fully qualified. They may well be students who have yet to complete their studies. These are the members of a team who will undertake a very wide range of activities during the life cycle of a project. They may assist in the design stages, create presentation materials, make models, do construction drawings, and so on. In many practices they are the largest group of individuals in the company.

The assistant architect position is generally seen as a stepping stone to a higher, more responsible position. Offices rely heavily on the assistant architect positions, as those filling them often display the most versatility. In smaller offices the assistant may be the only other role besides the principal. In such practices there will be a close working relationship between the assistant and the chief architect.

For those recently graduated from architecture school, or those taking time away from studies to gain work experience, the assistant role is ideal for developing a good understanding of how a project goes through its various stages, and for learning the different aspects of professional practice. The assistant architects will often be those who are completing their PEDR or IDP records in order to progress toward a professional qualification (see pp.60–1).

With almost every project, whether large or small, for a client or a competition submission, the presentation or visualization of design ideas is of paramount importance in communicating the design. Whether through traditional techniques of pen, pencil, marker, or watercolor, or through the use of computer-modeling and image-manipulation software, the ability to translate design concepts and ideas into a form that can be understood by others is a highly specialized skill. As with other roles, in a small practice the *visualization* of these designs will most likely be undertaken by one of the architects within the team or will be outsourced to a specialist firm. However, in larger practices there may be an entire team of staff who are specialists in such visualization. As with some other roles there is no specific requirement for these individuals to be architects, or even necessarily trained in architecture, but clearly a familiarity with architectural design and construction drawings will be necessary in order to fully understand and express the design team's aims.

Above, left and right
Assistant Architect
Assistant or junior architects will usually be those who have yet to complete the process of becoming a qualified architect. In many ways these individuals are the "backbone" of a practice. They will have a diverse range of skills, and are often the most versatile people in a practice. As they progress within the company, it is likely that they will begin to specialize in an area that is suited to their specific interest and skill.

Production architects

There are some instances in which the production of construction information (drawings and specifications) and the management of the project on site are undertaken by a different firm than that of the design architect. *Production/ construction architects* are engaged in cases where:

- The design firm is a practice of smaller size, and may not be able to undertake the production of a large set of documentation.
- The design firm may lack the experience of detailing and managing the construction of a large building project.
- The design firm may be from a different country or locality, and therefore not be familiar with local building techniques, materials supply, and availability, or building regulations—and may not speak the language.
- Local legislation may require that the *architect of record* (the individual or firm that is responsible for the project) is registered in the locality.

Even for cases in which the design firm is very experienced in the production of large documentation sets, a production/construction architect may be employed because of their local expertise and the potential cost savings that this familiarity may bring.

As we have seen, there are many roles and responsibilities within an architectural practice. While some practices may be large enough to include many or all of the roles that we have looked at, there are also a great many small companies in which each member of the practice may "wear many hats." However a practice may be structured (sole practitioner, partnership, corporation, or limited company), there are many different people with different specialisms, who will come together in order to complete a project.

The team

Regardless of the type and size of a project, the team that is assembled will need to be specific to the requirements of that project. For a small practice, this may often mean that it is a single member of the architectural practice alongside a series of consultants. For a large practice, working on a substantial project, the expertise may reside wholly within the practice or may involve many members of a number of other offices and professions. It is part of the architect's responsibility to give guidance to the client as to the make-up of the project team, and the relationships between the various consultants that may be involved.

The architect will often be referred to as the *lead consultant*, as they are usually expected to act as the conduit for information moving from the client to other consultants and back. Where there is a *project manager* who is separate from the architect there should be a close working relationship between these two.

Holzman Moss, ImaginOn: The Joe and Joan Martin Center, Charlotte, North Carolina, USA

East Seventh Street façade.

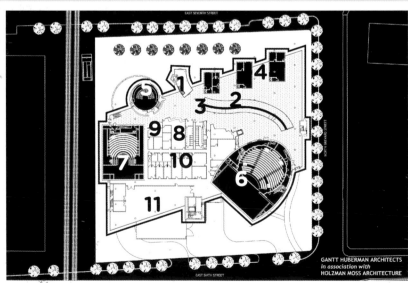

Main-Level Plan **1** Entry vestibule **2** Ramp **3** Main lobby **4** Children's library **5** Story room
6 550-seat proscenium theater **7** 250-seat studio theater **8** Circulation desk **9** Box office
10 Performers' support **11** Scene store

Architects often provide a range of services to a client: not simply the design of a building, but the interior layout and selection of furniture, fixtures, and fittings.

Often the relationship between the interior and the structure will be closely related in order to provide the project with a coherent overall vision.

ImaginOn is a unique coming-together of the Public Library of Charlotte Mecklenburg County and the Children's Theater of Charlotte. Building on a tradition of storytelling as a way of sharing experience and knowledge between generations, the project seeks to bring storytelling to a new environment and create opportunities for young people to engage with the library in new ways.

The building and interior of this new facility combine to create a story of their own. It includes a children's collection and teens' collection (located on the upper and lower levels respectively), as well as two performance spaces at opposite ends of the plan. The range of activities and services flow together along the circulation path.

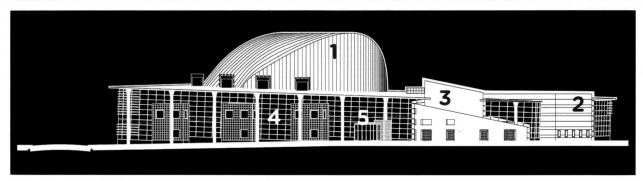

Elevation **1** Proscenium theater **2** Studio theater **3** Story room **4** Library **5** Entry vestibule

According to the architects, "ImaginOn was designed to provide the appropriate environment and setting for the various developmental stages ranging from Early Childhood, to School Age, to Teens." With its the differently sized furniture, soft sculpture games, and bright colors, the interior works with the building to create environments in which children and carers may spend time engaged in storytelling and learning.

Catering for school-age children, ImaginOn provides chalkboards to encourage self-expression, while a "Quiet Zone," with reference books and computer workstations, allows for study and homework. Teens are provided with a coffee-house atmosphere in "The Loft": a space in which they can gather, chat, and work together or relax. A video animation studio, complete with blue screen, allows teens to explore animation and film-making, using state-of-the-art equipment.

Since its opening ImaginOn has become a vibrant center for children, teens, and carers. It is a meeting place where families and children can spend time together in a range of activities that each may enjoy. This has been achieved through a careful consideration of the needs of different groups of users and a close coupling between architecture and interior.

Child and guardian areas.

Main lobby.

The "Quiet Zone."

Children's reading area.

The structure of a project team can be as varied as the kinds of architectural practice that exist. Each firm will have its own particular team structure and workflow that suits them. While there may be great variation, we will look at two of the most common.

A *departmental structure* will see a project move, more or less, in full from one part of the team to the next. There will be only minimal continuity of team members across the entire project, with possibly only the project leader staying with the scheme through all stages. For example, a project may be managed by an associate partner, having been initially established through the work of one of the principals. The associate will stay with the project throughout the workflow. To begin with, the design department, along with cost consultants, will consider the feasibility of the project and set down the overall design direction. They will further clarify the brief through contact with the client, in order to review design ideas and cost issues. When there is need for visuals specifically for a client (or other) presentation, the visualization/presentation department will come on board (although design will continue in parallel). Once the design has reached a possible fixed point the project will shift to the next department, which may be the production-information section. Initially they may prepare information for a planning application, with visualization, and the outcome of this may take that project back to the design department for more revisions. When the design is fully defined and will not change, then the production team can go into full swing in order to produce drawings and specifications. When a contractor is appointed and work begins on site, the project will pass to the site architect who will monitor operations on site through to completion.

As we can see, the *departmental* structure essentially has a team of people associated with each stage of a project. For such a structure to work well it requires that the person leading a project (in our case, the associate architect) be familiar with each phase in order to brief each department effectively as the project transitions between phases. There are clear benefits to architectural practices using this type of operation. By having departments that specialize it is possible to increase the "through-put" of a project, as each department concentrates only on its specific responsibilities. It also means that a practice may have many schemes at different stages, and each department is potentially able to manage their own input on a number of projects.

There are, however, some potential drawbacks to this model. Firstly, it is inevitable that the practice will have a large number of people in certain departments (such as production information) with fewer in others (such as design). At certain times there may be relatively few people in a large department who are actively engaged in work on a project. In terms of human resources, the success of each department will rely upon individuals with particular specialties; this may mean that there is less flexibility in the company overall. In addition, because each department will deal with a project only on a limited basis, some staff may find that the lack of ability to follow a scheme through from start to finish is less rewarding.

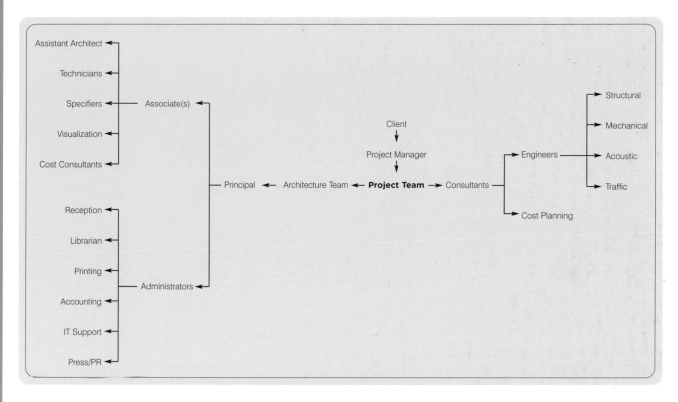

The other common form of practice structure is a *team-based* approach. In this model each scheme is allocated to a team who will work on that project throughout. For example, a team may be formed of an associate (who may have many different teams working under their leadership) and a group of assistant architects who have a broad range of skills. This team initially will carry out the work required for feasibility and design. The team will do the design work as well as any visualization needed for client presentations. They may also have within their ranks the cost-estimating expertise, or they may need the assistance of others within the company or an outside consultant for this part of the job.

Once the initial design is set and the client's brief has been further clarified, the team will then shift to undertaking further design development work as the project heads toward planning application. Again, the team will produce the drawings and visualization required for planning and further client meetings. When the project has completed the planning process and the design is fixed, the team will shift their energies toward the detailing and production of construction information. Now the individual members of the team will undertake the drafting of construction documents and will begin the specification. In terms of the specification, the "in-house" team may only develop the document as an outline (identifying broad categories of work, material, and process), which will then be further developed by an outside consultant. With the project completing the tender process and works on site beginning, members of the team may shift to become the site architects for the duration of the construction phase.

Above
A Project Team
The team of people that is engaged in an architectural project can range from one to hundreds, and include individuals from outside consultancies as well as from within the practice.

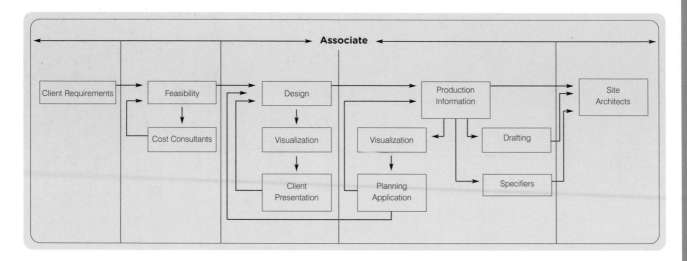

Above
Workflow in Departmental Project Structure.

What is clear from the team-based approach is that there is continuity throughout the project, because the same group of people will be involved throughout the project life cycle. For this to work there needs to be a broad range of skills available within the team; therefore, the hiring of staff within the practice must seek to maximize the skill-base of the individuals available for inclusion in project teams. For the individual team member it can be a more rewarding experience as they are able to follow a scheme from start to finish, exploring the different aspects of that project. The main drawback of a team-based approach is that if a particular skill is not held within the team, then there is a need to bring in others. This may mean that some members of one team get pulled into another team in order to fill such gaps. If this happens constantly, those individuals may feel that they are being used for a specific role rather than as part of a team. Essentially the maintenance of teams must be managed carefully in order that staff do not feel pressed into certain roles, rather than experiencing each project fully.

Workflow

Because architectural projects remain highly dynamic, with the potential for quite large changes to occur on a fairly frequent basis (particularly during the early phases of the project), the coordination of information between the various teams and individuals is a great challenge. When we consider the amount of information generated by a team working on a very large project, we can see that there are instances when the architects may have had to make design changes based, for instance, on information from the structural engineers—and if this information is not passed to the other consultants, then the project may begin developing in different directions. This can be costly both in terms of time (as the information will still need to be harmonized, but now there will be an amount of time that has been lost) and, potentially, money (if the project is on site with conflicting information between architect, client, and consultants).

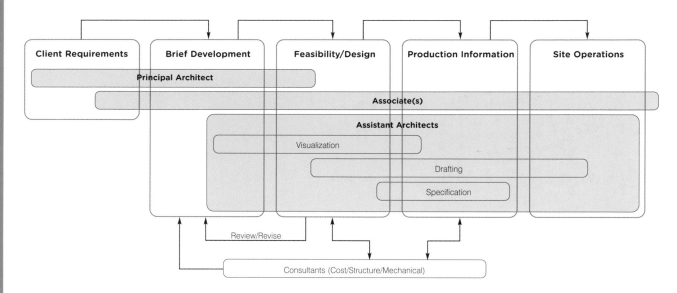

Client Requirements	Brief Development	Feasibility/Design	Production Information	Site Operations

Principal Architect

Associate(s)

Assistant Architects

Visualization

Drafting

Specification

Review/Revise

Consultants (Cost/Structure/Mechanical)

Above
Workflow in Team-Based Project Structure.

It is equally important to ensure that all parties are able to identify that they have the latest version of the information being discussed. Because a drawing may go through many *revisions*, it is important that each revision is noted and the changes are identified. There are many ways in which this may be done, from the simple (recording a date on the drawing and then highlighting those areas where changes have occurred) to the technical (some CAD/BIM software will keep a record of changes within the file, and these can be "rolled back" in order to examine the differences). Whatever the case, it is important that the architect (and the consultants) are able to identify that all are working from the same revision. For the architect it is also good practice to maintain copies of all previous versions of a drawing so that the sequence of changes can be tracked when necessary. Most practices will have very clear guidelines for staff in regard to the process of making changes to a set of drawings (whether CAD/BIM or traditional drawing-board-based work).

The effective management of information flowing into and out of a practice is handled in a number of ways. First, as we have already seen, there is need for specific individuals to act as liaison, so that all information flows through that person. In this way there is a better chance that a collective understanding is maintained. Second, there needs to be a system of documenting which information (particularly in terms of drawings, specifications, cost plans, etc.) has been released or received. To facilitate this most practices will have established a system of drawing-issue procedures. Whether these are simply a manual form or a computerized database, the principle is to record *what* has been released, *when* it was released, *to whom* the information was released, *who* released the information, and *why* it was released.

With the growth of the internet and the reduction in costs for high-speed connections, there has been a marked increase in the availability of collaborative project-management systems. A number of the major CAD/BIM software suppliers have developed systems that allow for a single repository of drawing files to be held in a single location, which can be accessed by

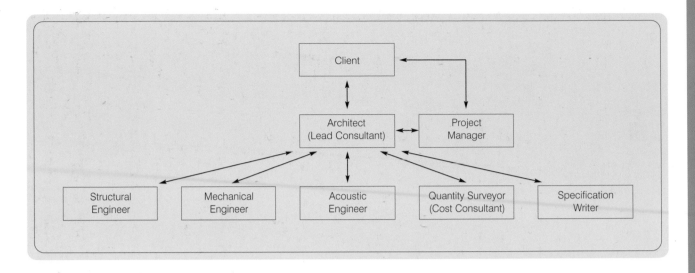

Above

Team Communication
To ensure that information is managed and integrated, all members of the team must have clearly defined lines of communication. Often, as "lead consultant," the architect will be the key member of the team.

architects and consultants. Similarly, there are now many specialist services available to the architect in order to manage the information forms. These systems rely upon the facility that many of the modern CAD/BIM systems offer of supporting collaborative working. With a large building, for example, the digital drawing or (in the case of BIM) the model will be divided into separate zones or parts (e.g. east wing, west wing, or floorplates, building envelope, structure). In this manner the architect may be making revisions to the floor plans while the structural engineer is working on the design of the structural system. Each will be able to see which changes the other is making and, therefore, either adjust their design or recognize that there is a potential problem to be addressed.

Some of these on-line project collaboration systems also include a *version control system* (VCS). This is a process whereby previous copies of digital drawings or models are stored after each session of work has been completed. This means that there is a continuous trail of all the modifications to the project (and to each of its parts). Once such a system is set up it will carry out this version management without need for further input from the users. These systems also use a "check-out/check-in" system (also called "file locking") in order to ensure that two people do not attempt to make changes to the same part of the design simultaneously. Thus, when one member of the project team opens a part of the building file to work on, this will automatically become unavailable to other members of the team until it has been "checked in" again. In this way it is possible for members of the project team to "hold" parts of the scheme while they make a body of changes and then "release" the updated part back to the rest of the project team. There is also the facility in many systems to notify all members of the project team that information has been released—in essence, it is an automated drawing-issue system.

One of the potential benefits of systems such as these is that they reduce the amount of printing required. In the past, when an architect released a set

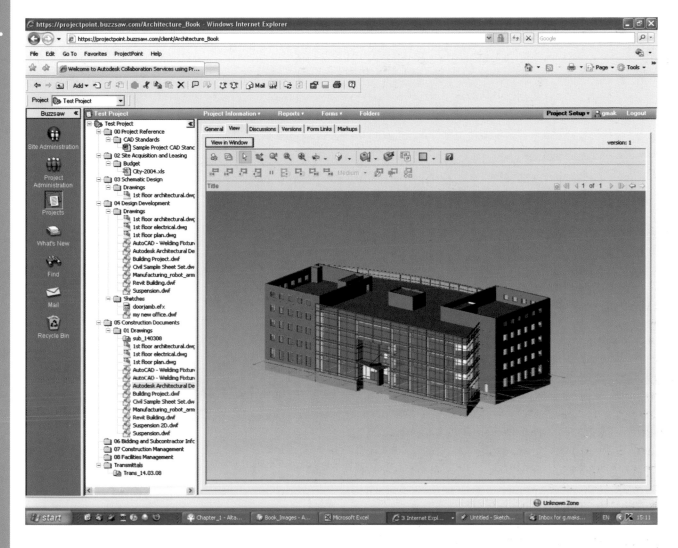

of drawings to consultants and a client they may have had to print hundreds of pages of drawings. While it might not have been the case that all of the drawings had changed, it was necessary that a full set be released in order to ensure that there would not be mistakes if people were trying to remove old drawings from one set to update with new drawings. With VCS and on-line collaboration, the members of the project team all have access to the full set of drawings/model and can print the information that they need, as they need it. While this does not create the "paperless office," it does help take us one step closer at least.

Only the smallest of practices can function without someone who manages the office itself. The *office manager* may or may not be an architect, but their primary role is to ensure the smooth operation of the firm as a whole. This may include issues to do with personnel and human resources, payroll, time planning, the supply of materials, and any other purchases. In well-run businesses the office manager may not be a particularly visible role, as when something is working well we tend not to notice it.

Above

Collaborative Online Environments
Autodesk Inc.—Buzzsaw—Online Project Management
The increasing speed of the internet, combined with low-cost servers, has seen a growth in the collaborative possibilities of project management and document management. Systems now allow large groups of designers, consultants, and clients to share drawings, specifications, and other project information easily and securely. Where the management software is able to link directly to CAD or BIM software, there can be a seamless process of working and sharing information across the world.

In larger practices the office manager may be the head of a team of people who work in many different ways to support the practice—taking the operational matters away from the creative parts of the practice in order to free them up to do their jobs more effectively. The office manager may also play an important part in maintaining the samples and supplier information for an architectural practice. This role should not be underestimated. Having someone in this post who is trained in architecture can be a great benefit, as they will be familiar with the process of design and building.

The office manager, as we have mentioned, may be the head of a team that deals with a very broad range of responsibilities. These may include:

- Reception and telephones
- Purchasing
- IT support
- Staff training and development
- Printing
- Personnel
- Library and samples
- Finance and accounting
- Press and publications

Whether in a small or large office, a good office manager can make a tremendous difference to the smooth running of a practice.

Specifiers (or *specification writers*) are tasked with the development of specifications for projects. As we saw in the previous chapter, the specification and drawings form the essential body of information that will take a scheme from design to realization. While there is no requirement that the specifier be a qualified architect or have an architectural education, there is a clear benefit to the progress of a project if they have this familiarity. The specifier will work very closely with the design team during the preparation of a project for tender.

Technicians (or *CAD operators*) are those who spend the majority of their time working on the construction drawings for projects. In some offices these may be assistant architects, but there are increasing numbers who specialize in the production of construction information. Not all of them will be trained in architecture, but they must have a good grasp of the building process. It is not necessarily the case that they will be using CAD, but it is clear that this is the direction in which the production of construction information is moving.

As with assistant architects, there can be many people employed in a large office as *architectural technicians*. Depending on the structure of the practice, they may have limited contact with the design team as it might be the case that when the project reaches a certain level of detail it is simply passed to the technical team to continue to develop the project after the design has been fixed. The technical team, particularly in large practices, will contain some fairly senior members of staff, whose role is to check that the drawings being produced are clear and accurate.

The technicians often will work closely with the specifiers to ensure that there is consistency of information between drawings and specification.

The specifiers may also be able to pass on the detail drawings (supplied by the product manufacturers), which need to be integrated into the drawings for the overall project. Similarly, the technicians will liaise with the design team in order to ensure that the construction documents and detailing are in keeping with the overall design aims.

In very large offices there may be a number of other non-architect members of staff involved in the work of the practice. As we have seen before, the success of an architectural project relies on the skills of many people—several will be providing non-architecture input yet, nonetheless, will be an important part of the team that will take a project through to completion. In smaller offices some of these roles may be combined with others, or the practice may seek outside consultants to provide these services.

Consultants

Whether for a small or a large building, the cost of construction is often one of the most debated and revisited aspects of any project. The client will have a budget in mind, and it is the architect's responsibility to bring the project to completion as close as possible to that budget. While some budget planning may be done by an architect, the detailed estimating of costs will usually be undertaken by a *cost consultant* (or *quantity surveyor*). These are individuals who are specifically trained to understand the complexities of building costs from the point of view of materials, construction methods, types of contract, land value, inflation, and many other factors. In large practices, there may be a team of cost consultants who work with the design team, specifiers, and technicians to ensure that project budgets are being managed at all stages.

There are many different types of engineering services that may be required in a building project or large development. Most projects, large or small, will likely have some structural works involved. The role of a *structural engineer* is to provide the design and specification of the system that will keep the building standing. For small projects this may be a relatively simple process of providing the sizes of steel or timber framing (including the mathematical calculations to support these sizings), concrete foundation details, etc. In large projects there may be complex structural systems which are to be custom designed in relation to the form of the building. For example, the structural system used in the "Turning Torso" building by Santiago Calatrava (see p.199) will have been specially engineered in order to achieve the design intention. In this case, as Calatrava is trained as a structural engineer as well as an architect, the design and structural solution are perfectly integrated.

Structural engineering is a specialized field, and its practitioners are part of a registered profession. As with the architect, the structural engineer will be appointed directly by the client. Their day-to-day contact, however, will almost always be with the architect, and they may have very little direct contact with

the client. Also, as with architects, there is a requirement for structural
engineers to have special forms of insurance for professional liability.

Mechanical engineers (ME), sometimes called *environmental engineers*,
consider the way in which the building is to be cooled, heated, and ventilated.
Whether through the use of mechanical or natural systems, the ME will seek
to develop a solution that provides for the greatest comfort of those who
will use the building. In larger projects the ME usually will design the water
supply, distribution, treatment, and waste-management systems as well.
In small projects (such as private residences) there may not be an ME
involved with this aspect of the project as it can be addressed by the
architect and contractor in liaison with the plumbing installer and the local
water-supply company. (The use of water is an increasingly complex issue
in relation to our environment.)

Left
Architectural Technician
Just as the computer has become an
indispensable part of the architect's office, so too
have the people who are able to make best use
of the ever-changing technology of CAD and BIM.
Technicians or CAD operators, who may often be
assistant or junior architects, will be tasked with
generating a majority of the information required
for construction. While for some this may be a
step in their career as they progress toward a
design or other role, it is increasingly the case
that such specialist skills are in high demand and
architects may train specifically to be technicians.
It is important to remember that architecture needs
many different types of skills, and each plays a
vital part in making ideas become realities.

With increased pressure on the building industry, the role of ME has become one in which issues of energy consumption are of great importance and many are now specializing in the design of systems that seek to have minimal impact on the environment. One of the greatest causes of environmental damage is the use of air-conditioning systems. Through the use of natural ventilation MEs are able to reduce the need for mechanical systems and thus conserve energy (reducing the need for fossil fuels).

The mechanical engineer will not simply be involved in the design of the "system," but will also advise on the use of materials that may help to create a suitable environment. For example, in the design of the Eden Project (by Nicholas Grimshaw), the use of an ethylene tetrafluoroethylene (ETFE) roof, which allows for the transmission of light and the capture of heat, has meant that the ME can support the design aims of the project while reducing its energy consumption. Further, the ETFE roof is a series of inflatable cells. By controlling the air pressure within each cell, the thickness of the roof can be changed—thereby allowing for variability in the way that the roof provides either insulation or the transmission of light and heat.

The design of the electrical system (light and power) for a building may be done by the mechanical engineer or by a specialist *electrical engineer*. Their role will be to design the system that will provide power to the building. In small projects this may simply be a question of using the existing electrical supply from a domestic power supplier. In fact, for many small projects the matters related to power supply will be handled by the architect and contractor (with their electrical subcontractor). However, with large projects there may be more power required than can be provided by the standard domestic supply. In these cases there will be a requirement for an electrical substation to be located on the site and for the necessary cabling to be integrated into the design. Furthermore, for some building types there may also be a requirement for back-up systems to provide power in case of

emergencies (the obvious example being a hospital or other care facility).
These higher-capacity electrical systems do not just require space within the
building, they also produce heat and (in the case of electrical generators)
exhaust emissions. Similarly, the design of a lighting system for a building
does not simply involve producing light for the use of those within the
building; these installations also generate heat—in some instances, very high
amounts of it—which needs to be dealt with. Therefore, a close relationship
between the electrical and mechanical engineers is necessary (which is often
the reason that these services are provided by the same firm).

Not every project will require an *acoustics engineer* (or *acoustician*), but
there are obvious examples where their services would be absolutely required
(theaters, performance halls, libraries, museums, etc.) because of the need
either to minimize the impact of sound within the space or to tune the way
in which sound moves through the spaces. Acoustics engineers may have
input into the form of the building and the materials and structural systems
proposed. In projects where an acoustic engineer is engaged there will be
issues related to sound from mechanical sound break-in (noise from outside
that comes in), sound break-out (noise produced within the building, or in

Left

Santiago Calatrava, "Turning Torso" Tower, Malmö, Sweden

The structural system used in the "Turning Torso," by Santiago Calatrava, will have been specially engineered to achieve the design intention. Calatrava trained as a structural engineer as well as an architect, and has created design and structural solutions that function together perfectly.

Left
Nicholas Grimshaw, Eden Project, Cornwall, UK
When the architect is able to work closely and
constructively with the other consultants, there
is an increased chance that the project will work
well. Mechanical engineers can offer innovative
solutions for challenging designs such as the
Eden Project, which required variable transmission
of light and heat to ensure the correct environment
throughout the year.

specific spaces within the building), and (in some cases) the way in which
sound behaves within the spaces. The aim of the acoustics engineer will differ
depending on the building type. If the project is to design a library, then the
need will be to create quiet spaces and to limit the amount of sound that can
enter the building. In the design of a performance hall the issues will be
related to the control of sound within the performance space (ensuring that
it is not too "live" or too "dead," that it does not echo, and that the full range
of frequencies can be heard within the space) and, to some degree, the
break-in and break-out of sound.

Interiors

There has always been a blurred line between architects, *interior architects*
and *interior designers*. The boundaries between interior architecture and
interior design are very indistinct; they may even—depending on whom you
ask—be identical. It is certainly the case that many architects engage in the
design and construction of interiors, either as a separate activity or as part
of larger building projects. For small practices interiors may be a very large
part of their business. It is often the case that young firms will work on
interiors projects until they get an opportunity to undertake substantial
building projects.

There is usually no legal requirement for an interior project to have an
architect involved. However, many clients choose architects for interior work
because they feel they understand what an architect can offer. For many,
there is less definition in the role of interior designer or interior architect. In
addition, architectural education involves the understanding of spaces—both

Opposite
Frank Gehry, Walt Disney Concert Hall, Los
Angeles, USA
Where a project may have a specific need for
managed sound, the client might appoint an
acoustic engineer. Inviting this consultant
to be a part of the design team can lead to a
stronger, more holistic design solution.

Left, top and bottom
MAKE Architects, Elephant & Castle Regeneration Area, London, UK
Urban regeneration within major cities is now an almost continuous process. Architects, working with a range of other professionals, may be engaged to masterplan a regeneration area. In such schemes the design may call for the redirection of traffic, demolition of existing buildings, and the introduction of a whole range of new structures that will provide housing, retail, office accommodation, and new green spaces for public use. The urban design does not seek to define the character of the buildings—or, in fact, to design the buildings at all. Rather, the aim is to design the way in which the area is used and the density of the urban fabric.

interior and exterior—which means that architects are able to undertake projects that are not necessarily about the design of a building, but the design of the space within a building.

We should not assume that architects will design the building and its interiors in every case. On the one hand, some practices are not particularly interested in interiors, while on the other hand some may specialize in interiors rather than buildings. In large projects—say, a shopping mall—the overall building may be designed by one practice but the many interiors (stores, restaurants, public spaces, etc.) may be designed by a number of separate firms. In some cases an architect is the most obvious choice to design an interior because the scale of the project or the need for some structural modification suggests that an architect's particular training would be the most appropriate.

Masterplanning/urban design

Just as architects are capable of designing interiors, they are also able to deal with the design of space at an urban scale. Again, most architectural education includes aspects of urban design—often in relation to placing a student's building design into a larger context. However, the design of cities is a complex undertaking. We should not assume that simply because someone has studied architecture they are completely conversant with the issues of planning and designing a city. While many architects, particularly those in large practices, engage in this field, there are also practices that specialize solely in the discipline of masterplanning. Equally, urban design is a field of study in itself (usually at postgraduate level) with its own history, theory, and practices.

Many of the basic principles of architecture (proportion, form, order) apply equally to urban design, but at a different scale. In very simplistic terms, urban design treats buildings as "blocks" rather than as a collection of spaces and functions. While the functions and activities associated with a building must be considered, it is at a "macro" level rather than a detail level. In terms of the design of urban space, this will often involve the design of buildings as urban forms (e.g. setting out the overall size and massing of the building) with little or no actual detail. The allocation of functions will be set out—again, at a macro level—such as identifying areas for commercial, office, and residential use.

Health and safety

Safety within buildings is an important part of the responsibility of the architect. Building regulations set down the basic minimum requirements to meet health-and-safety concerns for the users of a building. However, the safety of those who construct and maintain buildings is also important. There are materials that are heavy, sharp, and toxic. There are machines that, even

Architecture, Urbanism, and Landscape:
Bernard Tschumi, Parc de la Villette, Paris, France

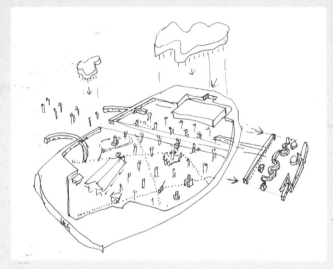

Concept sketch.

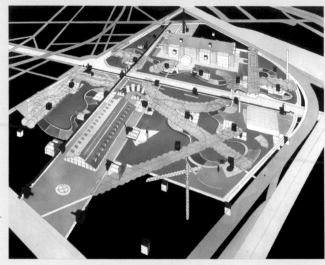

Overall site view.

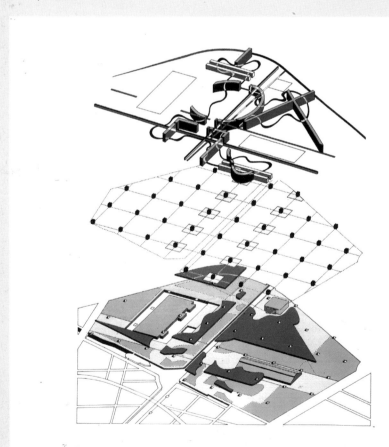

Exploded axonometric showing surfaces, points, and lines.

Architects often are engaged in projects that one might not typically think of as architecture. From the design of furniture to urban design, architects are called upon to engage in aspects of a wide range of design activities. In some projects the breadth of architectural practice is visible in challenging ways.

At one time La Villette was the central location for the butchery and distribution of almost all of the meat sold in Paris. The scale of this operation created employment for more than 3000 local residents. However, by the 1960s new refrigeration technologies made the need for such a centralized abattoir redundant and the area went into decline.

Parc de la Villette is the largest park in Paris, covering 123 acres (50 hectares) in the nineteenth *arrondissement*. The competition in 1983 to redesign the site called for the creation of a new park that would provide venues and spaces for music, science, art, and recreation. The winning entry, by Bernard Tschumi, is the most well-known project to be associated with deconstruction in architecture.

Tschumi has said, "Architecture only survives where it negates the form that society expects of it, where it negates itself by transgressing the limits that history has set for it." In the masterplan for Parc de la Villette Tschumi sought to transgress and disrupt the traditions and precedents of both architecture and landscape. Where nineteenth-century landscape designers might have aimed to create a "park in the city" (a green refuge of order

View of follies.

Detail of folly.

and pastoral beauty within the hustle and bustle of urban life), Tschumi has seemingly brought some of the chaos and uncertainty of the modern city into the park.

Through the creation of a design that defies a single reading or coherent meaning, the project challenges our perception of order and function. Based on a system of lines, points, and surfaces (none of which seems to correspond to the other), the park becomes a site of discontinuities. The surfaces provide areas of activity (playing fields, markets, leisure space). Lines are created by the combination of a 390-foot (120-meter) grid overlaid on the entire park as well as the paths that cut across the park—both axial (connecting the two transport interchanges near the park) and "meandering" (created by a series of thematic gardens with seemingly random curved paths). The points are established by a collection of follies that are all based on the same 32-foot-square (ten-meter-square) cube. The conjunction of these different systems creates opportunities for discovery and activity within the overall scheme of the park.

The built forms of the follies create a problematic element within the park. Their regularity (both in spacing and consistent basic form) suggests that they are part of an infrastructure. In reality, though, many have no obvious use. Where they do have function there is no clear relationship between the nature of the built form and the use. Here, again, Tschumi is attempting to deconstruct the relationship and hierarchy associated with form and function.

One of the most controversial aspects of La Villette is the apparent lack of coherence that the park suggests. At times one can be overwhelmed by the sheer number of fragments that are apparent within one's visual field. This, however, is an intention to create a space that is representative of modern urban space—charged with multiple meanings, divergent readings, and random events.

View along curved promenade.

when operated by trained professionals, are very dangerous to be near. There are high levels of loud noise. People may be working at a high level or far below ground. Given this range of potential hazards, architects must ensure that the design of a building and the processes required to construct it do not further exacerbate these risks. In some countries, the UK included, there is specific legislation that requires that a professional be appointed in order to review the design and construction methods and ensure that any risks are noted and that there are clear strategies to address these risks. This individual is also responsible for the compiling of all information related to the project that will need to be retained for the future. This includes copies of "as-built" drawings, certificates of compliance (for electrical installations, plumbing installations, mechanical services, etc.), and maintenance information for specific parts of the building. This project file will be handed to the client/owner and stays with the building (if the building is sold it must be handed to the new owner) so that any future work or repairs can be undertaken with a minimum of risk, based on a knowledge of the existing conditions.

Above
Temporary Structural Support
The safety of construction workers, as well as that of pedestrians below, means that scaffolding must be planned carefully. The safety of buildings is increasingly an important aspect of an architect's job from the earliest stages of a project.

7.

Architecture has never been a profession that remains static. As new technologies, new theories, and new challenges arise, architects seek to find ways to integrate a new view of the world with the way that they design. Just as the design of architecture responds to the world around us, so too does the profession of architecture change.

Predicting the future of anything is generally a futile effort. Most predictions will be downright wrong, or certainly off the mark, when we look back at them. However, sometimes it is good to look at where we are and where we might be heading. There are things happening today that give us some sense of what the future might hold.

Digital architectures

In the last decade, with the increasing computing power and graphics capabilities of desktop computers, combined with the growing speeds of the internet, the virtual environment has begun to expand. Where once an on-line "virtual world" was a slow, two-dimensional, cartoon-like experience, today we have on-line worlds that are rich in 3D content and allow real-time interaction. Second Life, an on-line virtual world created by San Francisco-based Linden Labs, boasts over 12 million "inhabitants," a real economy (with exchange rates between the on-line currency and the US dollar), and a system that allows residents to "build" within its virtual environment.

Most of the "buildings" of Second Life (SL) are often relatively crude, having been designed by non-architects. Equally, there are some very interesting structures and some that imitate buildings in the real world. Architects are beginning to explore what virtual environments such as SL mean to the way in which we experience architecture, the way that we may design, and what a "client" might wish to have designed. There are cases of architects providing design services to clients for the design and building of virtual homes in SL. Equally, some architects have used SL as space in which to model their projects and then allow their clients to walk through them.

If Second Life and other on-line environments continue to grow in popularity, we can imagine that there will be an increased demand for quality design services within the virtual realm. The challenge for architects will be to find a new architectural language in a space where the normal conventions of structure and form do not apply. At present much of the architecture of Second Life is still a mirror of reality. The possibility of a "virtual architecture" is intriguing when we consider the ways in which this phenomenon might begin to allow us to question real-world architecture.

For some this questioning is already taking place. The notion of an architecture based not on function or traditional notions of form and order may seem to run contrary to our conceptions of architecture itself, but there is an increasing exploration of architecture through computation. Already we see buildings being constructed based on this parametric method. Norman Foster's 30 St Mary Axe in London (often referred to as "The Gherkin" owing

Projects in Linden Lab's Second Life
Top
Avalon
Middle
Welcome
Bottom
Global Condo Center
With its ability to allow "residents" to build within the on-line "virtual world," Second Life (SL) has started a process that begins to question the relationship between architectural practice and the physical realm. In a world without gravity or construction cost, designers are beginning to question what architecture in virtual space might be like. From a practical point of view, some architects practicing in the real world are using SL as a low-cost way of testing design ideas. Building their project in the virtual world allows them and their clients to experience these spaces by virtually inhabiting them.

Iwamoto Scott Architects, Jellyfish House, Treasure Island, San Francisco, California, USA

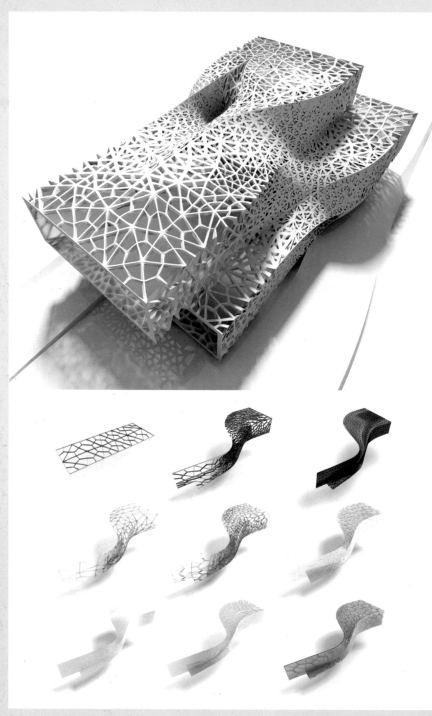

Structure and surface development.

Some architects have started to embrace technology to achieve designs that would, only a short time ago, have been impossible to realize. The use of high-powered computer modeling and rapid prototyping mean that computer models can be translated to physical models, allowing for the testing of new ideas of structure and form to be studied both digitally and physically.

The Jellyfish House is based on the idea that a house, like a sea creature, might coexist with the environment through a series of sense–response feedback loops. Like a jellyfish, which has no brain or central nervous system and consists largely of water, the house is an environmentally responsive system or network.

The house itself is only one part of a larger strategy for reclaiming the site—a decommissioned military base that has been left with toxic soil. Just as the Jellyfish House will be a responsive participant within the environment, the site strategy calls upon the regenerative and cleansing properties of some plants in order to "phytoremediate" the toxic areas. By introducing new wetlands the site will be cleansed of toxins and the wetland vegetation will, after the detoxification process has been completed, continue to filter rainwater run-off from the new housing areas that are to be developed.

The shell of the building is conceived of as a "deep," layered surface. Its patterns of openings and thickness change in order to address localized needs related to structural, functional, visual, geometric, or mechanical systems. These variations are based on complex calculations (Voronoi diagrams and Delaunay triangulation), executed within the software used for the design.

Just as a jellyfish relies upon water to exist, the house will tap into the wetland processes at the smaller scale. By capturing rainwater and gray water (the water used for bathing, handwashing, and dishwashing) the house itself will filter water through its "skin." In this the house is at one with the processes of the larger site.

This filtration at the building scale is also part of a heating-and-cooling strategy that sees areas of the building's skin act as a kind of "water jacket" in which the contents of fluid-filled pockets can be changed from liquid to solid in order to control the heat-loss and heat-gain of the building.

The Jellyfish House represents a fresh way of thinking about the possibilities new materials and technologies of building, linked to new ways of conceiving of space and form, can offer architects.

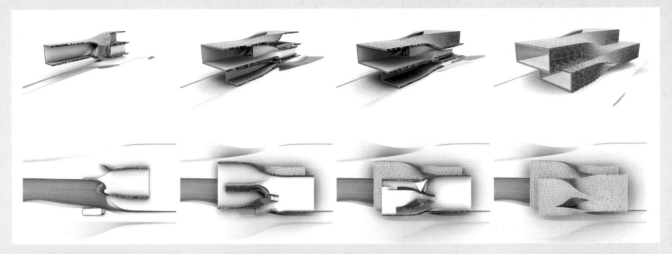

Section views (horizontal and vertical).

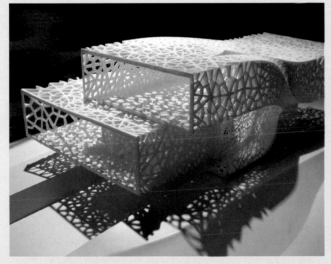

Rapid prototype model view of structure.

Rapid prototype model view of structure.

Site context view.

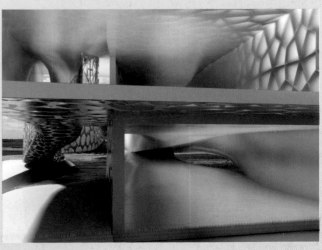

Entrance view.

to its shape) is based on a parametric equation that defined the façade and curvature of the overall building, optimizing the surface pattern to allow for the regularization of the façade elements and resulting in one of the most striking features of London's skyline. As computing continues to develop, and the use of software tools becomes further integrated into both education and practice, this strand of architecture is likely to grow.

Another technology that is gaining popularity is Google Earth. This application brings together geographic information systems (GIS), satellite photography, and 3D modeling to create the possibility of accurate, low-cost, 3D mappings of cities. Since the information that is available in the system can be added to, it is possible for architects and urban planners (and anyone else) to embed their designs into the system. Thus an architect is able to place their proposal within a larger context in order to explore the possible relationships between existing and proposed. This also allows clients to view their project within the context of what surrounds it, from any angle and any height. This is also invaluable to planning authorities and urban planners, as it provides an excellent way of viewing the impact of a large urban-regeneration project or a new tower in the heart of a city. The technology behind Google Earth is moving into the mainstream of CAD, and modeling software as well. Some of the industry-standard applications now allow the direct export of models to the Google Earth format, so architects are able quickly to put their projects onto the virtual site and share this with client, consultants, and others.

In Chapter 5 we touched on Building Information Modeling (BIM)—the systems that allow architects to design with "intelligent" models for both a visual understanding of the overall project and the production of construction

Above
Norman Foster, 30 St Mary Axe, London, UK
Some projects have already been built that are based on the use of computational models and parametric processes. The structure and skin of "The Gherkin," as it is commonly known, are based on calculations that allowed for the definition of the glass panels, lines of structure, and the overall form.

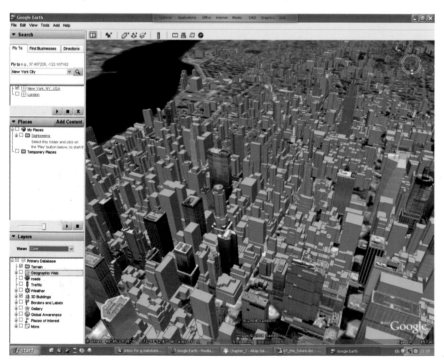

Left
Google Earth, View of New York City
Low-cost computers, of considerable power, combined with network computing, have opened up new technologies to a much broader audience. Google Earth brings together satellite imagery, computer modeling, and geo-referencing in order to provide a tool that can be used by professionals as well as the general public. With its simple interface and access to a huge library of publicly available data, it enables architects and urban planners to insert their proposals into models of cities and study the relationship between the existing and the proposed. Clients can "walk" down the street and see their project within a broader urban context. Some CAD and BIM software can now save models directly to Google Earth.

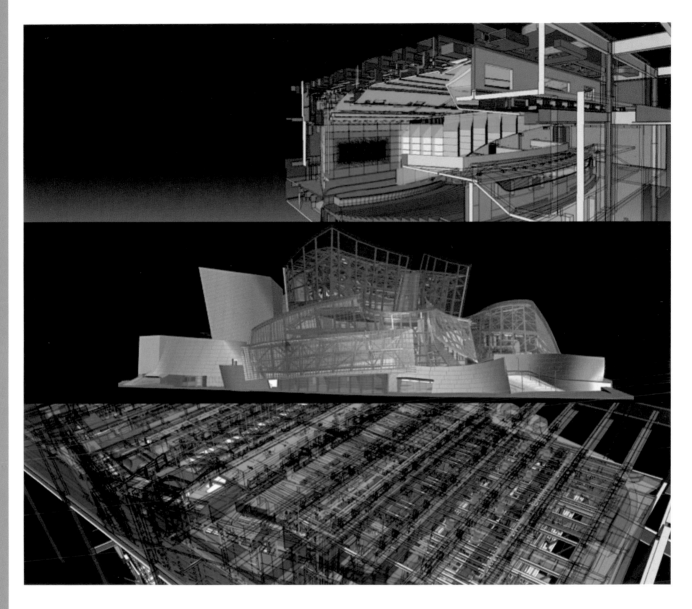

information. From both the current take-up of these systems within architectural practice and the efforts going into their continued development by software companies, this technology will continue to play a greater and greater role in architecture.

As these tools advance in complexity of function and ease of use we will expect to see buildings that could not in the past be realized (either economically or technically) become a reality. Architects such as Frank Gehry have embraced these technologies to the point where a new company, Gehry Technologies, has been formed, which is developing its own software platform to support the realization of complex projects. With most of the major CAD software companies either already producing a BIM application or adding BIM functionality to their existing products, this technology is clearly becoming embedded in the normal practice of architecture.

Above, all

Gehry Technologies, Digital Project using Parametric Design Software
An outgrowth of Frank Gehry's use of state-of-the-art software within his own practice, Digital Project is a new Building Information Modeling system that combines high-level modeling functionality with specialist architectural tools for structure, acoustics, mechanical systems, and specification. The continued development of specialist BIM software is changing the way in which architects carry out the design and development process—encouraging greater collaboration, minimizing conflicts between systems, and streamlining the production process. All of this is facilitated by the reliance on one model for all aspects of the project.

Professional development

The profession of architecture has changed considerably over the last 25 years, but there is more to do. At one level there is an increased recognition that architects cannot stand still in terms of their knowledge base. With new products, building methods, technologies, and materials emerging every year, there is a need for members of the profession to keep abreast of developments. Equally, with the pressures of climate change, building regulations are being updated to begin to address issues related to energy consumption and emissions, and architects must strive to keep up with these legislative changes as well. In short, architects must continue to learn.

Like many other professions, architecture has formalized the need for continued professional development. Organizations, such as the Royal Institute of British Architects (RIBA) and the American Institute of Architects (AIA), have established requirements for their members in relation to the types and amount of development activities that must be completed in a year. For these professional organizations Continuing Professional Development (CPD) is required of all members, who are expected to complete a minimum amount of recorded activities related to a suggested curriculum. There is a clear determination that much of the development activity be in those areas that ensure public health and safety. Although this may sound like a lot of work on top of the architect's normal practice, it should be noted that a good deal of CPD activities can be completed as part of that day-to-day practice. In most locales there is an allocation of the proportion of CPD time that must be through "formal" systems (lectures, seminars, training, etc.), while some can be carried out by reading the relevant publications and journals.

This notion of professional development has also begun to become a part of education, and will continue to exert influence on the higher-education syllabus. Many schools of architecture have established Personal Professional Development (PPD) elements within their curriculum. At its most basic PPD is a program of supporting students as they begin to explore their future professional lives, and identifying the things that they need to learn in order to meet their ambitions. Some of the activities normally considered to be a part of PPD are the acquisition of basic skills required for any professional context. These so-called *transferable skills* are those that help the student (or professional) in areas such as:

- Research and analysis
- Writing for professional uses
- Reflection and planning
- Time management

Teaching is increasingly a part of many architects' continuing professional development. The challenges to one's own sense of architecture when confronted with the need to critique and discuss the work of others is a very powerful way in which we can further define and update our own practices. In addition, the continuing drive for students to engage with practice as part of their education means that involving practicing architects in education is an ideal way of achieving this aim. It is not uncommon to hear and studio critics say that they learn as much from their students as their students learn from them. This reciprocal process keeps the profession enlivened by challenging the practitioners, and encourages students by bringing them into contact with those who are engaged with the profession daily.

Research

Research, both within practice and in education, will continue to be a vital part of the architectural experience. Again, with the rapid pace of developments in materials, technologies, building methods, etc., architects will find ample scope to engage in research.

For many practices the ability to differentiate themselves from other firms will be key to maintaining a successful position within a competitive market. To do this a practice must seek constantly to refresh its design ideas so that it may offer clients something that others cannot. The development of new ideas and new design directions can help a practice to define a unique character to its work, which can then be marketed differently from that of the competition.

In many cases such research is an ongoing and normal part of architectural practice—something that is done as part of every project. But, it can also be the case that practices will develop "internal" projects in order to look at specific aspects of their particular market. For example, a practice whose primary focus is on large-scale residential developments may recognize that a shift in the housing market suggests a demand for more varied forms of housing within a development. Therefore, it may undertake

Left
Lebbeus Woods, Berlin Free-Zone Project
Research continues to be an area of expanding interest for many architects. Whether through competitions, writing, or drawing and design, architects are continually exploring the nature of practice through projects that are intended not to lead to built form but to question the possibilities and future of architecture. In Woods's 1990 proposal for an abandoned government building in recently reunified Berlin, the role of space is explored for its potential opportunities following social and political upheaval.

internal design research in order to explore the implications of social changes, such as young people living at home longer or an increased elderly population. Such research, with design outcomes, might allow the practice to be more attractive to developer clients, as it would be "ahead of the game" in having solutions to some of the problems that those clients will be facing.

It should also be noted that a practice can benefit from theoretical research as well. While theory-based research may not be directly marketable to a client, it can help to define the design position of a practice. A developed body of theoretical research, published in journals or delivered through conferences, can help to raise the profile of a practice both within the architectural community and (to a lesser extent) the public. Such theoretical research can also help architecture, as a discipline, to expand its horizons. This form of research can take many different directions.

Some architects work almost solely in research. Lebbeus Woods has been researching, and teaching, architecture for 30 years or more. He is the director of the Research Institute for Experimental Architecture. His work—explored primarily through drawing, installation, and writing—continues to challenge the discipline by considering the ways in which architecture is engaged with, and influenced by, the world at large. Much of his work has looked at the design of architecture "in crisis"—the conflict between the old and the new. Where some theoretical architectures appear to be visions of a clean, perfect world, Woods's work has often felt unstable, fragile, and decayed. His designs engage deeply in a debate that includes politics, economics, and issues of war.

Such work challenges architects to consider the ways in which their practice touches upon the broader issues of society. Architects must continue to explore the boundaries of their discipline in order to be able to engage in the process of change that surrounds us.

Embracing diversity

Despite considerable advances, the profession of architecture is still largely dominated by white men. This must change if architecture is to reflect the society in which we live. A 2005 report in the UK found that Black and Minority Ethnic (BME) people still face obstacles to career progression and education in architecture. It was projected that BME people would make up more than half of the working-age population by 2009, and yet there is no suggestion that they are making up half of the occupations within the built environment.

There are also gender barriers. A study from 2003 found that while there was an increase in women studying architecture, this did not translate into the profession. Young women are more likely to choose a legal career—of law professionals in the UK, 37 percent are female, as opposed to 11 percent in architecture. Similarly a 1999 survey of interns (those either not yet fully qualified or recently qualified) by the AIA found that women and minorities were under-represented: only 10 percent of respondents were female, while 74 percent were white. Further, there remained a pay gap between the sexes.

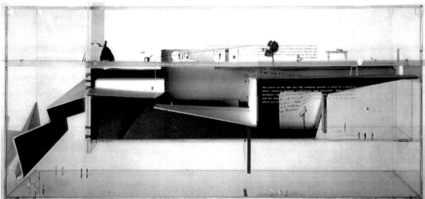

Above
MUF, Museum Pavilion, St Albans, UK
Left
MUF, Museum of Women's Art Project
Women and ethnic minorities are under-represented in the architectural profession. While the number of non-male, non-white practitioners has risen, it remains far below the level that would suggest that the profession is representative of the population as a whole. Ventures such as MUF, a collaboration between artists and architects, are perhaps representative of a new breed of practice. Its work spans art, architecture, exhibition design, landscape, and urbanism, and is often based on a close working relationship with the client or other stakeholders. It would be simplistic to suggest that as a practice established and run by women MUF has a different approach based on gender alone, but its breadth of practice and openness to alternative ways of working suggests a new and inclusive approach to design.

It is in education that we must begin to address issues of equality. This is equality of access *to* higher education as well as equality *within* education. It is often claimed that many members of BME communities do not enter into architecture as a field of study because they are not empowered to see it as a profession in which it might be possible for them to succeed. Equally, those who do enter into the study of architecture find that the curriculum can be too "Eurocentric" and does not engage with their own cultural history or identity.

Education must also seek to address issues of access and support for students from non-traditional education. These are students who may not have had the same learning journey as those who have entered architectural education in the usual way. Some of these students may have left formal education and been in employment for a period of time, or may have received a more vocational education (as opposed to a typically "academic" one). These students may have the necessary skills, but may lack the experience of formal higher education and may find it difficult to manage the expectations of an architecture school. Many universities have begun to address these students' particular needs by putting in place additional support to ensure that they have every opportunity to engage with their course and get the best results.

Increasingly students may have additional financial pressures that mean that they have to work while studying. In order to ensure that students are able to complete their studies, schools are exploring the possibilities of part-time study, work-based learning, and other ways in which students might continue to work while studying.

It is also the case that among some ethnic minority groups a young person may be the first generation of the family to have the opportunity to enter into higher education. Parents may not see architecture as an option for their child, as they may not understand the profession or the fact that their child might be able to succeed in it. There are few role models within architecture for ethnic-minority students to identify with and see as someone who shares their cultural experience. So, often, talented potential architects do not even enter the subject—opting instead for those areas in which parents are able to see a future, and which offer clear role models for success. If architecture is to speak to young people in BME groups then the message must be taken to primary and secondary education. Some schools of architecture have started to explore ways in which they might work with secondary schools in order to engage students in exploring architecture as part of their curriculum. The aim is to support students who may wish to progress to architecture at university level by assisting them during their time in pre-university education.

In professional practice the barriers to women and BME groups are as various as they are in education. It remains the case that there are clear issues in regard to racism both within the office environment and on site. Despite legislation for equal rights there is evidence that some members of BME groups do not get the same jobs as their white counterparts, do not achieve career progression at the same rates, and are discriminated against. Similarly, in an industry dominated by men there is still a pay gap between men and women in architecture. In addition there remains a "macho" attitude among many men (particularly on building sites), which can make it uncomfortable for women.

Addressing these issues is not simply a question of fairness and equality, although that is clearly a necessity. The profession suffers by not recognizing the potential benefit that would come from a more diverse and representative membership. If architecture is going to respond to the changes in our culture by creating buildings and spaces that can embody the diversity of that culture, then the people who are engaged in the design of those buildings and spaces should include the full range of gender, ethnicity, and mobility.

Left
The Architects' Collaborative, Clark Art Institute, Williamstown, Massachusetts, USA
Below
The Architects' Collaborative, JFK Federal Building, Boston, Massachusetts, USA
Collaborative work is part and parcel of architectural practice. Through combining the strengths and skills of a number of practitioners it is possible to develop more robust and effective design solutions. While collaboration may be a part of the fabric of the profession, practices are beginning to explore the ways in which collaboration with those outside architecture may enrich the design and experience.

Changes in professional practice

Just as architectural design changes in response to the broader context of social and economic influences, so too does architectural practice. There have always been some fairly unique types of architectural practice, but we are beginning to see forms of practice that are more complex, larger, or more varied. The future may well see a continued expansion of the types of practice that are engaged with architecture. In part this change will be in response to the types of projects that are on offer, and the desire for new solutions.

Architecture is a collaborative process. Whether a small practice or large, there are almost always a number of people involved in a project. There may be a team of designers or a single architect, but there will also be engineers, planners, interior designers, and other professionals involved. However, there is an increasing trend, particularly within smaller practices, toward involving people from outside of the traditional architectural scene.

Multidisciplinary practices are those that include non-architectural designers and creative practitioners in the design process. Whether it is a grouping of architects with artists, product designers, writers, or dancers, the integration of alternative forms of creative practice brings the potential of new design solutions to architectural projects.

There has long been a tradition of cooperation among small practices. As there are more young architects entering professional practice we may see an increase in this sector. Cooperatives are fluid groupings of professionals who, while maintaining separate company identities, share in the provision of resources and (at times) personnel. For example, a group may hire a receptionist to take calls on behalf of the different companies and to act as office support for each company. Similarly, the cooperative may purchase or lease equipment for the use of all members. Most of the time the various members of the cooperative will work entirely separately, but, given the opportunity, they may come together to work on a large project that a single member-company could not undertake on its own. For young practitioners a co-op can be the ideal way to move into practice on their own.

Alternative careers

One of the unique things about architectural education is that it prepares graduates not just to practice as architects but, potentially, for many related professions. There are, in reality, a significant number of people who graduate from architecture school but never practice as architects. This should not be seen as a weakness of architecture, education, or the students. Rather, we should celebrate the breadth of architecture as a field of study and embrace the range of occupations that can benefit from the graduates of architecture schools.

Visualization, film, and television

Visualization is one of the more common destinations, other than architecture, for graduates. By combining the skills of computer modeling and rendering with an understanding of architecture, graduates entering into the field have some advantages over those who are simply able to model and render. With a design education those involved in visualization are able to understand more clearly the architect's intention and seek to ensure that this comes through in their depiction of the project. The proliferation of visualization companies in the last five to ten years suggests that this is a growing area for the provision of services. As more students receive training in the more advanced uses of software for modeling and rendering we will continue to see a good number of candidates for employment in this sector.

Obviously there is a need for those in visualization to be able to use computer applications effectively and creatively in order to create 3D forms—but there are other skills that are important too. First, there is a need to be able to read and understand architectural drawings. If a visualization team is going to be successful in its work, it needs to be able to understand the nature of a given project and how it is to be constructed.

Second, there needs to be a fairly high level of understanding of materials in terms of their visual properties. When working with a design that might be using a new material the visualization team may need to recreate that material in digital form (often called a "shader") so that it can be applied to the digital model. This can be a very complex process, as there will be issues related to reflectivity, transparency, texture, finish, and much more. Each of these will need to be programmed into the shader. Much time can be spent developing a digital palette of materials to be used in a visualization.

Thirdly, a visualization expert will need to have a very good understanding of lighting—both natural and artificial. Many of the latest modeling applications include lighting systems that are based on real-world physics. Therefore the visualization specialist will need to be able to consider whether a 30-watt tungsten lamp in a downlighter fitting that provides a 60-degree throw will give the sort of lighting effect that best highlights the design. As with materials, there can be a good deal of time required to reach the correct lighting representation before doing final renderings. Finally, it is important that a visualization specialist understands perspective and composition, as

Above
CGI—Computer Generated Imagery
Training in the use of 3D-modeling and rendering software allows for the possibility that having studied architecture one may be suitable for working in a range of other fields. Film and animation has become an increasingly popular destination for architecture graduates. Not only do the graduates have capabilities in understanding buildings and form, and in using the appropriate software, they also have specific problem-solving skills that often allow them to approach a CGI task in ways that result in unique outcomes.

they will need to set up the views of the project for rendering. Whether considering an animated "walk-thru" or a still image, a good grasp of how to frame the view can make the difference between a merely good image and one that instantly captures the viewer's attention.

Visualization skills are not just in demand within the architecture and design fields. One need only think of the number of recent cinema films to have made use of CGI (computer-generated imagery) for character animation, special effects, or scene compositing, to realize that this tool is becoming mainstream in the motion-picture industry. While the design and creation of CGI characters is a highly specialized field, and is a subject area in its own right for higher education, the design and implementation of digital scenography and sets requires an understanding of form, space, and order. In essence the design of the environment for CGI or "composited" live-action filming is ideally suited to those with an architectural education. By possessing an understanding of design, structure, and form, as well as knowing the effects of sunlight on surfaces, the types of artificial lighting that might be found in a specific kind of interior space and a raft of other kinds of knowledge that are implicit in architecture, such practitioners offer the film and television industry a group of potential candidates to support the development of digital scenes.

Planning

One of the reasons architects sometimes find the planning process frustrating is because many of the people involved in planning departments are not trained in architecture or design, but they are (to some degree) making judgements about the value of design in certain situations. There is always a demand for people in the field of planning, whether as a member of the local authority planning department or as a planner within a practice or consultancy. In many ways planning has had "bad press" in the architectural community. Many see it as an obstacle, whereas if more people with an architecture/design training were to engage with planning as a career then there would, potentially, be a more reasonable relationship between the architect and the planning authority.

We should not assume planning is strictly a non-design or administrative role. Urban planning and urban design are very active professions and are increasingly in demand as regeneration projects are taken up in many major metropolitan cities. While urban planning and design are fields of study in their own right, there is a role for architects within these disciplines.

Project management

Not all architects are designers. There is a tendency to assume that architectural education is about becoming a design architect, when in reality there are many different roles that an architect might choose as their specialization. The process of design and building is one that requires a considerable amount of clear thinking and careful planning. The skills that allow an architect to manage a project in their office and on a building site

Opposite
Alsop Architects, Palestra Building, London, UK
For many small projects, and every large project, engagement in the planning or zoning process will be required. Where a project, such as the Palestra Building in London, is out of the ordinary and potentially challenges the published planning regulations, the process can require very close collaboration with planning officials. At present many of those working in planning do not have a design background, but are asked to make decisions that require design understanding. If those with architectural training were to work in planning departments it may create possibilities for real debate and discussion about the ways in which our cities and countryside will be developed in the future.

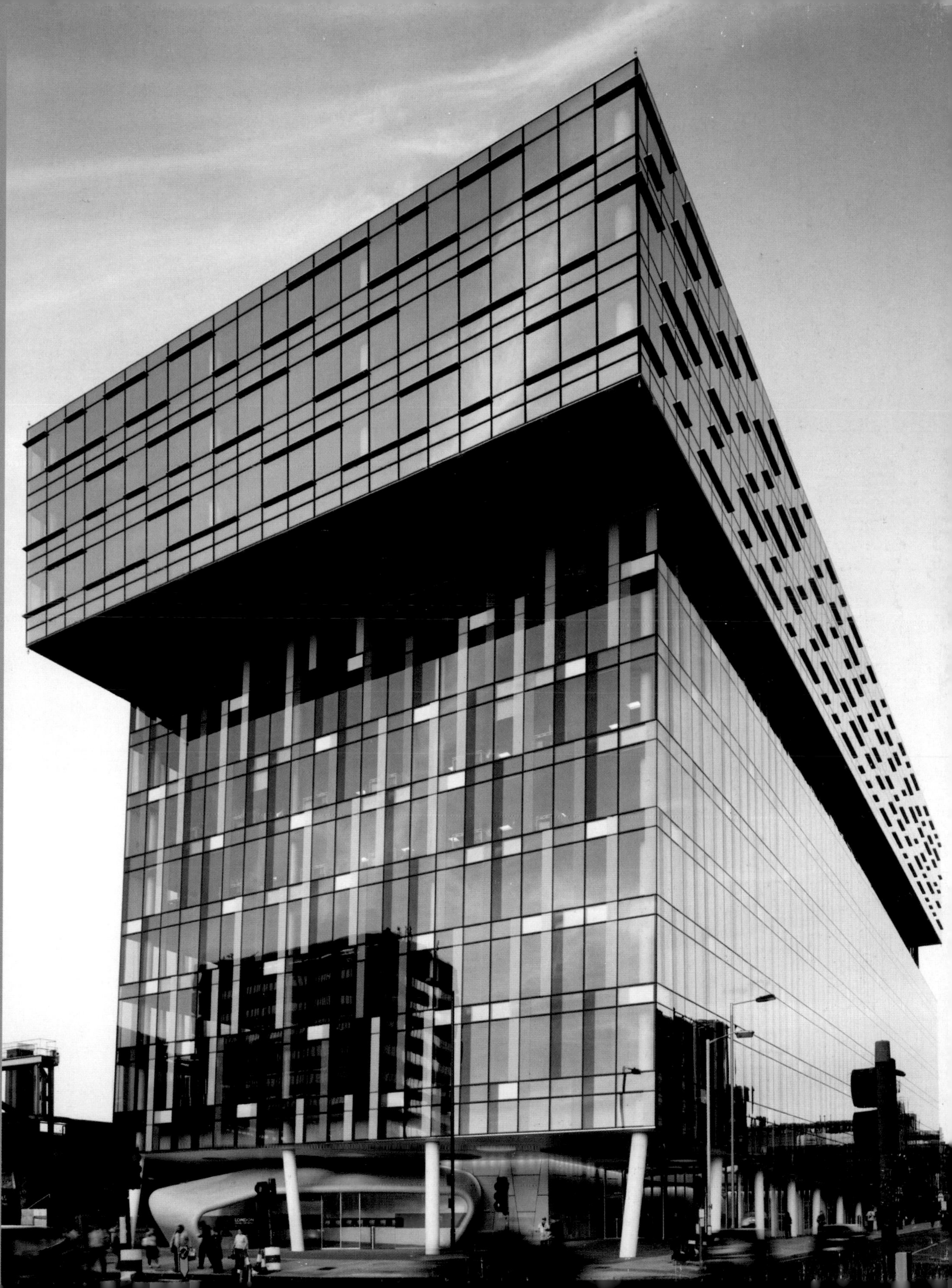

Tom Kundig (Olson Sundberg Kundig Allen Architects), Delta Shelter, Mazama, Washington, USA

Summer view with shutters open.

Hand crank to control shutters.

View toward entrance.

There are many approaches to designing with environmental awareness in mind. In previous chapters we have seen projects that seek to integrate technologies in order to address the energy consumption of a building, or that use materials that come from renewable sources or are recycled. There is also an approach that seeks to integrate physically with the environment, effectively becoming a part of the natural habitat that surrounds the project.

The Delta Shelter, by Tom Kundig of Olson Sundberg Kundig Allen, may initially appear incongruous in the landscape of remote Washington State. However, when one explores further it reveals itself to be a uniquely industrial but carefully considered intervention within its pastoral setting.

The site for Delta Shelter lies on the flood plain of an alpine river valley, so the building must respond to the possibility of regular flooding. Designed across three levels, the house is a weekend retreat for the owner—a chance to leave the city behind and be enveloped in nature. Essentially a steel-clad box on stilts, the house provides views in all directions while lifting itself above the 100-year flood level.

The lowest level of the dwelling is a carport and utility room. From this level a set of external stairs rises up to the middle floor, which comprises the entrance and two small bedrooms and bathrooms. The upper level is a single, open-plan space housing the sitting room, dining room, and kitchen. Balconies are cantilevered from the top and middle levels, providing further space for entertainment, relaxation, and enjoyment of the landscape.

Through its choice of materials and construction processes Delta Shelter embodies an approach to the environment that is both challenging and harmonious. The structure of the dwelling is based on four steel columns, which support the floors and roof. Much of the house (structure, roof, shutters, stairs) was prefabricated off site, allowing for rapid construction and minimal environmental impact as there was no need for high levels of traffic to and from the site for delivery of individual materials. This, combined with a material selection dominated by steel and timber (both of which are recyclable), further makes the project a sound environmental design.

However, what sets Delta Shelter apart as a unique environmental project is the way in which the building responds to nature. The large steel shutters, which are controlled by a sizeable handcrank within the house, serve to seal the dwelling against the elements during the harsh winters. These shutters also allow for control of solar gain via the extensive glazed areas of the house. Further, the steel responds to the elements through weathering and rust; in this way, the building continues to change and become richer by the literal exposure to its surroundings.

Delta Shelter shows us that there are different ways in which an architect can respond to the environment, ensuring that the work that we do does not have an adverse effect on the world around us, and that it integrates itself into the environment in interesting and sensitive ways.

Winter view with shutters open.

Winter view with shutters closed.

are such that they can be applied to many other types of project. The ability to work with a client and liaise with other consultants is a valuable service to offer clients. While this is not a design role, it is vital to the success of a project. With large schemes there is often a necessary role for a project manager to work directly with the client as an "interface" to the architect and other consultants. The project manager, in such circumstances, wields a considerable amount of power in terms of the implementation of design decisions. A project manager who is trained in architecture and design can be a valuable asset to both the client and the design team.

Specification writer

The construction drawings for a project are not always sufficient fully to explain the type and quality of materials to be used or the level of workmanship that is expected. For this we need specifications. Anyone can write a specification, but to write them well is a skill that takes time and effort to develop. Furthermore, specification writing is not simply a matter of typing things into a pre-existing template. Most of a specification writer's time is spent researching products, materials, suppliers, processes, and more. This research must relate directly to the design of the project, as it is the materials and products used in a building that will, to a great extent, determine the quality of its overall finish.

For many projects architects will be seeking to find new materials and new processes. Similarly, there are many practices that engage in continuous research into materials. Often the specification writers will be closely involved

Above
Richard Rogers, Lloyds Building, London, UK
For any project of great scale or complexity there will be numerous consultants as well as an architect, and it is often the project manager who will hold the overall scheme together. Having a training in architecture, an understanding of the design process, and an ability to work with diverse groups of people makes the project manager a key player in the realization of buildings. Architects are often called upon to act as project managers, either as part of an architectural service or as a separate consultancy service.

Left
Johann Otto von Spreckelsen, Grande Arche, La Défense, Paris, France
The difference between a successful project—one that is completed according to the architect's intention—and a project that falls short can be directly related to the quality of the specifications. While drawings can provide a wealth of information visually (about size, shape, and construction), they cannot give the depth of information about quality, manufacture, and assembly that is possible in a specification. The writing of good specifications is a highly developed skill and requires a wide-ranging understanding of architectural design, construction, manufacturing, and costing.

in such material-and-process research in order to understand the ways in which such new materials can be used in projects, what their properties are (in order to clearly specify them), and the wider issues associated with the material or process.

As environmental concerns become more and more embedded in the design of both buildings and spaces, the role of the specification writer will become increasingly important. The sourcing and the specification of materials and products that are environmentally sound will become a skill in itself. At present this is a relatively specialized area of the field of materials, but in the near future the knowledge of how to source and apply such elements within the whole building process will become increasingly valued.

Many large practices have a team of people dedicated to the writing of specifications. Specification writers will often work very closely with the design team in order to understand the aims of the design, and the production team in order to supply the necessary information to be integrated into the drawings. A specification writer who has studied architecture will be able far more readily to see the design intention and seek to provide specifications, materials, and products that support the design. Conversely, a good specification writer should be a source of information and inspiration to the design team. The designers may have an idea about a material, but it will often be the specification writer who has the research knowledge to be able to say whether the material is appropriate and, if necessary, suggest an alternative that might prove a better choice.

Site architect/contract administrator

For most people architecture is the buildings that they see. For clients it is the finished built form that is almost always their goal. The ability to move into a new house, start up business in a new office, enjoy a performance in a newly renovated theater, or to admire the skyline of a major city is the way

Left
Building Site
Site architects are often called upon to make difficult decisions and to sort out problems that might have tremendous impact on a project. It is a high-pressure role, but the rewards can be great. Seeing a project through an entire building process is an exciting prospect, and one that requires specialist skill.

in which people generally think of and experience "architecture." For this reason, managing the building process is one of the most important roles in construction. Unless managed carefully, a fantastic design can be completely ruined by poor construction.

Site operations are a very complex part of even the smallest project. On the one hand there is a need to establish clear working relationships with the contractors and their teams. On the other there is a need to have a very careful eye on both the overall and the detail. For large projects, as we have seen, there may be a team of architects that work on site to address issues as they arise. On smaller projects there might be weekly meetings on the site to review progress. In either case, the site architect must be able to ensure that the project is moving at the pace that is required to meet the completion date (this will also be the concern of the contractor and, of course, the client), while at the same time making sure that the quality of the work is of the standard that is expected and defined in the drawings and specification.

For some architects the process of building is the most exciting and interesting part of a project, and they may choose to specialize in this area. Such "site architects" or "contract administrators" will be particularly conversant in a broad range of building processes and techniques. In some cases they may specialize even further in a particular type of construction (e.g. steel-framed structures or timber framing). These will also be individuals who are able to deal with quite high levels of stress, because having a project on site can be a very tense experience. The pressures of completing things on time and in sequence can bring about heated discussions, and the site architect will need to be able to manage personalities as much as the project itself.

Through the collaboration of many different individuals, with particular specialisms, a team is able to define, present, articulate, quantify, specify, and inform the process of a project. Having studied architecture there is a broad range of fields that become career opportunities, and the nature of the education of an architect provides unique skills that can be applied across many different sectors.

Thinking architecture

In Chapter 1 we touched on architectural theory and explored, in brief, some of the recent trends in theoretical debates about architecture. This is a continual debate, and one that expands all the time as architecture becomes a site for discussion across many other areas. One can find discussions about the politics of architecture, architecture as a social function, architecture as an expression of power, and much more. Clearly a grounding in the study of architecture will allow one to consider the debate more closely and from an informed position.

It is vital that architects, and others, continue to challenge our conceptions and preconceptions of architecture and the role of the architect. A questioning

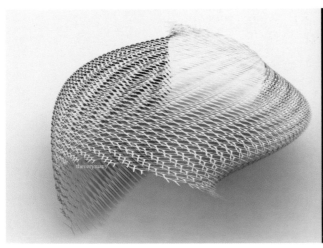
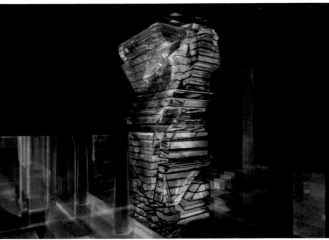

from within—architects examining and challenging architecture themselves—is crucial to the continued ability of the profession and its practitioners to respond to the world around us. For many architecture is a solid, stable, ordered profession that is based on a set of well-defined and well-understood principles (thinking back to Vitruvius' *"firmitas, utilitas, venustas"*). However, for others it is a shifting, unstable, open-ended profession that poses more questions than answers. Neither of these positions is necessarily correct or wrong. Instead, these are the poles of a wide-ranging discourse that enriches architecture for us all.

For many students of architecture the theoretical becomes a space in which they find the most enjoyment and most challenge. At postgraduate level (and beyond, to Ph.D. level), there are many opportunities to continue the theoretical debate. This is not a path that necessarily leads to architectural practice, although there are many examples of practicing architects who engage quite directly with the theories of architecture. Architecture, like many other creative practices, can be involved with the theoretical in different ways. One is through the making of architecture (whether built or un-built) and the other is through writing about the subject. Each is a form of debate and questioning of architecture, and each can bring about new ways of "thinking architecture" that inform and challenge architects and non-architects alike.

Sustainability and the future

Probably the most important issue that architects will face in the future is the question of sustainability. Already there are regulations in force that mean that architects must seek to minimize waste and energy consumption through the design of their buildings. We saw in Chapter 4 that architects can look to the environment as a design driver, and this will change the way in which we think of and construct our buildings. In the future, however, architects will need to take a much more proactive role in the minimization of energy consumption and waste management.

Above left
theverymany.net, 070808_XYCOMP
Above right
Michael Hansmeyer, Algorithms in Architecture
The increasing power of low-cost computer hardware, combined with the growing sophistication of modeling software, has allowed some architects to begin exploring the use of computation as a way of generating architectural form rather than simply as a way of representing it. The use of parametric systems, which allow for form to be derived through the interplay of defining parameters rather than from other, pre-existing forms or formal notions, means that the "architecture" that results is one in which dynamic change is built into the conception of the building—change one parameter and the effect may (almost literally) ripple through the entire design.

While the use of environmentally sustainable materials and renewable energy will help, there is a need to re-evaluate the way in which we design buildings. The average lifespan of a tall building is now estimated to be about 30 years. This means that as we look around our major cities anything built in the 1970s is now reaching the end of its life. Why? In some cases it will be because the building cannot support the kinds of new technology that modern businesses and residences demand. It is very difficult to fit large amounts of network cabling and electrical supplies into a building that was not designed to accommodate them. In other cases it may be that the quality of the building materials are such that they have now reached the point at which they are no longer effective in keeping the elements out, or that they have simply worn out and become unattractive. In some instances the layout of the building may be such that it cannot be reasonably adapted to a new use. Whatever the case, we have no effective way of dealing with the amount of waste that is generated by the demolition of buildings—particularly tall buildings. They produce massive amounts of material that cannot be reused. In addition, substantial amounts of energy and transportation are required in order to remove all the materials from the demolition site. Most of this material will not be reused but will go to landfill, where it will sit for thousands of years.

Architects must begin to consider ways in which the design of buildings can utilize more sustainable materials and allow for longer lifespans. Many of the large office towers that have been built around the world are based on very deep floorplates (i.e. the internal distance across the building is very large). This is effective for offices, as there are often areas of such buildings that do not require natural light and these can be clustered away from the windows. However, it means that these structures cannot be refitted for other uses, such as residential units, in which access to natural light is vital. The adaptation of buildings for different uses is one of the best ways in which to extend the lifespan of a building, but much of our built stock is locked into single use. Through rethinking the way that we consider the use of buildings, and seeking to design flexibility into our concepts, architects can assist in meeting the needs of the client today while still ensuring that a building will have a use when conditions change in the future.

Sustainability is not just about the environment, it is also about people. One of the great criticisms of social housing from the Modernist period was that it did not recognize the needs of the people that would live in it. These buildings, with a few notable exceptions, have long been seen as impersonal, cold, overbearing, depressing, dangerous, and dehumanizing. What is often forgotten is that many of them were designed with the best intentions, and based on the best sociological research at the time.

Our understanding of the way in which people live and the relationship between space and community has changed a great deal over the last 30 or 40 years. However, we must ask whether our approach to the design of communities has changed—and, if so, has the message reached all the

Above
Mumbai, India
As countries and cities develop and expand they place increased strain on the environment. Architects need to consider ways in which their projects can minimize this strain, while also supporting development.

people involved in the design of housing and communities? We are in a period of rapid growth in many cities (particularly in China, India, and South America), and massive change (through regeneration projects) in many large cities and towns in the West. To ensure that the designs of new communities do not fall into the same traps as their predecessors, architects must seek ways in which to engage the public in the design of their spaces. Consultation processes that actively bring the views of the public into the design process should be welcomed and facilitated. There is a tendency for many architects to think that they know best, having studied for five years and practiced. But, we must ask ourselves, do we know how these people will live? What are their aspirations? Surely the sensible approach is to engage, debate, discuss—and then design?

Above left
Shigeru Ban, Paper Tube Houses, India
Above right
Shigeru Ban, Paper Tube Houses, Kobe, Japan
Japanese architect Shigeru Ban had been working with paper as a building material for some time before the devastating earthquake that struck Japan in 1995, leaving many thousands homeless. Ban was able to apply his technological understanding of paper as a structural material to the design of low-cost, rapidly built shelters to meet the needs of those in crisis. This technique, and its accompanying technology, would be applied to other crisis situations in subsequent years. In each case the design attempted to allow some level of local vernacular to be achieved, while remaining a basic emergency measure.

Architecture for social change

As we have noted previously, architects are well trained in problem-solving. These may be new problems or they may be problems that have existed for a very long time. Architecture for Humanity, a charitable organization, is a network of architects and designers around the world working together to find architectural solutions to support people in developing countries or those in crisis situations (natural disasters, refugee crises, etc). By developing a worldwide network of interested practitioners, Architecture for Humanity allows individuals to utilize their design skills in pursuit of socially aware projects, which they might not have been able to undertake had they been working independently.

Others, such as Japanese architect Shigeru Ban, have sought ways to utilize design ideas from their practice to support people in crisis. As part of the Voluntary Architects Network, Ban has used ideas and technology based on paper tubes in order to construct temporary housing and community

Ben Spencer, Venilale Meeting Hall, Buacau, East Timor

Architecture, and architects, can play an important part in helping communities to develop. In areas where development has been stifled because of economics, war, or other problematic conditions, it is not enough for an architect simply to offer a building design; this would provide only a short-term solution. In such cases architects must be prepared to engage in a more holistic and integrated approach—working with local people to address local issues.

Between 2004 and 2006 architect Ben Spencer, working with the Peace Corps, lived and worked, along with his wife Jenn, in the village of Kota Ho'o in East Timor. Working with the Venilale Subdistrict Administrator, village chiefs, women's leaders, and youth groups, Spencer designed the Venilale Master Plan.

As Spencer explains, "the plan is aimed at regenerating Venilale's economy, social conditions, and ecology through the integrated development of education, industry/small business, ecotourism, forestry, agriculture, and health. The meeting hall will serve as the main gathering place for subdistrict-wide initiatives and the dissemination of information to the eight villages in the area."

In order to facilitate both the building of the meeting hall and to support the broader ambition of economic development, a series of bamboo workshops was organized. With the support of the Catholic Relief Services, the United Nations Industrial Development Organization (UNIDO), the Environmental Bamboo Foundation in Bali, and the Timorese Department of Agriculture, Spencer set up and ran tutorials on bamboo propagation, harvesting, preservation, and construction. These served to introduce Venilale's farmers to the possibilities available for using the fast-growing plant as a building material and commercial crop. There are further environmental benefits, in that bamboo can stabilize eroding agricultural soil, contribute to increased food security, help to replenish groundwater reserves, and act as a "bridge" for the re-establishment of other, slower-growing forest plants.

The Venilale Meeting Hall takes a "systems-based" approach to design. That is to say, it is based on a series of processes that, together, create the context for the project as well as the way in which that project will be implemented.

Exploded perspective with component systems.

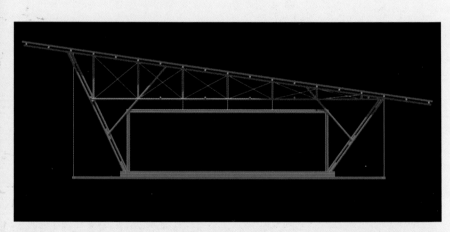

Section.

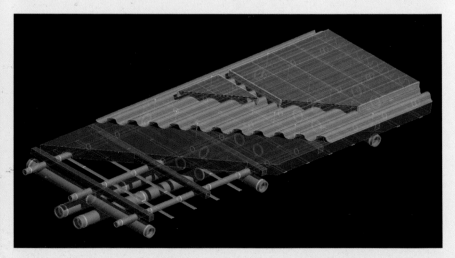

Detail of bamboo roof with solar panels.

View from approach.

Unfortunately, to date, the meeting hall has not been completed owing to the volatile political situation in the former Portuguese colony of East Timor. However, the Open Architecture Network (OAN) has allowed Spencer to maintain contact with organizations that will support the project to move forward when the situation in Timor settles.

The OAN is an initiative organized by Architecture For Humanity (AFH), a group founded by architects Cameron Sinclair and Kate Stohr in 1999. AFH was formed to provide architectural solutions to regions suffering humanitarian crises. The work of AFH is predicated on the notion that problems are local, so solutions should also be local. This means working closely with the people in an affected area, in order that the design solution meets their needs rather than simply the architect's idea of their needs.

The OAN was set up as an on-line "environment" in order to support the sharing of project information on humanitarian work. Some designers are using it as a project-management platform (sharing documents and information between designers, client groups, and builders), while others employ it as a means of sharing "best practice." No matter how it is being used, OAN continues to be a lifeline for architects working in the area of humanitarian projects. As Ben Spencer says, "I spent a lot of time on the OAN looking at projects other designers were doing across the world, learning from and commenting on them. It helped me stay in touch with what other designers were doing on international humanitarian work. It was kind of therapeutic."

Architecture can change people's lives. There is a strong and growing number of architects who are recognizing the value the unique problem-solving associated with architectural projects can bring to bear on humanitarian and development work. As Cameron Sinclair of AFH says, it is time to "design like you give a damn."

Interior view.

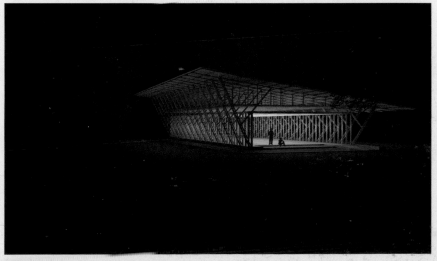

Night view.

facilities for survivors of the Kobe earthquake (Japan, 1995), for refugees in Rwanda, and flood victims in India. This technology, originally used in the project "Paper Arbor" (1989), began a process of research and development that resulted in a system that is low-cost and easily constructed.

The role that architects can play in the broader field of humanitarian aid continues to expand. Through organizations such as Architecture for Humanity and Voluntary Architects Network a new generation of architects is beginning to apply knowledge and problem-solving skills to help address issues around the world. It is also the case that education is becoming involved in these developments. As education and practice continue to explore ways in which architecture can move beyond the commercial, private, and corporate arenas, humanity becomes the client.

"All Change"

We have heard for a number of years that the pace of change in the world is accelerating. Technology has allowed us to achieve more in shorter periods of time—in some cases this has been a great advance, while in others we may be left questioning. It is unlikely that change will slow down, and we may not wish it to do so.

Architecture is both a part of this change and an anchor in what can seem turbulent times. Every day we can see new buildings rising up, old buildings being pulled down and, in those special cases, buildings that have stood the test of time becoming our landmarks and treasures. Architects have the privilege of being a part of this process. We design the new and, at times, attack the old in order to make way. If we are very lucky we may have the opportunity to design something that will last far beyond our own lifetime. Whether our work becomes a treasure for future generations is beyond our control, but we need only look around to see what we are a part of and what impact we can have on the lives of those around us.

For those who choose to enter into architecture as a field of study and a profession, there are challenges along the way. Some will be challenges that inspire and drive us forward. Others will be challenges to overcome. In either case the profession is one that offers great rewards. Perhaps the greatest of those rewards is the sense of achievement at seeing the finished work and knowing that, whether it is a small extension to a private residence or the building of a skyscraper, our efforts will have changed the lives of the people who visit and inhabit our work.

Glossary

Acoustical Engineer: an individual, or firm, dealing with sound and vibration; in relation to architecture their role is usually associated with the management of sound—how to reduce unwanted sound, how to enhance sound, how to reduce vibrations, etc.

Acropolis: most often refers to the Acropolis ("high city" in Greek) in Athens—an elevated plateau upon which a series of temples is located, including the Parthenon.

Aesthetic: most often refers to the study of sensory and emotional values; sometimes refers to the judgement of taste in relation to a work of art or other visual expression.

Ambulatory: the covered walkway around a cloister (the open courtyard found in many monasteries) or a walkway or aisle within a church that passes behind the altar, providing access to chapels.

American Institute of Architects (AIA): the professional organization within the United States that defines a professional code of conduct for members and acts to protect both the profession and the public.

Apprenticeship: a system in which a pupil (or protégé) develops the skills of a particular trade by working in close proximity to an established master.

Architect of Record: refers to the architect who is named, for legal reasons, as "the architect" of the building; all liability related to the project resides with this individual (or sometimes practice).

Architects Registration Board (ARB): statutory body in the UK for the registration of architects.

Architects Registration Examination (ARE): examination for professional qualification in North America.

Architectural Association: established in 1847, the oldest private school of architecture in the UK. In the 1970s it developed the "Unit System" of architectural education; remains one of the most well-known schools of architecture internationally.

Architectural Technician: an individual (who may have specific architectural training) whose primary role is in the development of technical drawing information to facilitate construction.

Arts and Crafts Movement: an art and design movement of the late nineteenth and early twentieth centuries in Britain and the United States that celebrated traditional forms of handmade works. Championed by John Ruskin, it is associated with an idealization and romanticization of handiwork in opposition to the industrialization of production.

Associate: within architectural practices, a person who has been promoted to a level below the principal or partners; often a practice may have many associates who manage projects and teams of employees.

Atelier: traditionally an artist's workshop or studio; in terms of education it refers to a relationship in which the student works under the supervision of the teacher (sometimes in their studio) in order to learn the way that the teacher works.

Axonometric: a form of 3D projection drawing in which parallel lines remain parallel; this allows for more than one side of an image to be visible in a view. Often used to show complex 3D relationships without losing detail through perspective.

Bachelors Degree: *see* Undergraduate Degree.

Bauhaus: school of art and design, lasting from 1913 to 1933, that became highly influential in the development of Modernist art, craft, and architecture (translates from the German as "House of Building" or "School Building").

Bid: *see* Tender.

Brief: the set of instructions, needs, or requests outlined by a client and developed by an architect; the aims of a project as articulated by a client; in education, the instructions given to students at the start of a project.

Building Code: *see* Building Regulations.

Building Control: the statutory authority in the UK that is charged with ensuring that design and construction are undertaken safely, as set out by Building Regulations.

Building Information Modeling (BIM): the process of generating and managing building data through design and construction; often undertaken using specialist 3D software that allows for the entire building to be developed in a single model or series of linked models.

Building Regulations: a set of guidelines that is intended to ensure that buildings are constructed safely and will continue to provide for safe use.

Cantilever: at its most basic a beam supported at only one end; in more complex constructions it may be a part of a building that is supported at one edge.

Carbon Footprint: measured in units of carbon dioxide (CO_2), it is the measure of the impact of human activity on the environment and the greenhouse gases that are produced by those activities.

Change Order: a written document from an architect to a contractor outlining the required changes to the design of a project while work is being carried out on site.

Charrette: in architectural education it is a period of intense design activity either as an individual or within a group; derives from the French term for a small cart, because students at the Ecole des Beaux-Arts would ride in the carts while completing their drawings on the way to classes.

Cistercian: founded in 1098, an order of Catholic monks dedicated to strict adherence to the Rule of Saint Benedict.

Cladding: typically any material used to form the outer surface of a building

Classical Antiquity: a broad period of history that encompasses the Greek and Roman civilizations, concerned mainly with the development of those empires centered in the Mediterranean area; also known as the "Classical era" or the "Classical period."

Classical Orders: usually refers to the system of design in the Classical tradition, based on rules of proportion and characterized by the details of ornament, typically differentiated by the column capitals and other elements. The Greek orders were known as Doric, Ionic, and Corinthian; later the Romans added the Tuscan and Composite orders.

Client: an individual or organization that commissions the services of a consultant.

Commission: to request the services of a consultant; in terms of a client, the process of appointing and briefing an architect or other consultant.

Competition: in architecture, a process of awarding a commission as a prize through a review of submitted designs or proposals from a number of architects or teams.

Computer-Aided Design (CAD): the use of computers for design, technical drawing, or visualization; often refers to the software used in such processes.

Computer-Generated Imagery (CGI): images or graphics produced using computer technology.

Concept: an underlying idea or principle that is embodied in the design of a project.

Construction Drawings (or Working Drawings): drawings produced for the purpose of explaining the way in which a project is to be built; typically these drawings are for providing information rather than giving an understanding of the way the project will look.

Constructivism: an art and design movement, primarily centered in the former USSR during the first decades of the twentieth century, in which art and design were seen as instruments for social reform. Work often challenged traditional forms and aesthetics, and was characterized by abstraction, bold forms, and simplicity.

Consultant: a person or firm hired to provide specialist services to a client or other professional.

Continuing Professional Development (CPD): a process through which a professional person enhances their understanding or skills through ongoing study or experience.

Contract: an agreement between parties, usually legally binding, that involves an offer, acceptance, and consideration (fee).

Contract Administration: in architecture the activities of the architect related to overseeing construction activity, as agreed in a contract between client and contractor.

Contract Packages: in "design-build" procurement projects the information released in stages to the contractor that relates to the phase of work that is required.

Contractor: the person or firm who is hired to construct or oversee others in the process of building.

Cost Consultant (or Quantity Surveyor): an individual or firm engaged in a project to provide information on the potential cost, and savings, of design and procurement decisions.

Cost Estimate (or Cost Plan): a document, usually produced through consultation between architect, client, and cost consultant, that aims to determine the potential cost of a project prior to construction.

Cradle to Cradle: a concept of sustainable design, developed by Dr Michael Braungart and William McDonough, that seeks to minimize or eliminate waste from the life cycle of a product.

Credits: in education, units of learning that are accumulated by the student up to a minimum required for graduation or progression; these units may be transferable between institutions.

Crit (short for Critique): see Tutorial.

Critical Language: refers to the use of terms and concepts in a critical discourse about a subject or work.

Curriculum Vitae (CV): sometimes referred to as a resumé, a structured document that lists an individual's skills and abilities.

Curtain Wall: a form of construction in which the outer skin of a building is non-structural.

Deconstruction: a form of critical analysis in literary criticism, social science, and philosophy that seeks to expose the inherent internal contradictions of literature and philosophy.

Deconstructivism: a style of architecture defined by Mark Wigley and Philip Johnson for their 1988 exhibition at the Museum of Modern Art in New York.

Defect Liability Period: the period of time (usually six months) during which a client will record any items that fail or wear unacceptably; at the end of this period the contractor will return to repair defects and a final completion certificate will be issued.

Design-Build: a form of building procurement process where the design and construction are awarded to a single entity (as opposed to a competitive tender process, sometimes referred to as "design-bid-build").

Developer: an individual or company who finances a building project in order to sell or rent the resulting building for a profit.

Dividend: a payment made to investors/shareholders in a company.

Doctor of Philosophy (Ph.D.): an advanced university degree, usually awarded upon the completion of a research-based project or dissertation.

Ecole des Beaux-Arts: a series of influential art schools in France whose curriculum was focused on Classical arts, architecture, and design; this model of education became the norm for most schools of architecture through the eighteenth and nineteenth centuries.

Electrical Engineer: an individual or firm engaged to deal with the design of electrical systems in buildings.

Elevation: a type of orthogonal projection drawing that shows one view of the outside of a building.

Embodied Energy: refers to the amount of energy that is required to manufacture, transport, and install an item or material in a building.

Environmental Design: the process of designing the environment of a building; typically includes issues of human comfort as well as systems and processes to conserve energy.

Environmental Engineer: sometimes considered the same as a "mechanical engineer;" a person or firm engaged to design the environmental systems of a building.

Ethylene Tetrafluoroethylene (ETFE): a form of plastic used in building for its high strength across a wide range of temperatures and for its resistance to corrosion.

Façade: usually the front face of a building (from the French for "frontage").

Feasibility: the preliminary phase of a project to determine whether the project is viable or achievable within the set parameters (as defined by the client and/or regulations).

Fee (or "Consideration"): a payment for services, usually defined through a contract.

Feng Shui: an ancient Chinese practice, based on astronomy and geography, developed to protect and gain positive energy; in design it involves the positioning of building elements based on a set of rules.

Flying Buttress: a structural element found on the exterior of a building that provides horizontal reinforcement to a wall; best known for its use in Gothic cathedrals, where its inclusion allowed for large areas of glass to be used in the outer walls of the cathedral.

Footing: a form of foundation, or sub-surface structure, that spreads a vertical load across a larger surface area.

Foundation: the structure of a building below ground; transfers the load of the building into the ground.

General Contractor: an individual or firm engaged to oversee the entire building program of a project and to manage the work of other subcontractors.

Gothic: in architecture a reference to a style that arose and flourished in Europe between the twelfth and sixteenth centuries, found most notably in the continent's great cathedrals.

Interior Architect: a person or firm engaged in the design and implementation of work within interior spaces; differentiated from interior design by the inclusion of structural understanding.

Interior Designer: a person or firm engaged in the design of interior spaces, usually not involving structural changes to the building envelope.

Intern Development Program (IDP): a part of the process of gaining professional qualification in the United States; a structured program of recording professional experience with the support of employers.

International Style: title of a book by Philip Johnson and Henry-Russell Hitchcock to record the "International Exhibition of Modern Architecture" at the Museum of Modern Art in New York (1932); one of the first times that European modern architecture was widely seen by the American public.

Isometric: a form of 3D projection drawing in which parallel lines remain parallel but right angles are distorted.

Jury: a form of group critique used in architectural education; typically a student will present their work before a panel of tutors/studio critics, practitioners, and peers.

Kitsch: usually refers to any work of art or creative endeavor that exhibits "bad" taste, often in reference to works that are inferior copies of an original.

Lead Consultant: in a project where there are a number of different consultancies, this is the firm or individual that acts as the primary conduit between client and consultants. In building projects it is often the architect who is considered the lead consultant and will coordinate the input of engineers, cost consultants, and contractor.

Liability: refers to the obligations of an individual or company in relation to past activities. In many countries architects are required to hold insurance related to professional liability in order to protect clients against possible problems that might arise from improper practice.

Liberal Arts: sometimes referred to as "classical education;" refers to a general educational curriculum that usually encompasses arts, sciences, and literature.

Light Emitting Diode (LED): a form of semiconductor that emits light when electrical current is applied; originally only used in situations where a low level of light was required, but technology now allows for LEDs with relatively high levels of light emission.

Live Projects: in education, refers to problem-based learning where the project worked on is intended for a real client.

Mapping: typically refers to the recording of cartographic information about an area or site, but may also refer to gathering information of transitory and non-physical information.

Master Plan: usually a large-scale urban plan for an area; may include location and overall scale information for buildings but usually will not consider detailed design.

Masters Degree: a university-level postgraduate degree that usually follows after the achievement of a Bachelors degree; may be completed in one or two years depending on the type of degree and institution of study.

Mechanical Engineer: an individual or firm engaged to design the systems within a building that control heating, cooling, water, and waste.

Mechanical Systems: the systems that manage the heating, cooling, and plumbing in a building.

Methodology: a set of procedures and practices specific to an activity or discipline.

Middle Ages (or "Medieval Period"): typically refers to a period in European history from the fall of the Roman Empire to the Renaissance.

Minimalism: refers to a stylistic expression, in art and design, where the work is stripped down to its most fundamental and basic elements.

Modernism: a cultural movement, in art, design, music, literature, and architecture, that reflects an embracing of constant change as well as a rejection of the Classical and Historicist movements of the nineteenth century.

Modular Program: a form of curriculum that treats individual elements as modules, each with a value (credit). Students assemble educational experience through the accumulation of credits by undertaking a series of modules that in some cases may be taken in any order, provided they add up to the requisite number of credits.

Multidisciplinary: in art and design this refers to the practice of working across or combining the activities or methodologies of different disciplines, such as an artist and an architect working on a project together, or an architect working in a fine-art practice.

National Council of Architectural Registration Boards (NCARB): the professional association of architectural registration boards in the United States.

Office Manager: a person whose main role is the overseeing of the operations of an office environment. Typically this will include the management of those staff who provide support services, purchasing and inventory of equipment and supplies, etc.

Office of Works: the organization set up by the English Royal Household in 1378 to oversee the construction of royal castles and residences. It became one of the first places where a systematic training of architects was developed.

Parametric: refers to the use of parameters (a mathematic function or equation that defines a property); in architecture it is most commonly used to describe a form of computer modeling.

Partnership: a form of company wherein a group of individuals shares the financial and legal liabilities, as well as the profits.

Pattern Books: used from the Middle Ages through to the nineteenth century, these were books (made either by an individual or later published and sold) that provided details and decoration that could be integrated into a design.

Personal Professional Development (PPD): an aspect of UK education that seeks to support students to develop and plan for their future professional careers; typically structured around the development of both subject-specific and generic professional skills.

Perspective: a form of projection drawing that represents objects in three dimensions and as the eye sees, with parallel lines converging toward one or more vanishing points.

Photovoltaic: a form of solar collector that converts light energy into electrical energy. The conversion process works as the photons from the sunlight excite electrons into a higher state and thus release electrical charge.

Plan: a drawing that shows a top-down view of a building or object, usually indicating the arrangement of spaces.

Planning: the process, in the UK, of gaining permission to build; administered by local government, it is a system of land-use management.

Pointed Arch (or "Gothic" or "ogive" arch): a form of masonry arch that is taller than it is wide; this geometry is more effective in transferring downward forces around an opening.

Portfolio: either a case for carrying drawings, sketches, etc., or a collection of work (drawings, sketches, models, etc).

Postgraduate Degree: typically any university, or tertiary education, degree beyond the undergraduate or Bachelors degree. Depending on the locale, this may be a one- or two-year degree.

Post-Industrial: a term that applies to cities, countries, or societies that have shifted from an economy based on industrial or manufacturing output to a service-based economy.

Postmodernism: a movement within literature, art, design, and architecture that was a reaction to Modernism. In architecture this was seen as a rejection of the Modernist aesthetic and an embracing of a more diverse and culturally engaged expression.

Practice Management: the professional and operational issues associated with the business of architectural practice.

Prefabricated: any building component or assembly that is made off site and can be installed and ready upon arrival at the site.

Primitive Hut: a notion of the "original" architectural form, popularized by Abbé Marc-Antoine Laugier, a Jesuit monk, in his *Essai Sur L'Architecture* (1753).

Principal: the lead architect within a practice.

Problem-Based Learning: a form of teaching and learning that sets the student a problem, based on real situations, such that through solving the problem the student will engage in the types of activities that model professional practice.

Procurement: in architecture the procedure of securing the completed project. A "traditional" procurement method would be an architect appointed to design the project, followed by a competitive tender process for the appointment of the contractor, who then undertakes the building process.

Professional Degree: usually refers, in the USA, to a one-year degree awarded after a Bachelors degree; the minimum level of architectural education in the USA necessary to meet professional qualification requirements.

Professional Qualification: the award of a qualification that confirms professional status; in architecture this is often a legal requirement in order to use the title "Architect."

•••

Project Manager: an individual or firm appointed to act on behalf of the client in overseeing the project; sometimes this may be an architect, but increasingly there are firms that specialize in this service.

Project: in architectural education this refers to a studio-based design assignment; in professional practice it is the general term for a body of work undertaken for a client.

Punch List: *see* Snagging List.

Quantity Surveyor: *see* Cost Consultant.

Rapid Prototyping: the general term for a range of technologies that are able to create physical objects from data supplied from computer files.

Referral: the process of getting additional work via the recommendation of a previous client.

Renaissance: a cultural movement, beginning in Italy and then spreading to most of Europe, from the fourteenth to seventeenth centuries; saw a rediscovery of the Classics (Greek and Roman) as well as the development of a broad Humanist philosophy.

Rendering: in computer modeling the process of generating an image based on the properties defined within the model.

Renewable Energy: sources of energy that are not depleted from reserves; usually refers to solar-, wind- or wave-power generation.

Request for Proposal (RFP): *see* Tender.

RIBA (Royal Institute of British Architects): the professional body within the UK whose members comply with a code of conduct; the organization also undertakes a validation program that forms part of the process of achieving professional qualification.

Romanesque: a style of architecture that developed during the Middle Ages in Europe; much of the details and formal arrangement was descended from Roman styles. Typically buildings were massive, with thick walls, rounded arches, and generally symmetrical.

Royal Academy (of Arts): founded in England in 1768 by King George III to promote "the arts of design." It was the first institution devoted to the promotion and raising of standards for visual arts, artists, and architects.

Schedule of Works: a listing of items of work in a project and the sequence in which that work will be undertaken; sometimes includes cost information.

Schedule: list of items of specific kinds (such as doors, windows, etc), providing detailed information related to the items.

Section: a type of drawing that presents a building or object as being cut through a specific plane; allows for information about the construction or arrangement of vertically stacked spaces to be indicated.

Self-Employed: a form of business practice where an individual works for themselves rather than for a company.

Semester: a division of an academic year, usually into two parts.

Sequencing: in construction the planning of work in order to ensure that access is maintained to existing parts of the building while other areas are completed.

Shares (often used interchangeably with "stocks"): a unit of account indicating the amount of capital ownership that an individual has in a company, entitling the holder to a portion of the profits of that company.

Site: the location for an existing or proposed building.

Site Administrator: a person, or firm, employed to manage operations during construction on site.

Site Architect: an architect whose primary role is to work on the site itself to ensure that construction follows the design and drawings and to provide additional information as the need arises.

Snagging List: a list of items of work that a contractor must complete before a project can be deemed complete.

Specification: a written set of requirements for a building or component; often defines specific attributes that must be met.

Statutory Obligations: typically refers to the need for planning regulation and building regulation approval, which are required prior to the start of a building project.

Structural Engineer: an individual, or firm, tasked with the design and specification of the structural system of a building.

Studio System: a form of architectural education where students work under the guidance of a studio critic/tutor on a common project during the course of a term or semester.

Subcontractor: an individual, or firm, appointed by a main contractor to undertake specialized work on a building project. Usually the client will have no direct contractual relationship to the subcontractor and the architect will have no specific administrative responsibility or relationship to the subcontractor under the building contract.

Survey: the process and outcome of measuring a site; the gathering of information (either physical or transitory) about a place.

Sustainable Design: the process of designing in such a way that the outcome, and consequences, of the project do not deplete the resources of an area.

Symmetry: a system of balance and harmony; a mirroring about a line. In architecture (and other visual mediums) it is usually associated with things that display similar or identical characteristics when viewed across an axis.

Technical Drawings: *see* Construction Drawings.

Tender: the process through which a project is awarded to a contractor by review of the submission of information; the offer to carry out work under a set of conditions (usually related to a fee). Also called Request for Proposal (RFP).

Term: in academic calendars usually a third of a year; sometimes referred to as a "trimester."

Tertiary Education: a period of education that follows secondary education or high school.

Tutorial: a method of teaching where the tutor/studio critic meets with an individual or group of students to discuss their work and provide feedback.

Undergraduate Degree: a university-level degree, usually taking three or four years of study.

Unit System: a form of architectural education, pioneered at the Architectural Association in the UK, where a small number of students work under the guidance of a tutor, usually throughout the entire academic year; often the projects undertaken within the unit will have a particular thematic relationship.

Urban Design: the range of activities associated with the planning and design of cities.

Valuation: the process, and subsequent document, that outlines the request by a contractor for payment in relation to work completed on a construction project.

Vaulting: the arched form of support for a ceiling, transferring vertical loading on the ceiling down to the ground.

Vernacular: refers to those things that are indigenous, or original, to a country or area.

Version Control System (VCS): a system that allows for the tracking of changes to digital files and in some cases can allow for changes to be reversed.

Visualization: the process, using either traditional methods or computer rendering, of presenting a building project through drawings or models.

Zoning: a form of land-use management that allocates use based on an overall view of the types and density of building in an area.

Further Reading

Chapter 1

Kenneth Frampton, *Modern Architecture: A Critical History*, London: Thames & Hudson, 2007

Spiro Kostof, *A History of Architecture: Settings and Rituals*, New York: Oxford University Press, 1995

Spiro Kostof, *The Architect: Chapters in the History of the Profession,* Berkeley, California: University of California Press, 2000

Neil Leach, *Rethinking Architecture: A Reader in Cultural Theory*, Abingdon and London: Routledge, 1997

Marian Moffett, Michael Fazio, and Lawrence Wodehouse, *A World History of Architecture*, London: Laurence King Publishing, 2008

Kate Nesbitt (ed.), *Theorizing a New Agenda for Architecture: An Anthology of Architectural Theory 1965–95*, New York: Princeton Architectural Press, 1996

Steen Eiler Rasmussen, *Experiencing Architecture*, Cambridge, Massachusetts: MIT Press, 1962

Tom Wolfe, *From Bauhaus to Our House,* London: Bantam, 1999

Chapter 2

Michael Chadwick (ed.), *Back to School: Architectural Education—The Information and the Argument (Architectural Design)*, San Francisco: John Wiley & Sons, 2004

John Hejduk, *Education of an Architect: Irwin S. Chanin School of Architecture of the Cooper Union*, New York: Rizzoli International Publications, 1988

David Nicol and Simon Pilling (eds.), *Changing Architectural Education: Towards a New Professionalism*, London and New York: Spon Press, 2000

Simon Unwin, *An Architecture Notebook*, London: Routledge, 2000

Lee Waldrep, *Becoming an Architect: A Guide to Careers in Design*, San Francisco: John Wiley & Sons, 2006

Chapter 3

Sue Carmichael, *A Guide to Successful Client Relationships (Small Practices)*, London: RIBA Publishing, 2002

Rolf Fehlbaum, *Visionary Clients for New Architecture*, Munich: Prestel Verlag, 2000

David Hyams and David Chappell (eds.), *Construction Companion to Briefing*, London: RIBA Publishing, 2001

Frank Salisbury, *Briefing Your Architect,* Oxford: Architectural Press, 1998

Chapter 4

Kenneth Allinson, *Getting There by Design: An Architect's Guide to Design and Project Management*, Oxford: Architectural Press, 1997

Geoffrey Baker, *Design Strategies in Architecture: An Approach to the Analysis of Form,* Abingdon and New York: Spon Press, 1993

David Chappell, *Contractual Correspondence for Architects and Project Managers*, Oxford: Blackwell Publishing, 2006

Francis D.K. Ching, *Design Drawing*, San Francisco: John Wiley & Sons, 1997

Stephen Emmitt, *Architectural Technology*, Oxford: Wiley-Blackwell, 2002

Ronald Green, *The Architect's Guide to Running a Job*, Oxford: Architectural Press, 2001

William Lidwell, Kritina Holden, and Jill Butler, *Universal Principles of Design: 100 Ways to Enhance Usability, Influence Perception, Increase Appeal, Make Better Design Decisions, and Teach Through Design*, Beverly, Massachusetts: Rockport Publishers, 2007

Sarah Lupton, *Architect's Job Book*, London: RIBA Publishing, 2000

Roland Phillips, *The Architect's Plan of Work*, London: RIBA Publishing, 2000

Chapter 5

Charlotte Baden-Powell, *Architect's Pocket Book*, Oxford: Architectural Press, 2001

Bert Bielefeld and Tim Brandt, *Tendering (Basics Series)*, Basel: Birkhauser, 2007

Roy Chudley and Roger Greeno, *Building Construction Handbook: Incorporating Current Building and Construction Regulations*, Oxford: Butterworth-Heinemann, 2006

Andrea Deplazes (ed.), *Constructing Architecture: Materials, Processes, Structure (A Handbook),* Basel: Birkhauser, 2008

Mark Hackett, Ian Robinson, and Gary Statham, *The Aqua Group Guide to Procurement, Tendering and Contract Administration*, Oxford: Wiley Blackwell, 2006

Hartmut Klein, *Project Planning (Basics Series)*, Basel: Birkhauser, 2007

Branko Kolarevic (ed.), *Architecture in the Digital Age: Design and Manufacturing*, Abingdon and New York: Taylor & Francis, 2005

Jan Krebs, *CAD (Basics Series)*, Basel: Birkhauser, 2007

Willem Kymmell, *Building Information Modeling: Planning and Managing Construction Projects with 4D CAD and Simulations*, New York: McGraw-Hill Professional, 2008

David Littlefield, *Metric Handbook: Planning and Design Data*, Oxford: Architectural Press, 2007

Charles George Ramsay, Harold Reeve Sleeper, and Bruce Bassler (eds.), *Architectural Graphic Standards*, San Francisco: Wiley, 2008

David J. Wyatt and Hans W. Meier, *Construction Specifications: Principles and Applications*, Florence, Kentucky: Delmar Cengage Learning, 2008

Chapter 6

American Institute of Architects, *The Architect's Handbook of Professional Practice: Student Edition*, San Francisco: John Wiley & Sons, 2002

Bauman Lyons Architects, *How to Be a Happy Architect*, London: Black Dog Publishing, 2008

Simon Foxell, *Starting a Practice (Good Practice Guide)*, London: RIBA Publishing, 2006

Sarah Lupton (ed.), *Architect's Handbook of Practice Management*, London: RIBA Publishing, 2002

Management Consultant Faculty, *Practice Management Guidelines*, Coventry: Royal Institute of Chartered Surveyors (RICS Books), 2003

Peter Piven and Bradford Perkins, *Architect's Essentials of Starting a Design Firm (The Architect's Essentials of Professional Practice)*, San Francisco: John Wiley & Sons, 2003

Chapter 7

Kathryn H. Anthony, *Designing for Diversity: Gender, Race, and Ethnicity in the Architectural Profession*, Champaign, Illinois: University of Illinois Press, 2008

Architecture for Humanity (ed.), *Design Like You Give a Damn: Architectural Responses to Humanitarian Crises*, Los Angeles, California: Metropolis Books, 2006

Alastair Fuad-Luke, *The Eco-Design Handbook: A Complete Sourcebook for the Home and Office*, London: Thames & Hudson, 2005

John M. Levy, *Contemporary Urban Planning*, London: Pearson Prentice Hall, 2008

William McDonough and Michael Braungart, *Cradle to Cradle: Remaking the Way We Make Things*, Emmaus, Pennsylvania: Rodale Press, 2003

Elizabeth Wilhide, *Eco: The Essential Sourcebook for Environmentally Friendly Design and Decoration*, London: Quadrille Publishing, 2004

US Magazines & Periodicals

Architect
Architectural Record
Azure
Dwell
Environmental Design + Construction
Frame
Harvard Design Magazine
Log
Metropolis
US Architecture

UK Magazines & Periodicals

Abitare (UK and Italy)
The Architects' Journal
The Architectural Review
Blueprint
Building Design
Domus (UK and Italy)
Frame
Icon
Quaderns (UK and Spain)
RIBA Journal
Square
*Wallpaper**

Online Resources

www.an-architecture.com
This Austrian blog site provides timely postings on a range of issues related to architecture in Europe.

www.archidose.org
Blogs and project profiles; the "book of the week" provides a review of a recent architecture book, while the "dose of the week" is a review of a project.

www.archidose.blogspot.com
This is the "daily" offering from Archidose—a collection of blog posts and images.

www.archinect.com
Dedicated to making architecture "more connected and open-minded;" provides news and features from the fringe as well as mainstream architecture.

www.archinnovations.com
Articles, news, blogs, and project profiles from around the world; includes competition listings, links to related sites, and feeds from other architecture sites.

www.archis.org
The website of the Archis Foundation, an architecture and spatial "think tank;" provides information on the activities of the Foundation as well as the "network" of related groups.

www.architectmagazine.com
Online version of the US magazine *Architect*; provides additional resources including product information, practice portfolios, and job listings.

www.architectsjournal.co.uk
News and information site related to the UK magazine *The Architects' Journal*; keeps abreast of news, product information, and job offers in the UK.

www.architecture-page.com
Provides information about architects and projects; anyone can publish their work.

www.architectureweek.com
US-based online magazine that pulls content from a variety of different sources; provides news as well as technology-related listings.

www.arcspace.com
A collection of project profiles, images, and a unique series of blogs ("kk Letters" and "Travel").

www.bdonline.co.uk
Online version of the UK weekly architecture and construction magazine *Building Design*; as well as news, provides job listings, project profiles, event listings, and commentary.

www.bldgblog.blogspot.com
This blog brings together some of the most interesting commentary on contemporary architecture and urbanism, with art and design thrown in too; interviews, project reviews, and news feeds make this a continuously refreshing place to visit.

www.floatingpodium.com
This is your "one-stop-shop" for news and blogs related to architecture and design, pulling in information from sites around the globe.

www.inhabitat.com
One of the best "green" blogs for architecture and design, this site brings together a wealth of information for architects and designers; the Friday feature on "sustainable homes" often provides a look at interesting projects from around the world.

www.interactivearchitecture.org
This blog aims to provide information on the merging of digital, virtual, and real spatial practice; with postings on London-based, as well as international, events and projects the site provides info on some of the most challenging of contemporary practitioners.

www.o2.org
Website for the O2 global network, linking like-minded people in support of good design that is also sustainable; links to book reviews, news, and people.

www.rematerialise.org
A resource site for "eco-smart" materials, managed by Kingston University in London.

www.treehugger.com
A US-based media outlet dedicated to providing information on sustainability; as well as news and information there are interviews and blogs that explore issues of sustainability from a wide range of viewpoints.

www.world-architects.com
A collection of practice and project profiles from around the world, categorized by country, as well as international job listings.

www.worldarchitecturenews.com
Provides news and information on architecture from around the world; includes job listings, bookstore, podcasts, and newsfeeds.

Useful Addresses in the USA

American Institute of Architects (AIA)
1735 New York Avenue, NW
Washington, DC 20006-5292
www.aia.org

*The AIA is the main professional membership body
for architects in the United States. It works to
uphold the profession while also supporting
education and clients. Its aim is to "serve as the
voice of the architecture profession and the
resource for our members in service to society."*

**Association of Collegiate Schools of
Architecture (ACSA)**
1735 New York Avenue, NW
3rd Floor
Washington, DC 20006
www.acsa-arch.org

*The ACSA serves to promote and support
architectural education, in the USA and Canada,
through advocacy, liaison, and communication with
similar organizations around the world. The
organization includes 250 schools of architecture
in the USA and Canada, and works with students
and faculties of those schools to support the
continued development of architectural education.*

Construction Specifications Institute (CSI)
99 Canal Center Plaza
Suite 300
Alexandria, VA 22314-1588
www.csinet.org

*As the national association that aims to create and
promote standards in construction documents, the
CSI provides a range of services to the building
industry. In addition to maintaining the standard
format of US construction specifications, it also
provides professional certification programs for
specification writers.*

**Graham Foundation for Advanced Studies
in the Fine Arts**
4 West Burton Place
Chicago, IL 60610-1416
www.grahamfoundation.org

*This Chicago-based organization provides financial
grants for the development of projects that expand
and challenge the role of architecture in the arts,
culture, and society. Each year the Foundation
awards funding to a range of projects that span
historical studies to cutting-edge digital research.*

International Code Council (ICC)
500 New Jersey Avenue, NW
6th Floor
Washington, DC 20001-2070
www.iccsafe.org

*The ICC is a membership association that works to
develop building codes for the safety and security
of the public. Most of the building codes used
across the United States are based on those
developed by the ICC.*

**National Council of Architectural
Registration Boards (NCARB)**
1801 K Street, NW
Suite 700-K
Washington, DC 20006
www.ncarb.org

*NCARB is the national body that protects the health
and safety of the public by regulating the process
of testing and registration of architects in the
United States. It sets the basic requirements for an
individual to become a qualified architect in the
USA, with the specific process being undertaken at
state level.*

U.S. Green Building Council (USGBC)
1800 Massachusetts Avenue, NW
Suite 300
Washington, DC 20036
www.usgbc.org

*The USGBC is a non-profit organization that aims
to promote the use of sustainable building in the
United States. Comprised of 15,000 organizations
from across the industry it works to support
research and testing, as well as certifying the
Leadership in Energy and Environmental Design
(LEED) program.*

Useful Addresses in the UK

Architects Registration Board (ARB)
Ability House
7 Portland Place
London W1B 1PP
www.arb.org.uk

The ARB is an independent statutory regulating body in the UK for the protection of the consumer and safeguard of the reputation of architects. The organization provides services in support of architects in the form of managing and maintaining the list of registered architects, as well as promoting standards in education and professional practice. All those wishing to practice architecture in the UK must be ARB registered.

The Architecture Foundation
Somerset House
South Building
London WC2R 1LA
www.architecturefoundation.org.uk

The Architecture Foundation is the UK's premier independent architecture center. Located in London it provides a venue for exhibitions, lectures, debates, and talks, as well as sponsoring competitions and promoting contemporary architecture to the wider public.

Building Research Establishment (BRE)
Bucknalls Lane
Watford
Herts WD25 9XX
www.bre.co.uk

The BRE Trust Companies provide a range of research, testing, and consultancy services related to building in the UK. Based on their work they publish a range of technical documents to support the building industry and to establish codes.

The Commission for Architecture and the Built Environment (CABE)
1 Kemble Street
London WC2B 4AN
www.cabe.org.uk

CABE is the UK government's advisor on architecture and urban development. Through its work it encourages UK policy-makers to support design that is safe, beautiful, and sustainable. It supports education programs at all levels and regularly sponsors events throughout the UK.

Design Council
34 Bow Street
London WC2E 7DL
www.designcouncil.org.uk

The Design Council is a UK government-funded organization that aims to promote the use of design in business and public services. Its role is to help the business sector to recognize the value that design brings and to promote UK design throughout the world.

National Building Specification (NBS)
The Old Post Office
St Nicholas Street
Newcastle upon Tyne NE1 1RH
www.thenbs.com

Part of the RIBA Enterprises group of companies, the NBS provides documents, tools, and services related to the production of consistent specifications for the UK building industry. This includes software for scheduling and specification writing, as well as paper-based specification forms.

The Royal Institute of British Architects (RIBA)
66 Portland Place
London W1B 1AD
www.architecture.com

The RIBA is the UK body for support and promotion of architecture and the architectural profession. In addition to working with the government to improve the design quality of buildings, it also provides services for clients and students.

Shell LiveWire
Design Works
William Street
Felling
Gateshead
Tyne & Wear NE10 0JP
www.shell-livewire.org

Supported by Shell Oil, this UK (and international) organization can help small businesses get started through the provision of free advice, information packs, and access to a "social network" of related business startups.

UCAS
Rosehill
New Barn Lane
Cheltenham
Gloucestershire GL52 3LZ
www.ucas.ac.uk

UCAS is the primary access route into Higher Education in the UK. Its website provides information on all university courses in the UK.

UK Green Building Council
The Building Centre
26 Store Street
London WC1E 7BT
www.ukgbc.org

The mission of the Green Building Council is to "dramatically improve the sustainability of the built environment." Through the promotion of good design and planning the organization supports the industry to move forward toward a more sustainable future, through research, campaigns, and publications.

Index

Page numbers in **bold** refer to picture captions